Politics and Ethnicity on the Río Yaqui: Potam Revisited

Observers of Yaqui Indian society and culture in southern Sonora, Mexico, inevitably return to the theme of ethnicity. Yaquis have maintained their distinct identity through centuries of interaction—frequently violent—with the surrounding society. Renewed confrontations in the 1970s over the control of the marine resources and the productive farmlands along the lower Río Yaqui offered the opportunity to study the role of ethnicity in regional politics. Although the tribe was not fully successful in these struggles, the strength of Yaqui ethnic identity remains undiminished. Contributing factors to the persistence of the ethnic group include the uncoerced nature of individual participation in Yaqui political and religious institutions, the ascriptive foundations of group membership, and the role of audience—Indian and non-Indian—in fostering Yaqui interest in a distinctive ceremonial system.

Politics and Ethnicity on the Río Yaqui: Potam Revisited

THOMAS R. McGUIRE

The University of Arizona Press

TUCSON

About the Author

THOMAS R. MCGUIRE since 1983 has been an anthropologist with the Bureau of Applied Research in Anthropology at the University of Arizona, where he received his Ph.D. in 1979. He has been involved in assessing economic development opportunities for Indian reservations in the Southwest, and in the study of state and national policies toward Indian water rights. He has also pursued an active interest in the history of Native Americans in the region, conducting studies on the White Mountain Apache Reservation, the Gila River Reservation, and the Ak Chin Indian Community.

THE UNIVERSITY OF ARIZONA PRESS
Copyright © 1986
The Arizona Board of Regents
All Rights Reserved

This book was set in 10/11½ VIP Baskerville.
Manufactured in the U.S.A.

Library of Congress Cataloging in Publication Data
McGuire, Thomas R.
Politics and ethnicity on the Río Yaqui.
(Profmex monograph series; 1)
Bibliography: p.
Includes index.
1. Yaqui Indians—Ethnic identity. 2. Yaqui
Indians—Government relations. 3. Indians of
Mexico—Sonora (State)—Ethnic identity.
4. Indians of Mexico—Government relations.
5. Yaqui Indians—Water rights. 6. Indians of
Mexico—Sonora (State)—Water rights. I. Title.
II. Series.
F1221.Y3M35 1986 323.1'197 86-11445
ISBN 0-8165-0893-3 (alk. paper)

Contents

ILLUSTRATIONS

Figures

Maps

TABLES

Preface

Sonora's Yaqui Indians have been passionately concerned, through much of their known history, with survival and persistence as an ethnic group. To the residents of the Zona Indígena, the tribal reserve along the lower Río Yaqui, questions of ethnic identity are no longer terribly interesting. The present study seeks to understand the causes and consequences of this situation.

Clues may be found by looking at those issues that did elicit attention from the Yaquis in 1975 and 1976, the convulsive end of Luis Echeverría's presidency in Mexico. Some of these issues were purely local: a bitterly contested election for pueblo governors; a successful campaign by Yaqui women to close down the cantinas and pool halls of the river towns in the zona; a seemingly inordinate rash of sickness and death through the winter; a common concern with shortages of farm credit, irrigation water, and functioning outboards to motor the fishing cooperative's boats. Other local issues preoccupied the nation as well: the violent surge of agrarian politics after several decades of relative quietude in the countryside was ignited by the shooting of Mexican *campesinos* at San Ignacio, Río Muerto, a few kilometers from the Yaquis' reserve. To be sure, some of the issues addressed by Yaquis in 1975 and 1976 did have implications for the analysis of ethnicity, the study of social and cultural persistence. But these issues were addressed in ways that did not explicitly attempt to shore up ethnic boundaries or enforce the allegiance of individuals to the received traditions and values of Yaqui society.

Questions of ethnic identity—the "sum total of feelings on the part of group members about those values, symbols, and common histories that identify them as a distinct group" (Royce 1982:18)—are unin-

teresting to contemporary Yaquis because that identity is largely un-
problematic. In his major synthesis of Yaqui society, history, and culture (1980) Edward Spicer speaks briefly of a "clarity of definition"
regarding Yaqui ethnic identity now. Much of his professional career
has been devoted to observing and explaining the processes Yaquis
employed to construct this definition. Key to Spicer's thinking on
ethnicity is the "oppositional process." Persistent identity systems are
formulated through time by continuous antagonism. The internal
content of the identity system may change, as the succession of historical events is endowed with new meanings. But the fact of opposition to
the dominant society, at times militant, at others passive, remains.

Oddly, Spicer seldom challenged other views of ethnic persistence
with his own. Uncontentious by temperament, he did not engage
himself actively in the theoretical debates of the 1970s. And with the
exception of Anya Peterson Royce (1982), few third parties have juxtaposed Spicerian notions of ethnicity to others of the decade. This
monograph pursues an indirect route to such comparison. It is not a
rigorous essay in theory, but rather an effort to understand Spicer's
archetypal persistent people, the Yaquis, in the context of contemporary anthropological thinking on ethnicity.

AN OVERVIEW

Chapter 1 addresses some preliminary observations on Yaqui
ethnicity to the dominant anthropological theories of the 1970s,
specifically, the ideas of Fredrik Barth on the maintenance of ethnic
boundaries and those of numerous authors on the instrumentality of
ethnic identity, represented best in a programmatic statement by Leo
Despres. The chapter retains something of the combative tone of its
original drafting in 1978, both against these two writers and against
Spicer's writing on the oppositional process. The argument against
Spicer stemmed from my feeling that he allowed insufficient flexibility
in what it means to be a Yaqui. His 1980 statement on "clarity of
definition" now removes many of my objections, once the implications of
this statement are pursued. Problems with Barth and Despres remain.

The important essay by Barth (1969) redirected anthropological
research on ethnic groups. Like Spicer, he acknowledges that, in
Royce's words, "ethnic identity is more often the product of increasing
interaction between groups than the negative result of isolation"
(Royce 1982:40). This provides a necessary antidote to assimilation and
acculturation theories, by which increasing contact inevitably led to a
demise in traditional values and behaviors of previously distinct groups
and individuals. But unlike Spicer's emphasis on the historical development—through opposition—of an ethnic group, Barth is more
concerned with the microsociology of boundary maintenance. He

looks at the behavioral strategies that generate and preserve distinct ethnic identities of groups in contact. In doing so, Barth appears to overstate the case. His actors are almost consumed with concerns of ethnicity, of behaving according to appropriate ethnic standards, preserving those standards from dilution by outsiders.

Leo Despres (1975) is also concerned with ethnic groups in contact. He examines how ethnic identities are used, not simply maintained. They can be used effectively, he suggests, in the political struggle for resources, and in such use the salience of ethnicity to group members is enhanced. Despres, however, does not fully explore the implications of this idea: what happens to the content and use of ethnic identities when the political demands fail? Moreover, what is it about the larger arena that accounts for the failures and successes of ethnicity-based political action?

In its evaluation of these writings, chapter 1 becomes somewhat tortuous. The discussion could be simplified by resorting to the idea of the "fixed-membership group." James Clifton, in a 1965 article, draws upon earlier work by Leonard Plotnicov (1962) to characterize the Southern Ute Tribe as a political and social entity. Primary attributes of the fixed-membership group are: (1) social relations that are regarded as "permanent or as lasting indefinitely"; (2) group membership that is based on ascription, thus "largely irrevocable"; (3) reluctance on the part of the group to lose or expel members; and (4) a "membership, because of the value given to the permanence of their relationships, [that] is able to and does in fact freely experiment with cultural novelties" (Clifton 1972 [originally 1965]:488).

For the Southern Ute and—as I argue throughout this monograph, in somewhat different terms—for Sonora's Yaqui as well, the characteristics of the fixed-membership group derive inevitably from corporate political organization. Despres, with his interest in ethnic group politics, comes close to making the same argument. But he turns most of his attention to the external uses of the ethnic polity, not to the internal implications of political organization on group membership and behavior. Barth, as noted above, is predisposed to looking at ethnic identity as a performance. Achievement, not ascription, forms the basis for group membership.

I take much of the blame for ignoring the relevance of the fixed-membership group to the arguments presented in chapter 1. Part of the responsibility, however, should go to the stimulation of theoretical advances in the 1970s. John Bennett talks of "the new ethnicity" that characterizes the work of Barth, Despres, and other writers:

The "newness" implies something new in the world—or at least something newly noticed by anthropologists: the proclivity of people to seize on traditional cultural symbols as a definition of their own identity—either to assert the Self over and above the impersonal State, or to obtain the resources one needs to survive and to consume (1975:32).

In accounting for these realities, theoreticians cast aside most of the elements of "the old ethnicity." The concept of the fixed-membership group was one such element that was largely ignored, if not rejected. It regains some merit now for understanding groups such as the Sonoran Yaquis which have already won a measure of political autonomy from the state.

Chapter 2 begins the effort to situate Yaquis within the regional context and to characterize the nature of Yaqui political organization. The period under discussion is the crucial one for understanding contemporary Yaqui polity and economy: the early decades of the twentieth century. With the mapping and construction of irrigation canals from the Río Yaqui, the lower valley was transformed, at least incipiently, into what it is today. In the nineteenth century, the regional drama of power and politics was typically staged in one or another of the indigenous pueblos on the river. Battles continued to be fought there for land and water in the twentieth century, but the opening of new farmlands south of the river inevitably altered the scene. The concentration of water and wealth in this Valle Nuevo worked to the economic detriment of the indigenous Yaquis, but not to their political detriment. In a fashion similar to the formation of Indian reservations in the United States, Yaquis were granted some measure of political autonomy on residual land, close to the economic activity of the valley, but they were not to become full beneficiaries of that development.

The events of this transformation are treated cursorily, for they are discussed by others. Claudio Dabdoub's *Historia de El Valle del Yaqui* (1964) remains the definitive treatment. Several North American historians have recently turned their attention to the archives of the region and the period. The complex story can now be found in a conjunctive reading of Hu-Dehart (1984), Voss (1982), and especially, Clifton Kroeber's *Man, Land, and Water: Mexico's Farmland Irrigation Policies, 1885–1911* (1983).

The succeeding two chapters try to make sense of disparate observations on the behavior of the Yaqui ethnic group. Congruent with the notion of the fixed-membership group, the argument is that the ethnic identification of individual Yaquis is based on ascriptive criteria, not on performance or achievement. Primary evidence comes from fieldwork in and around Potam in 1975 and 1976, but the argument is also motivated by the recorded life histories of Yaquis in *The Tall Candle* (Moisés, Kelley, and Holden 1971) and *Yaqui Women* (Kelley 1978). Numerous Yaquis characterized in biographies appear to have little concern with the core elements of Yaqui culture, or, through their own actions, with the perpetuation of that culture. Casual about their ethnic

performances, these Yaquis do not thereby lose their group membership. Emphasis on ascription, not achievement, seems to account for
this, but it does not answer the question of why an active and costly
ceremonial system persists in the Yaqui Zone. I argue that Yaquis
participate in ceremony precisely because they are not coerced into
participation. Ritual, in turn, communicates to Yaquis and non-Yaquis
alike the meaning of Yaqui ethnic identity.

Three chapters then explore the limits of Yaqui political action.
Together, they form a loose test of the proposition that the strength of
ethnic identity varies directly with the political success of the ethnic
polity. Empirically, the proposition fails. Yaqui shrimp fishermen, as a
group the least "ethnic," were, during the 1970s, the most successful in
the politics of resource control. Farmers from the historic pueblos of
Río Yaqui pressed their perennial demands for more land during the
decade, but these claims went virtually unheard. Chapters 5, 6, and 7
seek reasons for these differentials of success and failure.

Some answers are to be found in the larger ecology, economics,
and politics of fishing and farming in Mexico's northwest. Chapters 5,
6, and 7 depart rather widely from a concern with the persistence of
the Yaqui as an ethnic group. The concluding chapter returns to this
theme, through a simple model of Yaqui ethnic action. The model
orders the primary variables in the persistence of the group: the
corporate polity, the ascriptive basis for ethnic group membership, the
continued participation of Yaquis in complex ceremony, and the communication of ethnicity through that ceremony.

These were all key elements in Professor Spicer's interpretation of
the Yaqui as a persistent people. But, because of the time period that he
worked on the Río Yaqui, he structured these elements differently.
Spicer conducted fieldwork during the 1940s, and his modest ethnography, *Potam: A Yaqui Village in Sonora* (1954), has not received the
professional acclaim of his earlier *Pascua* (1940), nor of the synthetic
Cycles of Conquest (1962). Nonetheless, *Potam* is rich enough in detail
and interpretation to warrant a "revisit"; the subtitle to this monograph
purposely invokes the anthropological controversy between Robert
Redfield and Oscar Lewis. Lewis restudied Redfield's Tepoztlán (1930)
in Morelos twenty years later, and found Redfield's picture of harmony
to be a reflection of interpretive bias, not ethnographic fact. I conclude
with some brief observation on this controversy and on the ethnology
of Redfield's student, Edward Spicer.

Over the decade in which this study has taken shape, debts have
accumulated and I welcome the opportunity to acknowledge if not
repay them.

I am most appreciative, first, of those individuals and organizations
that allowed me to pursue my own leads on the story of contemporary

Potam. The National Science Foundation funded what was supposed to have been an entire dissertation on the Yaqui fishing cooperative. Richard Henderson, Richard Thompson, and the late Edward Spicer, of the University of Arizona's anthropology department, supervised the discrepant results. It was characteristic of Professor Spicer's scholarship and ethics that he encouraged my work because, not despite, of the fact that I was writing on a subject and people so close to his own interests. The late Thomas Hinton, who was passionately curious about Sonora, generously supported the initial stages of research through a departmental travel grant. Two other students of Yaqui society, Rosamond Spicer of Tucson, and Jane Holden Kelley of Calgary, have been equally unselfish in their intellectual encouragement for the research reported here. Douglas Schwartz also helped substantially by allowing me to use the facilities of Santa Fe's School of American Research, under a fellowship from the Weatherhead Foundation.

Others assisted by giving me the flexibility to return, when necessary, to thinking and writing about Yaquis. Special thanks go to Sara Kiesler of Carnegie-Mellon University, and Carlos Vélez-Ibañez of the Bureau of Applied Research in Anthropology, University of Arizona, who provided material and moral support for the project. María Rodríguez and Betty Leavengood, also of the bureau, struggled to bring my grammar and spelling into conformity with commonly accepted standards. Michael Meyer, the editor of the PROFMEX series, gave me indispensable advice and support, and Charles Sternberg drafted the maps and figures for the monograph with his customary precision.

Families play a key role in an endeavor such as this. One will remain unnamed—that of my landlord and host in Potam. This family appears frequently in the pages to follow, in vignettes which I hope will not seem unbecoming. My parents have been a constant source of encouragement on their frequent trips to Tucson from their home in Ithaca. To all of these individuals I am grateful.

T.R.M.

CHAPTER ONE

The Political Organization
of Ethnicity

Past ethnography and historiography of the Yaqui left me strangely ill-equipped to understand the contemporary situation in southern Sonora. I was struck, early in my stay, with several impressions about Yaqui society that seemed logically disconnected to the interpreted Yaqui past of intense, organized, often violent opposition to the encroaching Mexican economy and polity. I was struck, first, with the apparent stability of interpersonal relations across ethnic lines. Little overt ethnic tension surfaced during my fieldwork. Indeed, there was much evidence of cooperative, even friendly interaction between Yaqui and *yori* (Mexican) in and around the Yaqui Zone. I was impressed, too, with a surprising lack of ethnic assertiveness on the part of most Yaquis I came to be associated with; in the idiom of contemporary social theory, Yaqui ethnic identity seemed largely "undercommunicated." Finally, I became increasingly convinced of a wide gulf between norm and action. A variety of Yaqui customs, abstract values, and prescriptions for the conduct of mundane life seemed to be observed in the breach.

None of these impressions—of apparent intergroup stability, of the undercommunication of identity, of the differentiation between norm and action—could be easily reconciled to the dynamics of Yaqui-Mexican confrontation in the past. Nor did they comfortably fit with the hard facts of the present. Economically, Yaquis are now tightly bound to a system of commercial agriculture, dominated by outsiders who control all of the essential factors of production and distribution save the land. But culturally, contemporary Yaquis are adamantly persistent; the complex ceremonial schedule, voracious as it is of human energy, time, and money, is still actively carried on.

Ritual persistence in the face of economic domination and market involvement is something of a paradox (see Smith 1977a). More problematical is the reconciliation of ritual persistence with intergroup stability, undercommunication, and differentiation. One would expect, at first glance, to find ritual going hand in hand with this association, reinforcing but also deriving from a close correlation between actions and norms. We would expect distinctive ritual to provide reasons and ammunition for interethnic conflict. And we would expect ritual to yield ample symbols and opportunities for the active communication of ethnic distinctiveness. One of my tasks is to understand why these expectations are not fulfilled in contemporary Yaqui society.

A second task, around which the solution to the first will largely hinge, is to understand the current role of the Yaqui polity. Here again, traditional expectations are not directly supported by reality. Yaquis are as politically autonomous as they are economically dependent. On some issues, too, Yaquis are as politically unsuccessful as they are politically united.

Anthropologists have devoted considerable attention to issues of politics, ceremony, and ethnicity over the last two decades. Two guiding propositions have dominated this literature. In *Ethnicity and Resource Competition in Plural Societies* (1975), Leo Despres concludes that ethnicity is above all an instrumental phenomenon. Ethnic identities and their symbolic accouterments can be manipulated. They are, in a sense, political resources, bases for organizing groups so as to enhance political or economic power. Thus, he introduces the following proposition:

By definition, ethnic boundaries express some organization of status identities to which status claims of one type or another are attached. With respect to material resources, to the extent that these status claims confer competitive advantage upon populations who assert them, social boundaries supportive of categorical ethnic identities will persist. Conversely, when such claims confer no particular advantage in this regard, ethnic boundaries weaken and the assertion of ethnic identities appears to diminish (Despres 1975:199).

Partisan to his own position, Despres expresses at the same time an increasing dissatisfaction with the second theoretical trend in the study of ethnicity, the program set forth in Fredrik Barth's (1969) *Ethnic Groups and Boundaries*. Barth views ethnic identities not as instrumental political phenomena but as categorical and subjective ones. The key issues to Barth are not how ethnic identities can be used, but how ethnic groups form and persist, how individuals subjectively categorize themselves and others as members of discrete groups, and how these discrete groups are preserved despite, and because of, numerous individual interactions across group boundaries.

These differences aside, Despres attempts a summary framework that will align his own concerns in the politics of ethnicity with those of Barth in the ascription and achievement of ethnic group membership. Despres acknowledges that ethnic phenomena ought to be analyzed simultaneously in terms of "cultural systems, organized groups, and individual transactions" (1975:194). Thus, he suggests some covariant relationships among these several dimensions of ethnicity. For example, when ethnic group membership yields no special advantage in the competition over resources, boundaries will weaken and the assertion of ethnic identities will diminish. Equally suggestive and tentative is another potential covariant: ". . . ethnic populations are one type of structural phenomena and ethnic groups are quite another, and each type may differentially influence the system of interethnic relations that might obtain among individuals" (Despres 1975:196). Without following through on all of its ramifications, Despres is making a critical distinction between population aggregates and corporately organized groups. *Ethnic populations* are aggregates of individuals that show determinate boundaries and membership based on categorical identification. *Ethnic groups* may share these features of boundaries and membership, but they differ from ethnic populations in being politically organized: "Internally, they reveal governmental processes; externally, they generally reveal a determinate set of political relationships" (Despres 1975:196).

The corporate organization of an ethnic population, Despres suggests, may enhance that group's chances of success in the competition for resources. Characteristically possessing "a common estate, a unitary set of external relations, a relatively exclusive body of common affairs, and procedures which are more or less adequate to the administration of these affairs" (Despres 1975:196), corporate organizations would presumably have the legitimacy and the personnel to, in a sense, speak with one voice. They would have the potential to enter into legal negotiations when appropriate, and perhaps to mobilize mass support when negotiations collapse.

With his explicit concern for relations of power, Despres curiously neglects a systematic analysis of the conditions under which *ethnic populations* become—are allowed to become—politically organized *ethnic groups*. Likewise, he fails to systematically explore the actual outcomes of corporately expressed demands for resources: he does not sufficiently acknowledge the potential for failure in the face of overwhelming political and economic power.

Ironically, corporate ethnic organizations have been treated most successfully by anthropologists working in urban Africa, where such groups are frequently absent. Abner Cohen deals with two crucial problems: the potential efficiency of formal, corporately organized groups, and the conditions under which formal organization is precluded. Following Max Weber, Cohen suggests that formal groups, "rationally planned on bureaucratic lines," are a most effective and efficient type of organization. This efficiency can be seen most easily by juxtaposition to informally organized interest groups (or "aggregrates" in Despres's terms) which attempt to articulate interests along diffuse lines of kinship, friendship, and ritual. Cohen notes:

> This strategy of organizing a group on the basis of different types of obligation which are not consciously adopted or planned, is likely to be wasteful in time and energy, and is not as efficient in achieving the group's ends as formal organization. For example, instead of organizing an official meeting for the members of the group to discuss a current problem, the informal group will attend a ceremonial during which the problem is only informally and unsystematically discussed, amidst a great deal of what for the achievement of the ends of the group are irrelevant symbolic activities, though these activities may at the same time satisfy some important personality needs (1974:68).

Formal organization may thus be markedly more efficient than informal organization. It may also be very difficult to achieve and maintain.

This realization leads Cohen to an examination of the changing organizational fortunes experienced by the Nigerian Hausa under colonial and independent regimes. A colonial policy of indirect rule allowed and fostered corporate organization of tribal entities. With independence, the politics of nationalism overtook those of tribalism. Distinctiveness and corporateness of ethnic groups lost official sanction. Hausa organization in Ibadan was directly and swiftly undermined:

> Their community was no longer officially recognized as an exclusive 'tribal' group and the support which had been given by the colonial government to the authority of the Hausa chief was withdrawn. The weakening position of the chief affected not only the organization of the functions of communication, decision-making, and co-ordination of policy within the quarter, but also the very distinctiveness of the community because it was no longer possible for the chief to coerce individuals to act in conformity with the corporate interests of the group (Cohen 1974:103).

In the power context of independent Nigeria, the Hausa were prevented from retaining their polity. They turned, with a vengeance, to ritual. The majority of Ibadan Hausa were initiated into a mystical Islamic sufi brotherhood, halting, according to Cohen, the "disintegration of the bases of the exclusiveness and identity" (1974:104) of the

Hausa. Thus, a new "myth of distinctiveness" was created: "The community was now a superior, puritanical, ritual community, a religious brotherhood distinct from the masses of Yoruba Muslims in the city, complete with their separate Friday mosque, Friday congregation and a separate cemetery" (Cohen 1974:104).

Politically marginalized groups—at least Cohen's Hausa—resort then to traditional or nontraditional symbols for the articulation of political and economic interests. We can logically expect the converse: corporately organized groups need to rely less on the manipulation of symbols. In a sense, the organizational "weight" is taken off traditional institutions of ritual, kinship, and friendship. What happens to these traditional, normative institutions—which may once have served very forcefully to articulate political interests and maintain group boundaries—when such organizing weight is removed, placed instead on a corporate polity? This question will be one of my central concerns and will be matched with a second. How does the corporate polity of an ethnic group fare in the arenas of resource competition in southern Sonora? What are the outcomes of contests joined between the Yaqui and an array of local, regional, and national interests?

THE STUDY OF YAQUI ETHNICITY

Trained observers invariably agree that Yaquis have successfully battled repeated attempts by Spaniards and Mexicans to destroy their ritual expressions, co-opt their political institutions, and control their productive land (see Spicer 1954, 1961; Beals 1945; Erasmus 1967; Bartell 1965). Indeed, Sonoran Yaqui society is the archetype for Spicer's (1971, 1976) concept of the "persistent identity system." Spicer outlines two major facets of such systems: first, a "coherent sense of collective identity" (Spicer 1976:6), and second, the individual's relation to, or participation in, this collective identity (Spicer 1971:799). The first involves the realm of public symbols and their meanings. In persistent identity systems, as Spicer notes, "the meanings of the symbols consist of beliefs about historical events in the experience of the people through generations" (Spicer 1971:796). The second facet is a necessary complement to any theory of symbolic behavior:

> What we are dealing with here are beliefs and sentiments, learned like other cultural elements, that are associated with particular symbols, such as artifacts, words, role behaviors, and ritual acts. . . . The display and manipulation of the symbols calls forth sentiments and stimulates the affirmation of beliefs on the part of the individuals who participate in the collective identity system (Spicer 1971:796).

Spicer thus lays the theoretical groundwork for the examination of the relation between collective symbols and individual sentiments. In his scheme, however, more emphasis is placed on the historical development of identity systems than on contemporary symbolic action. This focus is codified in his primary definition of symbols as "beliefs about historical events." He identifies the historical transition through which these beliefs crystallize and acquire sanctity: the "oppositional process" of ". . . continued conflict between these peoples and the controllers of the surrounding state apparatus. The conflict has occurred over issues of incorporation and assimilation into the larger whole" (Spicer 1971:797).

Ironically, the very success that Yaquis have shown in resisting assimilation and incorporation into Mexican society may render Spicer's analytical approach to ethnic persistence inappropriate to an understanding of contemporary Yaqui society and culture. Spicer acknowledges this possibility in *The Yaquis: A Cultural History* (1980). By the mid twentieth century,

> . . . the development of the Yaqui sense of identity had proceeded to a point of clarity of definition such that its persistence no longer necessarily depended on the continuation of the type of community, and hence of tradition transmission, which had existed throughout their history from the 1600s to the late 1900s (1980: 303).

For most contemporary Yaquis this ethnic "clarity of definition" is undeniable. But to focus on the symbolic consequences of the oppositional process, as Spicer is inclined to do, gives insufficient attention to the structural consequences of that process. The Yaqui struggle in southern Sonora was simultaneously a fight for cultural integrity and for political autonomy. Subsequent sections of this chapter will develop some theoretical guidelines for analyzing the complex phenomena of ethnicity. Despres's hypothesized relation between competitive advantage and the persistence of identities will form the basis for examining Yaqui belief and behavior in the volatile political arena of southern Sonora.

ETHNICITY AS A CATEGORICAL PHENOMENON

Transactions and Identity

In *Ethnic Groups and Boundaries*, Fredrik Barth (1969) shaped a dominant trend in anthropological studies of ethnicity: the scrutiny of structured interaction across ethnic boundaries, joined with an examination of criteria for ascribed and achieved membership in ethnic groups. The key tenet in Barth's investigations of ethnic identity and group boundaries—the theory of transaction—is to be found in his earlier programmatic work, *Models of Social Organization* (Barth 1966).

In *Models*, Barth defines *transactions* as "those sequences of interaction which are systematically governed by reciprocity" (Barth 1966:4). The strategy that governs transaction or interaction between individuals is the attempt of each party to ensure that the value gained for himself is equal to or greater than the value lost. Broadly, transaction refers to material or immaterial "items" or "prestations," for example, animals, food, labor, power, prestige, or trust (see Kapferer 1976:1). Formally stated, Barth's claim is that

where for actor A, $x < y$, and for actor B, $x > y$ (see Barth 1966:13).

For Barth, the utility of the transactional model lies in relating individual choice to the constraining circumstances of statuses, obligations, and values. He employs transactions in two manners: first, as a device for understanding how stereotypic role behaviors are produced by individual choice as well as by the obligations inherent in statuses, and second, for comprehending how disparate values may be altered through choice and interaction.

Erving Goffman's (1959) early work provides the impetus for the first use of transaction by Barth. Recognizing the static nature of status and the dynamic nature of role, Goffman argues that actors, in the initial stages of successful interaction, must reach consensus on a definition of the situation. This agreement is essential for selecting which of a person's many statuses is applicable to the situation. And, in the process of defining the situation and closing in on the appropriate statuses, regular stereotypic forms of behavior are generated. These forms of behavior, which Goffman and Barth term "roles," are thus not direct outcomes of status obligations. Rather, they are the outcomes of the process of communicating one's own definition of the situation to other actors. Here Goffman introduces the strategy of "impression management," whereby individuals, in any given situation, act so as to overcommunicate relevant statuses and undercommunicate inapplicable statuses.

Goffman deals primarily with the first use of transaction noted above: the transition from status to role. Barth is more interested in the second potentiality: the feedback process by which "instances of transaction affect in turn both the canons and distribution of values, and in part compel the 'correction' of these values" (Barth 1966:15).

The self-regulating function of transaction is the most important theoretical claim put forward by Barth, structuring his entire approach to ethnic boundaries and their maintenance. It is also a vulnerable tenet, leading to the conclusion of total or near-total functional and conceptual integration of culture.

Barth initially defines integration as the "extent to which phenomena constitute a system, share determinacy and consistency in relation to each other." The phenomena he scrutinizes are values, defined as "people's principles and scales of evaluation, as well as . . . such abstracted amounts or ratings of preferences which appear to be relatively stable over time" (Barth 1966:12). More specifically, values are "views about significance, worthwhileness, preferences in/for things and actions" (Barth 1966:12). Thus the problem becomes one of understanding the process by which consistency is created among possibly disparate evaluations and preferences.

Key to this process, as might be expected, is the operation of repeated transactions. Barth's argument here is crucial, so it is necessary to quote extensively:

> The offer or performance of such a transaction has two aspects which concern us here. Firstly, prestations 'x' and 'y' are made transitive to each other, in the sense that they must be compared and made commensurate and interchangeable both by 'A' and 'B'. This means that the values of 'x' and 'y' must be compared. If their significance and worthwhileness cannot be judged by the same canons, some overarching value principle between those disparate canons must be constructed. This constitutes a step in creating consistency of values. . . . Whatever the basis for the transaction may be, through it the parties receive information indicative of each other's principles and scales of evaluation. Through repeated transactions I would argue that these aspects are reinforced, and that the values applying to those prestations which flow between parties become systemized and shared. They become systemized because when, and only when, we are faced with the repeated necessity of choice, are we forced to resolve dilemmas and make some kind of comparison between, and evaluation of, the alternatives with which we are presented. They become shared, or institutionalized, because in groping for a solution to the dilemmas, we prefer to use other people's experience as our guide rather than risk the errors implied in a trial-and-error procedure. Thus we adopt their principles of evaluation, and collectively grope towards a consistency of values (Barth 1966:13–14).

For transactions between actors to occur, the "items" must be commensurable since, by definition, each actor has to receive something of equal or greater value than that which he offers. Where items are not initially commensurable, they must be made so by the construction of a covering value. Thus, through repeated transactions, increasingly consistent preferences and evaluation scales are formed.

Anthony Wallace has effectively challenged the fundamental premise underlying Barth's theory of transaction and cultural integration: that successful and continued interaction demands a mutual agreement on values (Wallace 1970; see also Paine 1974:18–23; Salisbury 1976). From the results of field and clinical research Wallace is led to the conclusion that many social systems "simply will not work if all participants share common knowledge of the system." Cognitive nonuniformity serves two crucial purposes. First, it allows for the development of a more complex social system than can be comprehended by any and all of its participants. Second, it relieves participants of the burden of discovering and understanding each other's cognitions and motivations. All that is required for successful interaction, Wallace claims, is that individuals be able to predict the behavior of others under various circumstances, "irrespective of knowledge of their motivation." Thus predictable, the behavior of others can be "predictably related to one's own actions," calling forth appropriate responses (1970:35).

Wallace's conclusions still need to be adequately tested. Nevertheless, they demand a skeptical response to Barth's contention of inevitable and more-or-less rapid integration of values through interaction. One must, in turn, be cautious of Barth's approach to ethnic boundary maintenance, for it is integrally founded on the transaction-integration thesis of *Models*.

In his programmatic introduction to *Ethnic Groups and Boundaries*, Barth (1969:17) structures his theory around three elements. First, ethnic identity is viewed as a status and as such "implies a series of constraints on the kinds of roles an individual is allowed to play" (Barth 1969:17). As a status, ethnicity has both ascribed and achieved aspects: an individual's identity is often, for example, ascribed to him by virtue of his "origin and background" (Barth 1969:13). The second key element in Barth's theory is that an individual's ethnic identification demands validation by others. This process of validation requires a "sharing of criteria for evaluation and judgment" (Barth 1969:15) of a person's role performance by other members of the ethnic group. Thus, over and above the ascribed factors of origin and background, an individual must achieve his ethnic status through the requisite performances. As Barth argues:

> Since ethnic identity is associated with a culturally specific set of value standards, it follows that there are circumstances where such an identity can be moderately successfully realized, and limits beyond which such success is precluded. I will argue that ethnic identities will not be retained beyond these limits, because allegiance to basic value standards will not be sustained where one's own comparative performance is utterly inadequate (Barth 1969:25).

These first two elements of the thesis serve to define ethnicity as a categorical and subjective phenomenon. Individuals come to be defined, categorically, as belonging to one ethnic group or another, and this dichotomization is founded on the measurement of an individual's actions against subjective criteria of evaluation and judgment.

To this point, Barth's theory is largely indistinguishable from more traditional views of ethnic groups as dichotomized populations whose members share a set of values or cultural configurations. The appendage of a third element, drawn directly from his earlier *Models*, does differentiate his theory, however. Barth concerns himself with the logical implications of transaction and integration in situations of interaction between members of different ethnic groups, sharing different sets of values and evaluations. Thus, ". . . where persons of different cultures interact, one would expect these differences to be reduced, since interaction both requires and generates a congruence of codes and values—in other words, a similarity or community of culture" (Barth 1969:16).

It follows from this assumption that the entire process of ethnic boundary maintenance is one of careful structuring of contact and interaction situations. Structuring, according to Goffman (1959), is governed by a systematic set of rules prescribing and proscribing the content of interaction. These rules allow for ". . . articulation in some sectors or domains of activity . . . preventing interethnic interaction in other sectors, and thus insulating parts of the cultures from confrontation and modification" (Barth 1969:16).

To the extent that the claims of Anthony Wallace (1970) are valid, we should find little evidence of such a systematic set of interaction rules. Alternatively, if Barth's theory of transactions and value integration is correct, these insulating rules will be paramount. Presumably, the most crucial parts of culture that must be so insulated are the sets of evaluations and judgments pertaining to ethnic identity. If these facets were to become subject to transaction, they would inevitably be modified in the direction of consistency across two societies. Ethnic differences would then disappear; ethnic boundaries would evaporate.

Pivotal and Peripheral Attributes
of Ethnic Identity

While Barth's program affords a variety of suggestive approaches to ethnic identity and boundary maintenance and has indeed stimulated excellent empirical work (see essays in Barth 1969; Braroe 1975; Hicks and Kertzer 1972), it is not entirely adequate for an understanding of Yaqui ethnic identity. Sonoran Yaquis have little concern for the achievement of ethnic status through successful performance. Rather, Yaqui identity is essentially ascribed, on the basis of "origin and background." Failure to perform adequately has little effect on the ethnic status—the rights and duties—of individuals.

A more productive approach to Yaqui identity may be built around the insights of S.F. Nadel into the structure of roles. Roles, to Nadel, are "interconnected series of attributes." These attributes, however, are "not all equivalent or of the same order . . . any roles series has a definite structure, of a hierarchical kind, in which the various attributes occupy places of graded relevance" (Nadel 1957:31). He distinguished three grades of attributes:

(1) *peripheral:* their variation or absence does not affect the perception or effectiveness of the role which is being performed; in other words, they are understood to be optional or to admit of alternatives.
(2) *sufficiently relevant:* that is, sufficiently firmly entailed in the series, for their variation or absence to make a difference in the perception and effectiveness of the role, rendering its performance noticeably imperfect or incomplete.
(3) *basic or pivotal:* their absence or variation changes the whole identity of the role, and hence the interaction it would normally provoke (Nadel 1957:32).

The immediate methodological problem, as Nadel recognized, is to identify the pivotal attributes of roles. He suggested that the "simplest and quickest way to decide what a role 'basically' means is to refer to the semantic content of the conventional role name" (Nadel 1957:33). The difficulty with this approach, quickly acknowledged by Nadel, is that role names are "shorthand symbols for the array of properties which the entity named is presumed to possess" (Nadel 1957:33). This "array" logically subsumes sufficiently relevant and peripheral attributes as well as pivotal ones.

An alternative approach to identifying pivotal attributes of roles is suggested by Ward Goodenough (1969). More specifically than Nadel, he ties the concepts of role and status to rights and duties: "As used in jurisprudence, rights and duties are two sides of the same coin. In any relationship A's rights over B are the things he can demand of B; these same things are what B owes A, B's duties in the relationship" (Goodenough 1969:313).

For the analysis of Yaqui ethnic identity as a status, I will take these rights and duties as primary. Thus, basic or pivotal attributes of this status will simply be those which, upon empirical examination, serve to allocate the rights and duties of Yaqui ethnic status to individuals. In other words, the rights and duties attendant upon Yaqui status are allocated to individuals by the fact that they evidence certain pivotal attributes. In this sense, Nadel's sufficiently relevant and peripheral attributes are of the same order. Presence of these attributes has no effect on the allocation of the rights and duties of a given role or status.

Nadel proceeds to define two types of roles: *recruitment* and *achievement*. The first encompasses roles where "the governing attribute is an inevitable or fortuitous state in which the individuals find themselves; it then entails the 'further characteristics'—all the other attributes in the series—as consequences or concomitants" (Nadel 1957:36). In achievement roles, on the other hand, "the governing property is a behavioral attribute . . . which individuals are free to choose as a goal or objective, the 'further characteristics' are entailed in it either as necessary preconditions or again as consequences and concomitants" (Nadel 1957:36). Essentially (Nadel's subtle arguments to the contrary [1957:37−41]), his recruitment roles are identical to Barth's "ascribed statuses," roles founded upon properties over which the individual has no control: "They may be physiological characteristics (sex, age), semantic features, [or] qualities of descent and extraction . . ." (Nadel 1957:23).

With these equivalencies, Barth's emphasis on ethnic identity as an achieved status (or role) can be rephrased in terms of Nadel's framework: Barth views the "governing property" of ethnicity as lying in the realm of "sufficiently relevant" (and perhaps even "peripheral") attributes. A "noticeably imperfect or incomplete performance" of these attributes, Barth would imply, dictates that one's claim to a specific ethnic identity will be abrogated. The alternative approach, more useful in understanding the Yaqui case, is to give primacy to the recruitment or ascription facet of ethnic identity, in which "origin and background" serve as the pivotal attributes around which rights and duties are allocated. Neither sufficiently relevant nor peripheral attributes have important effects on the allocation of rights and duties of Yaqui ethnic status.

Classifying and the Nature of the Observer

Reducing ethnic identity to pivotal attributes, to rights and duties, to ascription, neglects the important function played by secondary attributes in the perception of ethnic groups and in the ready classification of specific individuals to discrete ethnic groups. To accept Barth's ideas on the careful structuring of interaction across ethnic lines so as to prevent the "integration," and hence loss, of distinct values systems is unnecessary. Individuals must classify their interactants for purposes of generating appropriate behavior and predicting responses. And, empirically, it may be determined that "the reciprocal recognition of ethnic differentiation is a prominent factor in many critical spheres of human relations" (Thompson 1974:106). Likewise, categorizing processes proceed at a group level, in the construction and maintenance of ethnic stereotypes. Discussing ethnicity in Yucatan, Richard Thompson suggests:

In reality, there may be few objective differences between a given Mestizo [Indian] and Catrín, perhaps no more than the minimal difference in clothing style or footwear. In addition, each may have kinsmen in both ethnic groups. But ethnic stereotypy is a persistent conditioning force in interpersonal relations. It provides the individual with a structured set of preconceptions that may not change much under the pressure of reality (Thompson 1974:108).

While Thompson relates stereotypy to processes of individual interaction across ethnic lines, it is equally functional for noninteraction. For the Canadian plains, Niels Braroe observes:

> To Indians, strictly White spheres of action are mysterious, dark places where vaguely specified but nefarious things go on. . . . In Short Grass, the Indians' ignorance of White ways of life make it possible for them to construct fantasy pictures of White impurity. They can thus rescue a degree of self-worth to the extent that they deny it to Whites; and this is made possible by the absence of conflicting information about Whites. Thus ignorance is stabilizing, that is, it averts open conflict (Braroe 1975:182).

Categorization, then, may proceed for a variety of purposes, from the assignment of membership rights and duties, to behavioral predictions, to stereotyping of group characteristics. At each level, we can expect corresponding differences in the nature of information processed by the classifier.

We may also expect an interplay between the locus of the observer and the information processed in classification—the attributes of ethnic status which the classifier attends to in placing specific individuals into discrete groups or constructing stereotypes. We need, in short, a typology of classifiers to correlate with typologies of attributes and of categorizing motives.

Shibutani and Kwan (1965:40–41) provide an easy typology of observers with their distinction between "ethnic category" and "ethnic identity." The former refers to the "way a person or persons defines or describes a collection of *other* people." It thus includes the labeling procedures by which outsiders categorize ethnic units. Elements of the label may include readily observable traits such as clothing, housing, language use; labels may also be founded on less apparent markers, perhaps racial or national origin in phenotypically nondiscrete groups. Ethnic identity, by contrast, is the characterization made from within, the group's own definition of self. But ethnic identity, like ethnic category, may apparently cover the gamut of ethnic status attributes, from pivotal to secondary markers.

A more discriminating typology of observers and observed may be founded on Erving Goffman's (1963:51) concepts of "personal identity" and "social identity." Conceiving of identification "in the criminological and not the psychological sense"—discovering "who" rather than "what" one is—Goffman is most precise about the nature of personal identity. This comprises the ". . . positive marks or identity pegs, and the unique combination of life history items that comes to be attached to the individual with the help of these pegs for his identity" (Goffman 1963:57). Personal identity, in other words, is the collection of biographical information that one individual, the observer, has regarding another person. Some observers—the "unknowing," the utter strangers—inevitably maintain no personal biography of a given individual. Thus, such observers recognize or categorize individuals on the basis of social identity. Unlike the idiosyncrasis of personal identity, social identity comprises the more structured realm of role repertoires and the rights and duties pertaining to those roles (Goffman 1963:63–65). Hence, an observer, an "other," when faced with the task of recognizing and categorizing a given individual, will focus on that individual's social identity when this "other" has no personal biography on the individual. From the perspective of the individual to be classified the range of "others" is divided into those who "know him," or maintain a personal biography on him, and those who do not know him but can recognize him on the basis of social information, information indicative of the individual's role repertoire. However inelegantly, I will term these two sets of observers as "personal others" (or biographical others") and "social others."

Goffman's classification of "others" provides an important modification to Shibutani and Kwan's typology of in-group and out-group observers. For Goffman's "personal others" can clearly belong to either the in-group or the out-group, to one ethnic group or another. Likewise, "social others" may belong to one group or another: information on a given individual may cross-cut ethnic lines.

Observers, Attributes, and Purposes

To highlight the importance of the observer, I return briefly to Nadel's discussion of the internal structures of roles. Nadel conceives of role (P) as a series of attributes including pivotal ones (p), sufficiently relevant ones (a,b), and finally, peripheral attributes (I,M,N), admitting of alternatives or options $(/)$. Thus the internal structure of any role can be symbolized as

$$P = p,a,b,. \ldots .I/M/N \quad \text{(Nadel 1957:31)}.$$

Actual roles differ widely in the degree of entailment among attributes; however, "not all attributes are equally good ones, either because they are not sufficiently exclusive to a given role or because they are not sufficiently firmly integrated ('entailed') in the series" (Nadel 1957:30). For example, an ethnic ascription, based on parentage, may in fact have no sufficiently relevant attributes associated with it, no attributes

Table 1.1   Elements In the Ethnic Classification Process.

Purpose of Classification
  a. stereotypy: group-level moral evaluations
  b. interpersonal relations: individual-level classifications for purposes of interaction
  c. categorical group membership: individual-level identification for purposes of allocating rights and duties

Relationship of Classifier to Object
  a. personal other: of same or different group as object
  b. social other: of same or different group

Nature of Role Attributes Uses as Information in Classification Process
  a. pivotal or basic
  b. peripheral or secondary

Degree of Entailment of Role Attributes
  a. strongly entailed
  b. weakly entailed

Basis for Categorical Group Membership
  a. ascription
  b. achievement or performance

that are firmly entailed. Such a role may, however, entail weakly a series of peripheral attributes, largely optional and variable. The fact that these peripheral attributes *are* entailed, if weakly, allows them to be used as markers of an individual's ethnic ascription. But, by definition, they are not pivotal"; they do not serve as governing properties of the role, and hence cannot be used exclusively and with certainty to classify individuals into discrete groups. Thus, when the allocation of rights and duties of ethnic membership is at stake, weakly entailed attributes are unreliable.

The process of ethnic classification is, in short, multifaceted. Table 1.1 summarizes the complexities involved in this process. Chapter 3 will draw loosely upon this scheme for an understanding of Yaqui ethnic categorization.

THE INSTRUMENTALITY OF ETHNIC IDENTITY

If ethnicity implicates processes of categorization, it also is an instrumental phenomenon. Ethnic categories are drawn and maintained for a purpose. Some anthropologists appear sufficiently satisfied that the instrumentality of ethnic identities lies in the very process of classifying. Braroe, quoted above, reads purpose into the stereotypy process. Barth views classification and consequent structuring of interaction as preservers of cultural integrity. Leo Despres, on the contrary, seeks to treat ethnic identities and ethnic boundaries as virtual epiphenomena of resource competition. It is worth reviewing his central thesis:

With respect to material resources, to the extent that these [ethnic] status claims confer competitive advantage upon the populations who assert them, social boundaries supportive of categorical ethnic identities will persist. Conversely, when such claims confer no particular advantage in this regard, ethnic boundaries weaken and the assertion of ethnic identities appears to diminish (Despres 1975:199).

Despres awards primacy to the corporate organization of ethnic groups for political and economic purposes. Dependent upon this organization are two "residual" phenomena: the categorical ethnic identities of population aggregates, and the ethnic ascriptions of specific individuals. Thus, if corporate organization along ethnic lines offers no competitive advantage, the ethnic identities of populations and individuals become deactivated, superfluous.

Current social reality amply attests to the pervasiveness of political-economic motivations among ethnic groups. Diverse groups, in urban and rural settings, in developing and developed countries, are employing ethnic symbols in the attempt to overturn inequities in the distribution of resources (see the essays in Bennett 1975). The results have been varied, leading in some cases to increased control of resources and eventual economic improvement, to increased ethnic solidarity with little alteration of dominant-subordinate political and economic structures, and in other cases to ethnocide in contexts of overwhelmingly superior and intractable political power. The diverse outcomes result from many factors, affording ample scope for empirical investigation.

Despres's claim constitutes a useful working hypothesis for the analysis of ethnicity, due to its grounding in social reality and to its parsimonious ordering of the several dimensions of ethnic phenomena: corporately organized groups, individual ethnic ascriptions, and the categorical identity of population aggregates. It is, however, nothing more than a working hypothesis. Can ethnicity, and particularly Yaqui ethnicity, be adequately interpreted in a political-economic framework—one which gives primacy to the interplay between organized ethnic groups and the economic and political structures which encompass them?

Before Despres's position can be juxtaposed to Sonoran Yaqui society, some immediate difficulties with his proposition must be addressed. Despres takes inadequate account of the range of circumstances determining the *effectiveness* of resource competition. Effectiveness lies in part in the group's ability to organize itself and express its demands, that is, in its ability to become a corporate group. Equally important, however, is the nature of the surrounding political and economic structure. Focusing on such "encapsulating political structures," on politically dominant states, F. G. Bailey provides a useful typology for understanding the differential successes of ethnic movements. Encapsulating societies manifest, in Bailey's terms, a "composite interference variable," including the "determination to interfere," as well as the "resources to make interference possible" (Bailey 1969:152). Thus, apparently dominant states ". . . might not have the resources to interfere within the encapsulated structure, even if they wished to do so; or they might not consider it worth their while because the payoff for successful intervention might exceed the cost of the intervention" (Bailey 1969:150).

Several outcomes, differing both in determination and capability for interference, can be delineated. At one extreme, "encapsulation is merely nominal, merely, one might say, a matter of geography" (Bailey 1969:149). This situation may arise when the dominant structure cannot or will not intervene in the politics and economics of encapsulated societies for lack of adequate resources or acceptable payoffs. The second possibility is one of predation, where leaders of the dominant polity "do not concern themselves with what goes on inside Structure A [the encapsulated structure] so long as the people who live under it pay the revenue" (Bailey 1969:150). This possibility also implies a limitation on the capability of the dominant society to interfere more radically.

A third type is indirect rule, founded upon "an agreement to leave intact the broad structure of A, providing this does not do violence to certain fundamental principles . . . which are embodied in Structure B [the dominating polity]" (Bailey 1969:151). Such an option, Bailey argues, may result from a limit on Structure B's determination to interfere, on a "moral conviction that people are entitled to their own beliefs and should be allowed, as far as possible, to preserve cherished institutions" (Bailey 1969:151). Or it may derive from an assessment of costs and payoffs of intervention: "indirect rule is cheaper than a radical reorganization of the political structure of A. To reorganize means to create conditions of uncertainty, to risk explosions and to incur for certain the expenditure of resources involved in re-training people, even when this is possible" (Bailey 1969:151).

The final possibility, at the extreme from nominal encapsulation, is integration, a radical transformation of the dominated society. Of this possibility, Bailey notes:

> The basis for such a decision [to force integration] is likely to be compounded of many elements: moral repugnance for what goes on in Structure A is certainly one, often phrased in terms of the removal of iniquitous 'feudal' institutions and their replacement by socialist democratic institutions: allied with this goes another kind of moral attitude, that the people of Structure A should devote their energies to a wider polity than their own parish group. This is in fact a judgment that the costs of incorporating the personnel of

Structure A into Structure B will be more than offset by the resources which they put into Structure B. This position is adapted by
virtually all the developing nations: they seek, with varying degrees
of determination and success, to put an end to casteism or com-
munalism or tribalism or regionalism and to make a united nation
(Bailey 1969:151; see also Geertz 1973:255–310).

By examining the variable capabilities and determinations of
dominant structures to exert themselves over encapsulated groups,
Bailey helps us to understand the differential success experienced by
dominated ethnic groups in competition for resources. Ethnic groups
may attempt to gain increased control of resources and increased
autonomy, yet may fail in the face of opposition from a highly determined and capable state. Alternatively, limitation on the capabilities
and determination of the dominant group may set the stage for a
successful effort by an encapsulated society to increase its control over
resources.

Further difficulty with Despres's proposition lies in his narrow
definition of "resources" as environmental components such as land,
water, technology. Implicit in Bailey's discussion of encapsulation,
though, is a more expansive notion of resources: human and material
items which, when controlled by a leader, serve to enhance his power.
But neither Bailey nor Despres deals adequately with an additional
arena of control and power, the *system of exchange and distribution*.
Analyzing the genesis and maintenance of stratification, Carol Smith
focuses on such "differential access to or control over the means of
exchange." Thus

> . . . variation in stratification systems is related to types of exchange
> between producers and non-producers as they affect and are af-
> fected by the spatial distribution of the elite and the level of com-
> mercialization in the region and beyond. This approach is found to
> be particularly useful for understanding certain colonial and
> neocolonial cases of stratification where neither landholdings nor
> other productive means are alienated from the peasant producers
> and yet "surplus value" is clearly extracted from the peasantry
> (Smith 1976:310).

Smith applies this perspective to colonial and contemporary Guatemala, noting that Indians retain ownership of productive resources—
essentially land and labor. Yet, she observes, "while land and independent Indian labor are the only significant productive resources in the
region, landless Ladinos are clearly wealthier than landed Indians"
(Smith 1975:116). The Yaqui region of Sonora replicates in many
regards the area of Smith's work in northwest Guatemala and points to
another factor in the competition for resources. To the extent that
enclaved ethnic groups control the networks of distribution (and they

seldom do), they reduce the capability of dominant states to interfere locally.

In sum, we can increase the comparative utility of Despres's hypothesis by taking explicit account of conditions under which resource competition by a corporately organized ethnic group is likely to be successful. Simply put, competition is more likely to be successful under conditions of low determination or the low capability of the dominant political group to interfere. Thus, although corporate organization of an ethnic group is no mean accomplishment, it may nevertheless lead to insignificant changes in the structure of domination. It may be ineffectual in reducing the control exerted by a highly determined and capable state.

Ethnic Boundaries and Resource Competition: Summary

In the preceding sections questions were raised about two dominant approaches to the anthropology of ethnicity: that of Barth on the categorization process and that of Despres on the instrumentality of ethnic identity and ethnic group organization. To balance Barth's emphasis on the achievement or performance aspect of categorization, I have tried to resurrect the importance of ethnic ascription. To Despres's focus on instrumentality, I have argued for a closer examination of the external context. The nature and strength of outside interference may determine both the type of organization allowed to an ethnic enclave and the success or failure of the enclave in the struggle for resources.

These additions and modifications by no means destroy the basic theoretical designs of Barth or Despres. They do, however, seek to make the treatment of categorization and instrumentality more amenable to an analysis of Yaqui ethnicity, politics, and resource competition. They seek, in short, to provide the conceptual frame for responding to the questions raised previously: how does the Yaqui corporate organization work in the struggle for resources in Sonora, and what are the ramifications of this polity for other aspects of Yaqui ethnicity?

CHAPTER 2

Society and History
in the Yaqui Valley

The District of Guaymas is the richest in agricultural resources; containing as it does the great valley of the Yaqui river, comprising nearly one million acres of highly productive lands, on which may be grown readily cotton, sugar cane, coffee, oranges, limes, lemons, and all tropical fruits, tobacco, wheat, corn, beans, tomatoes, peas, in fact almost any product of the torrid and temperate zone. A large irrigation company has just completed a great canal forty miles long which carries water sufficient to irrigate six hundred thousand acres of land. The company is arranging to colonize these lands with colonists from Europe. They are located on the south side of the river. On the north side private land owners have smaller irrigation works which cover tracts of land sufficiently large to assure the dignity of principalities were they in Europe. Such is the tract in the vicinity of Potam, which Messrs. Charles and Frank Cranz are preparing to plant to cotton. On both sides of the river are the "pueblo" lands of the Yaquis, set apart for their use and accepted by these Indians in the recent treaty of peace signed at Ortiz in May, 1897. The lands comprise some forty thousand acres than which no more fertile can be found anywhere in the world. With their well known industry the Yaquis will soon bring all that great area to a high state of productiveness, and their frugality will make the seven "pueblos" into which they are divided, the richest communities of the kind in the world (J. R. Southworth 1897).

John Southworth's optimism in 1897 was firmly grounded on a vast stretch of rich alluvial soil, an impressive river running incongruously through the Sonoran desert, and a development-oriented Porfirian elite whose local representatives were in tight control of state politics. The Yaqui delta had incontestable potential at the end of the nineteenth century and would later become the locus of Mexico's agricultural revolution. But Southworth's enthusiasm was premature. He perceived the themes that would dominate the valley in the twentieth century: economic expansion, ethnic survival, and the unequal development of the north and south sides of the river—known locally as the *margen derecho* and *margen izquierda,* the right and left banks, and more recently as the Zona Indígena of Yaqui farmers and the Valle del Yaqui of Mexican growers and their rural proletariat. Southworth simply failed to foresee how these themes would be played out. Had he written *Sonora Ilustrado* a few years later, he might have been more prescient. By 1899, Yaquis were again fighting for their lands along the river. The Peace of Ortiz was simply an interlude in a long struggle, and the conflict has yet to be fully resolved.

Spicer has reconstructed and analyzed the sweep of Yaqui history, under the Jesuit mission system of colonial New Spain and under the garrisons and haciendas of independent Mexico (Spicer 1961, 1974, 1980). Syncretic Yaqui ritual no doubt crystallized with Jesuit guidance in New Spain and had persisted in its essential form into the twentieth century. Yaqui polity and economy were likewise structured in the mission communities but were not fully tested until Independence. The history of Sonora under Mexican rule is one of *caudillos,* of technocrats, and of foreign investors, all grappling with the problems of economic modernization and political stability. Yaquis were prime actors in these struggles as well, and the present Yaqui organization must be understood in this historical context.

RIVER TOWNS AND THE FIVE YA'URAM

The fighting that preceded the Peace of Ortiz quickly resumed after the treaty. For most Yaquis the struggle was directed toward preservation of the physical and organization bases of the Ocho Pueblos, the eight Indian towns along the lower river. Physically and socially, these pueblos took shape as Jesuit mission communities, suffered recurrent assaults in the nineteenth and early twentieth centuries by Mexican officials and North American colonists, and ultimately, under presidential decrees of Lázaro Cárdenas in 1937 and 1940, achieved a degree of territorial and organizational integrity. Several of the original townsites were lost years ago to Mexican settlers. Yaqui refugees from Cocorit now live in nearby Torocoba and Loma de Gaumuchil, and the Yaqui officials of the former pueblo of Bacum now conduct affairs from Bataconsica. The remaining six Yaqui towns are situated in the vicinity of the original missions. Torim sits amid wheat fields close to what is now the dried-up bed of the Yaqui River. Further down the river, Vicam pueblo remains a political center, but its resident population is vastly overshadowed by the Mexican commercial and military outpost of Estación Vicam, along the highway and railroad between Guaymas and Ciudad Obregón. Potam is now the largest center of Yaqui population; educated guesses by local residents place its population between five and nine thousand persons, Indian and Mexican. Rahum, Huirivis, and Belem (relocated to Pitahaya) have fully functioning civil and religious systems, but struggle to survive at the lower reaches of the canal network. Two substantial villages of Yaqui fishermen have developed at opposite ends of the Yaqui coastline: Guásimas near the northern boundary, and the seasonal shrimp camp of Lobos in the southern region. And, in the formidable Sierra Bacatete, numerous ranchos and communities of Yaquis are producing beef, cheese, and liquor for regional consumption (see map).

All villages now have electricity—a point of pride to Mexican development officials, but something of a humorless joke to local residents who find themselves forced to pay for poles, wire, and the circuitry needed to run current off the main pueblo avenues. The pueblos also have government clinics available to residents who qualify for Mexico's health care. And Potam, as the largest indigenous settlement, has its own Mexican police commissioner. He records births and deaths and presides over the parades of Independence Day.

The Mexican army, once garrisoned in the major Yaqui towns, is now consolidated at Estación Vicam, along with branch offices of the government bureaucracies. The Vicam army serves mainly as a check against drug smuggling, and its exercise yard has taken on the look of a motley air museum of confiscated planes. Lackadaisical infantry patrols along Federal Highway 15 no longer arouse the hatred of once-belligerent Yaquis. Local residents were shocked at the virulence of these troops in 1975, when campesinos invaded the wheat lands around San Ignacio, Río Muerto.

Within the eight Yaqui pueblos, a complex and intertwined political and religious organization carries out the affairs, civil and ceremonial, of the tribe. Five "realms of authority" or *ya'uram* predominate: the civil government, the military society, the church, *fiesteros,* and the *kohtumbre ya'ura,* "protectors of the traditions" (Spicer 1954:89).

The civil government of each town consists of a set of governors and their assistants and an informal body of elders. Through their spokesman, the *pueblo mayor,* elders transmit opinions and complaints of residents to the governors. In addition to the "first governor" and his assistants (usually four), there are several other civil positions of importance. A *secretario* acts as scribe, drawing up official documents for signature by the first governor. With the governor, pueblo mayor, and secretario two other signatures appear on important documents: the *capitán,* head of the military society, and the *comandante,* who is said to have jurisdiction over people and resources outside the pueblo proper, but within the traditionally recognized territories of each town.

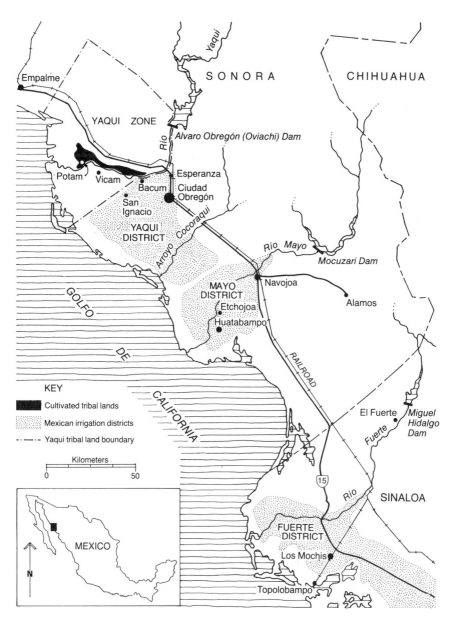

The Coast of Northwest Mexico, 1975

These five signatories conduct the daily civil affairs of the town. Important town or tribal matters receive an airing at open Sunday meetings in front of the *comunila* or *guardia*, a structure housing the civil offices. When such meetings are called, any member of the pueblo is free to speak, and decisions are made once the discussion moves toward consensus.

Each pueblo is theoretically autonomous and no single tribal "chief" is acknowledged by Yaquis; however, an incipient tribal hierarchy has developed. Informants speak of Vicam Pueblo as *primera cabecera*, "head pueblo," and of Potam as *segunda cabecera*, "second." The governors of Vicam Pueblo are, indeed, frequently asked for advice and consent by governors of other pueblos and important matters concerning the entire tribe are brought before a general assembly in Vicam Pueblo, with the governor of that town presiding.

The military society, in addition to participating in civil decisions through the office of its capitan, plays a major ritual in government. Its members, once responsible for mobilizing an effective Yaqui fighting organization, now function primarily as guardians of the civil authorities (Spicer 1954:70). They open and close meetings with a ritual maneuvering of flags and drums, they stand watch over the comunila housing the paraphernalia of civil authority, and they perform the Coyote dance, formerly a victory dance, but now carried out primarily at ceremonies honoring deceased members of the military society.

More elaborate than the military society, the Yaqui church organization is headed by varying numbers of *maestros*, those knowledgeable in Catholic liturgy. Maestros conduct all important religious observances in Yaqui territory. They are invariably accompanied by female *cantoras* who assist in the singing of hymns. The church organization also includes persons who tend the images and look after the church. Finally, the *matachines*, a dance group of extreme ceremonial importance, fall under the auspices of the maestros.

The remaining two ya'uram, the fiesteros and kohtumbre, are responsible for the organization and operation of important calendrical ceremonies. Fiesteros conduct the elaborate fiesta held yearly in honor of the patron of the pueblo's church. In Potam, the Tiniran fiesta (Day of the Trinity) in late May or early June occasions a ritual reenactment of the battle between Christians and Moors. Large amounts of food are collected and consumed and the surplus is distributed to local residents. Following the three-day event, fiesteros seek replacements to begin preparations for the next year.

The kohtumbre ya'ura have similar responsibilities of organization and conduct for the complex set of ceremonies during Lent and Holy Week. Two societies compose the kohtumbre: the *Kabayum* ("caballeros," horsemen) and the *Fariseos* (Judases, Pharisees). In the involved acting-out of the Passion during Lent, Fariseos are "bad soldiers" led by

Pilate, pursuing Christ. The kabayum, in turn, are the "good soliders," supporters, and protectors of Christ.

A final group of ritual specialists are autonomous from the five ya'uram but play crucial and highly visible roles in most Yaqui fiestas. The *pascola* dancers, "old men of the fiesta" (Spicer 1954:75), with their associated musicians and deer dancer, operate as ceremonial hosts. By joking, dancing, and recounting stories, they draw crowds, entertain, and heighten interest in religious observances.

THE CORPORATE YAQUI POLITY

Corporate polities are, as Abner Cohen and Leo Despres suggest, administratively efficient and, more often than not, politically successful. But the corporate organization of ethnic enclaves may also be difficult to attain and may vary in strength as a reflex to the dominant politics of nation and region. The nature of the present Yaqui civil government can be viewed in analytical terms borrowed from Despres (1975). The balance of this chapter will outline the larger economic setting for Yaqui polity and society—the Yaqui delta as it came under the control of Mexican and North American settlers.

Corporate political organizations are a complex of traits. Despres notes four: a common estate, a unitary set of external relations, a relatively exclusive body of common affairs, and a set of governmental procedures adequate to administer these affairs (Despres 1975:196). Drawing selectively from Max Weber, a fifth trait can be added: the extent to which the corporate group is either "autocephalous" or "heterocephalous." Autocephaly, to Weber, "means that the chief and his staff act by the authority of the autonomous order of the corporate group itself" (1947:148). When those leaders derive their legitimacy from outsiders, the corporate group may be characterized as heterocephalous. More so than Despres's flexible criteria for the presence or absence of corporate groups, this distinction allows a comparison of Yaqui government at different points in time. Since the Independence of Mexico, and most likely well before that time, Yaqui organization has been corporate. Since Independence, though, it has undergone cycles of autocephaly and heterocephaly, and it is in these cycles that the peculiarities of the Yaqui corporate polity are to be found.

Common Estate

Meyer Fortes has defined the characteristics of an estate as "a body of rights and duties related to property that is held by the corporation and transmitted by succession" (1969:293). With the Yaqui, such an estate exists at present on two levels. First, within each pueblo, land is held in common and distributed through the offices of the pueblo governor. In theory and frequently in fact, a Yaqui must petition the town officials for the right to settle a homesite and the right to plant farmland and utilize the wild resources of the *monte* (desert) and coast for purposes beyond family subsistence. The authority of pueblo officials over the land is in turn validated by Mexican officials. Irrigation agencies have a mandate to decide on the feasibility of watering and farming sections of pueblo land, but Yaquis desiring to farm such land must obtain the consent of their own town officials. At a tribal level as well, a common estate has existed legally since the presidential decrees of the late 1930s, which defined the territorial boundaries of the Yaqui Zona Indígena. Within this reserve, Mexican entrepreneurs can reside and work only at the sufferance of tribal officials, and the wild resources of the zone can be exploited by outsiders only with the permission of pueblo officers.

Unitary External Relations

Tribal policies toward the outside—toward the current array of development officials and the historical succession of claimants to Yaqui land and labor—have been complex. And such policies have seldom been strictly unitary. In fact, through the 1970s, full-scale factions existed in most of the river pueblos. One group, engagingly dubbing itself the *comunistas* after its seat of power, the pueblo comunila, included the holders of Yaqui government positions and their supporters. Their opposition revolved around the backers of an aborted attempt in the early 1970s to oust the Potam governors. Ideologically, the groups differed over the amount of external aid needed to develop the tribe's resources. The opposition, by and large, sought a full-scale development of agro-industry in the Yaqui Zone: local plants to mill wheat and process the oil-seed, *cártamo* (safflower), as well as Yaqui-controlled export facilities and direct marketing connections to foreign buyers. The comunistas feared the influx of Mexican technicians and entrepreneurs that such economic expansion would bring to the zone. They sought a more limited involvement in export agriculture—a continuation of the system of capitalization and distribution of farm products, coupled with demands for increased acreage under Yaqui control.

In 1975 and 1976 the two factions contested bitterly over the offices of several pueblos. But the passion of the dispute belied some important common interests. Opponents fully supported the pueblo governors in their political struggle to regain tribal territory lost to Mexican colonists. In turn the comunistas were entirely cognizant of the need to continue heavy reliance on outside financial aid and technical assistance—if such dependence could be maintained on terms favorable to the pueblos.

The factional struggles of the 1970s were real, but by no means new to the Yaquis. Charles Erasmus has reviewed the conflicts that arose in the late 1940s while the zone was still under the jurisdiction of the Mexican military. General Guerrero, chief of the garrison, attempted to impose his hand-chosen governors on the pueblos, hoping thereby to gain control of land revenues from the zone. His collaborators, *Yaquis militarizados,* were quickly opposed by a second faction of *Yaquis tradicionales,* and the pueblo governorships were contested for almost a decade. Erasmus recounts the dénouement:

> In 1958 a plebiscite was held by the federal government to determine which set of Yaqui leaders would be officially recognized in each pueblo. The traditionalists won in five pueblos and the collaborators in three. However, in the annual elections for 1959 the traditionalists returned to power in all of the eight pueblos (Erasmus 1967:26).

The factional dispute of the 1970s was equally intense, but it arose less from external interference than from internal differences of opinion, less from an aborted attempt to impose heterocephaly than from the growing pains of the autocephalous corporate group. The contestants in the 1970s fought narrowly over the question of *means* of economic development, not over the *ends*. Both groups professed allegiance to an ideal of tribal autonomy, to the integrity of Yaqui lands and Yaqui *costumbres,* to their culture. The opposition leaders sought to preserve this through full economic development. The incumbent governors sought it through limited adjustment to the existing situation of economic dependence.

An Exclusive Body of Common Affairs

Pueblo governors and their assistants retain a number of areas over which they alone have decision-making power. They have the authority to allocate land within the pueblos, to decide on the membership status of individuals in the tribe, to permit and tax the exploitation of wild resources by outsiders, to appoint officeholders and to negotiate as official representatives for the tribe with Mexican governmental agencies. And the pueblo governors, with the counsel of ceremonial leaders, are the final arbitrators in civil disputes among Yaquis within tribal territory.

In this preserve of exclusive affairs, Yaqui officials are currently autocephalous. As Weber suggests, autocephalous officials obtain legitimacy from within, by recognition of the members of the corporate group. Periodically, this legitimacy has been challenged. When questioned in 1976, the incumbent governors, involved at the time in tense negotiations with Mexican officials, refused to give up office. But this challenge was easily deflected. The officials stepped down as the immediacy of the outside negotiation slackened. Several months earlier, the governors had been challenged by disgruntled opponents demanding general pueblo elections. The governors sought to retain the traditional method of selection by ceremonial elders and active officeholders. Tribal autonomy in this case was upheld from the outside, by the commander of the Mexican army in Vicam. Both sets of Yaqui contenders took their cases to him and in a reasoned argument devoid of the opportunism of previous commanders in the zone, he ruled that he had no authority to judge such a dispute. Urging cooperation and understanding on both factions, he returned the issue directly to the tribe.

Adequate Administrative Procedures

Logistically, the pueblo and tribal governments have proven adequate to conduct their affairs. Regular and open meetings of the village officials—civil and ceremonial—are held at the guardias on Sundays. Complaints can be aired, and when the case warrants, village elders and officials will attempt to settle the issues by consensus. On matters affecting the entire tribe, extraordinary meetings of all Yaqui officials are convened in Vicam pueblo. At such gatherings delegations are selected to carry the Yaqui demands to the state offices in Hermosillo, to federal representatives at agency offices in Estación Vicam and Ciudad Obregón, and directly to the presidential offices and ministries of Mexico City.

For the last century, and indeed for the hundreds of years of contact preceding, Yaquis have struggled to preserve and strengthen this corporate polity. The history of this fight is now well known (Spicer 1961, 1974, 1980; Gouy-Gilbert 1983). At times, the tribe has lost its common lands, has been fractured into competing interests, and has been deprived of its power and authority to conduct its own affairs. At other times, under other circumstances, the corporate polity has waxed strong. This complex history is beyond the scope of the present report. Of more immediate need is to examine the development of southern Sonora's export economy. The fate of the contemporary Yaqui polity is rooted directly in this evolution.

ECONOMIC EXPANSION IN THE YAQUI VALLEY

When John Southworth observed Sonora in the final years of the nineteenth century, strategies to turn the Yaqui Valley into a major region of export agriculture had already been mapped. A railroad stretched from Nogales to Guaymas in 1883, providing roundabout connections between Mexico City and stations in Arizona and Texas. It was not until 1927 that a direct linkage to central Mexico—through the treacherous mountains of Nayarit—would be completed. Canal networks laced the plats of surveyors and land concessionaires in the valley. Construction would await the financing of North American entrepreneurs after the turn of the century. An adequate water supply to flood the canals would come much later.

By the end of the nineteenth century, a variety of crops had been tested and found productive in the valley, although they did not have the diversity claimed by Southworth at the time. The full potential of the alluvial soils would not be unlocked until the very expensive products of recent research were applied. By 1900, farm plots had been laid out for speculation, with provisions that 25 percent of the colonists would be North American. But settlers who would produce for the market were reluctant to come. Much of the land in the valley had remained in the hands of land companies and cattle-ranching hacendados. Full colonization of the river awaited a more stable peace with the Yaquis.

All of these factors were integral to the rise of export agriculture in southern Sonora, and some must be traced in more detail. They begin to explain how Yaqui society and economy came to be what they are at the present time.

Railroads, Land Speculation, and Revolt

In the nineteenth century, long before the development of national highways and motorized transport, railroads were the key to export economies. They reduced the costs of transportation considerably, opened isolated rural areas to distant markets, and made the ownership of land more lucrative than ever before (Coatsworth 1974:49). And in Mexico, racked by costly wars of regional separatism and foreign invasion in the decades following Independence, railroads afforded an entrée to international investment. Even after the Mexican Revolution of the twentieth century, the rewards to such investment were baldly acknowledged in U.S. government reports:

> The West Coast of Mexico was the scene of the last great railroad construction undertaking by the line of American transcontinental railway builders, the extension of the Southern Pacific Railroad from Guaymas to Tepic, down the West Coast, being due to the vision of men like Epes Randolph, who, with others, interested the late E. H. Harriman in the construction of this line and the development of this new empire, which combines so many potential opportunities for American enterprise and capital. Revolution in Mexico stopped construction through to Guadalajara, but the West Coast was given its first adequate transportation, and

stagnant communities received their stimulus of modern commerce and development by contact with the rest of the territory
and with the outer world (Bell and MacKenzie 1923:45).

In a more recent assessment of the social impact of the Mexican
rails, John Coatsworth is less positive:

A simultaneous process of integration and marginalization occurred, with some regions adjusting to new opportunities while
others declined into more or less permanent backwaters. In either
case, transport innovation was the cause of important shifts in crop
structure, estate management, labor arrangements, land tenure
patterns and rural welfare. Rural populations shared few of the
benefits of this modernization and frequently suffered as a result.
Often the only benefit the railroad brought was increased mobility,
the opportunity to escape the railroad's effects on rural social life
(Coatsworth 1974:49).

Beginning with the first Sonoran railroad concession in 1875, the
Yaqui Valley witnessed the full impact of these processes. In 1877, after
the initial concession was revoked for failure to commence construction, a new award was made to the Atchison, Topeka and Santa Fe
Company for a line connecting Guaymas to Nogales. The company
worked rapidly after 1880, and the Sonora Railway was completed,
reaching the port in 1883. An additional concession had already been
awarded to the North American, Robert Symon, to extend the rails to
the Río Yaqui. It was Symon's intent, according to Mexican ministry
reports, to open up the "immense coal lands" in the vicinity of the river.
His surveyors encountered logistical problems, and Symon requested
an extension. As the official reports summarize, however, "new
difficulties were presented by the incursions of barbarous Indians into
the state of Sonora, and by the state of insurrection of the inhabitants of
the Río Yaqui" (Coatsworth 1974:62). Symon never built his railroad. It
was not until 1907 that a connection with Navojoa across the Yaqui
River was completed (Bell and MacKenzie 1923:48). Mazatlán was
reached by 1909, and Tepic in the Sierras of Nayarit by 1912 (Bell and
MacKenzie 1923:48). The most difficult stretch, the one hundred miles
between Tepic and La Quemada near Guadalajara, was not finished
until 1927, finally completing the West Coast route from Nogales to
Mexico City.

Archetypal to a pattern throughout early Porfirian Mexico, the
continuing Yaqui resistance under the Indian leader Cajeme corre-
sponded closely to the activities of the railroad concessionaires
(Coatsworth 1974:49). But encroachment onto Yaqui lands, and consequent Yaqui resistance, were not inaugurated by the railroad surveys
of the 1870s. At intervals throughout the nineteenth century, Yaquis
took up arms to preserve their territory. At times, they battled indis-

Table 2.1 Claims to Terrenos Baldíos in Sonora.

Year	Hectares Claimed
1875	2,126
1876	29,255
1877	30,639
1878	42,973
1879	28,507
1880	99,377
1886	245,782
1888	244,797

Source: Coatsworth 1974:68.

criminately against the haciendas, mines, and ranchos ringing the Yaqui Valley. On other occasions, they joined the armies of state caudillos, with the purpose of exchanging military aid for the recognition of territorial integrity. By midcentury the policy had been relatively successful: Escudero (1849:100) estimates that only twenty *familias blancas,* or non-Yaqui families, were living in the eight pueblos. With mounting intensity, though, Sonoran militias and colonists assaulted the valley. In 1867 a force of five hundred Sonorans was established at Médano, where the Yaqui River flows into the Gulf of California, to patrol the Yaqui and Mayo valleys. A year later, the Yaqui force at Cocorit was defeated, and the survivors were murdered in the church of Bacum. Yaqui resistance was broken for nearly a decade (Acuña 1974; Stagg 1978; Spicer 1961, 1974, 1980; Hu-Dehart 1984).

In 1875, Jose María Leyva, known as Cajeme, precipitated a Yaqui and Mayo uprising against the haciendas and ranchos in southern Sonora. Aided by a civil war over the right to occupy the state governor's office, and by continuous Apache depredations in northern Sonora, Cajeme prolonged his leadership for more than a decade. In the spring of 1886, his Indian forces were finally routed by the Mexican general, Marcos Carillo, at two Yaqui strongholds—El Añil along the river and, two months later, at Buatachive in the sierras. Cajeme himself escaped to the Mayo region, to be captured a year later and executed on the streets of Cocorit.

The railroad concessions of the 1870s may have been little more than irritants contributing to this renewal of Yaqui resistance; rails would not bridge the Río Yaqui for years. But the repercussions of those awards were felt quickly throughout the state. "Vacant public lands," the *terrenos baldíos,* were claimed at a rapid rate. In 1875, petitions were made for only 2,000 hectares in Sonora. As the rail lines took shape, these claims rose sharply (Table 2.1).

The fate of "Baldío 8," one such grant in the Yaqui region, in the foothills north of Bacum, is instructive. The land was first deeded to

Messrs. Quaglia and Teruèl by the Secretary of Public Works in 1885, and to the commercial house of Luis Huller and Company in 1886. These two tracts were consolidated into a unit of 43,000 hectares and turned over to the Compañía Internacional Mexicana later in 1886. That company was also buying up lands in Lower California and the Isthmus of Tehuantepec. In 1889, the Mexican Land and Colonization Company of Connecticut took over the business of the Compañía Internacional and thereby acquired Baldío 8. Again in 1902, the still undeveloped land changed hands. Some 35,200 hectares of the baldío were transferred to the Yaqui River Land and Development Company in London. Over half the shares of stock in this company were owned by the Constructora Richardson, so Baldío 8 was added to Richardson's massive acquisitions in the valley (Compañía Constructora Richardson 1904–1927).

The Richardson Construction Company was but one of the land operations speculating in Sonoran properties, and its predominance in the Yaqui Valley would not come until late in the rule of Porfirio Díaz. With the defeat of Cajeme in 1886, however, the stage had been set for foreign occupation of the Yaqui River.

Canals and Colonists in the Valle Nuevo

Speculation in Sonoran lands continued as the rails were laid through Guaymas and down the coast. Yaquis in the river pueblos faced more immediate problems after Cajeme's execution. Two delegations came to the valley in 1887. The first, under the direction of Lorenzo Torres, had instructions to organize the defeated Yaquis into villages with town councils. Torres also received a mandate from the state government to "protect the rights and property of the tribes against the encroachments of the Mexicans and to favor them in any dispute arising between the two antagonists" (Beene 1972:139). A second commission was chartered to survey and divide the river lands among the Indians. Each of the pueblos organized by Torres would receive a block of land, 7,500 hectares in area, to be parceled into individual lots of 35 hectares for each family head. _Agostadero_, pasture land, was to be reserved for each pueblo as well. The remaining lands, unclaimed by Yaqui farmers, would be opened to colonization by non-Indians (Beene 1972:139–40; Dabdoub 1964:255–56).

War-weary but intensely suspicious of the government plans, Yaquis for the most part refused to accept the offered parcels. Lorenzo Torres quickly became proprietor of more than 15,000 hectares of river land, and much more went into the hands of commission members and Mexican colonists. Several of these new owners began to run feeder canals off the lower river to their farms (Dabdoub 1964: 253–55).

The remainder of the Yaqui delta was given to Carlos Conant of Guaymas in 1890. With the financial backing of Walter S. Logan, a New York attorney who would later fund William Greene's copper operations in Cananea, near the Arizona border (Sonnichsen 1976), Conant established the Sonora–Sinaloa Irrigation Company of New Jersey. For the next ten years, Conant and his engineers surveyed the lands south of the river, blocked out lots of 400 hectares, constructed access roads, and built the first twenty-six miles of canal from the diversion dam at Los Hornos, up the Río Yaqui.

By the end of the nineteenth century, Conant had spent between $600,000 and $900,000 on the project that would open 400,000 hectares of the valley to irrigated farming (Dabdoub 1964:259–93; Hu-Dehart 1974:76). By 1901, however, only 800 hectares had been sold to colonists, and the Sonora–Sinaloa Irrigation Company went into receivership (Compañía Constructora Richardson 1904–1927). Conant's bankruptcy can be attributed to renewed Yaqui activity through the 1890s. The droves of settlers expected by Conant and demanded by Porfirio Díaz and his representatives in the state offices had refused to come, fearing Yaqui depredations.

Under the leadership of Tetabiate in the 1890s, Yaquis left the river towns, then occupied by the Mexican army, and retreated to the Sierra de Bacatete and to haciendas throughout the state. From their rugged mountain stronghold, they carried out a nagging guerrilla campaign against delta settlements and ranchos. A peace treaty signed at Ortiz in 1897 proved to be transitory. Guerrilla activity began again in 1899. A more lasting peace was achieved—apparently—in 1900 when state troops killed four hundred Yaquis and took eight hundred more as captives in the Battle of Mazocoba. The government proclaimed the formal end of the Yaqui campaign in August 1901 (Hu-Dehart 1974:79).

Less than a year later, Governor Rafael Izábal found it necessary to design a new Yaqui policy, for the raids continued. Izábal ordered all peaceful Yaqui laborers to obtain passports from the district prefects, and sought out the active rebels in their mountain camps. All "Yaquis found wandering without passports would be considered rebels and subject to arrest, and maybe even to deportation from the state" (Hu-Dehart 1974:80).

Of his options, Izábal quickly found that only deportation would work effectively. Between 1903 and 1908, some two thousand Yaquis, by conservative estimate, were forcibly deported to southern Mexico and hundreds more took asylum in Arizona (Hu-Dehart 1974; Spicer 1961). Large landowners in the Guaymas valley, traditionally reliant on Yaquis as hacienda laborers, protested vigorously. But Izábal's policy was ultimately successful. The Yaqui delta had been brought under Mexican control, and was finally safe for colonization.

By 1908 the Yaqui Valley had largely passed into the ownership of the Compañía Constructora Richardson of Los Angeles and New York City. On the strength of a concession for the railroad across the Yaqui River from Guaymas, Davis Richardson raised the initial capital of $150,000 for the territory, from Los Angeles businessmen in 1904. A year later, Richardson sold the railroad concession to the Southern Pacific Railroad and began to acquire the lands held by the creditors of Conant's enterprise. By 1906 he had acquired rights to 100,000 hectares in the valley, with the extant network of canals and diversion dams on the left bank, for a price of $300,000. Following more purchases, the company owned 225,000 hectares of land by May 1907. The railroad was completed in the same year, and Richardson opened the valley to colonization. By April 1909 some 12,000 hectares had been sold in average plots of 100 hectares to three hundred farmers from California, Arizona, Canada, and Sonora. In the same year, the company obtained additional funding of $1 million and a $12 million bond issue for purposes of expanding the canal system. A contract was drawn up between the Mexican government and Richardson, giving the company rights to import without duty the machinery necessary to build and operate the irrigation system, and to expropriate lands under private ownership which were needed for building the system (Compañía Constructora Richardson 1904–27).

With the official sanction of the Revolutionary government, the Richardson engineers designed a network of canals and drains that would hypothetically irrigate some 300,000 hectares of alluvium on both sides of the river. On the ground, work went slowly. In the peak season of 1912–13, only 11,000 hectares received water. And, as the Mexican Revolution continued through the decade, disrupting transportation links and construction schedules, and as renewed Yaqui attacks on the Richardson colonists made farming uncertain, the acreage declined.

Frustrated by the politics of revolution and the depredations of Yaquis who had resettled the pueblos, the Richardson Company directors made plans to fold late in the decade. As Herbert A. Sibbett would recall:

> When the new constitution of 1917 was published prohibiting any foreigners from acquiring land within 100 kilometers of the border or 50 kilometers of the coast, and prohibiting anyone, foreigner or Mexican, from owning more than 100 hectares of agricultural land anywhere in Mexico, it was evidently time to sell out (Compañía Constructora Richardson 1904–27).

By 1927, the transfer was complete: for 6 million pesos, Alvaro Obregón, on behalf of the Mexican government, purchased the Richardson Company. For their "extraordinary services" to the development of the valley, Sibbett and William Richardson (the latter had

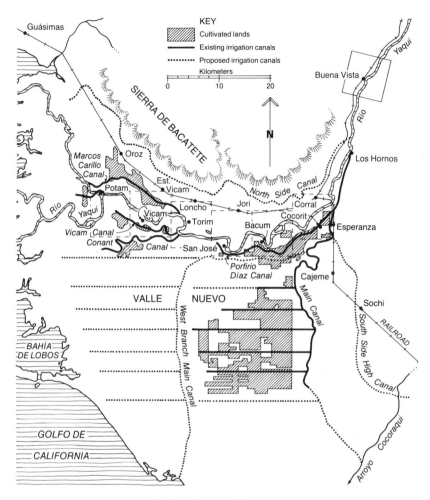

The Yaqui Delta, 1917

succeeded his brother as company president) were allowed to retain 200 hectares of land near Esperanza and an additional 2,000 hectares of pasture in the delta (Compañía Constructora Richardson 1904–27).

Railroads through the Yaqui Valley, connecting the region to North American markets and eventually to central Mexico, had determined the fate of the Sonoran coast as a zone of export agriculture. Initiated by Carlos Conant and extended by the Compañía Constructora Richardson, the network of canals added to the infrastructure necessary for making the region viable. But the canals had an additional impact: they determined to a large degree the geography of conflict in the Yaqui Valley (see map). Before the infusion of North

American investment, the zone of contention centered on the Yaqui pueblos, and the earliest canals, built after Cajeme's defeat, ran through old pueblo land. Conant altered the face of the land by running his main ditch down the left bank of the river, out onto the flat expanse of monte below the Yaqui towns. Richardson continued Conant's vision and pushed the main canal further south toward the Gulf of California. Yaqui pueblos along the river were marginalized. The future of the delta lay in the Valle Nuevo to the south. For the Yaquis, the social and economic consequences were mixed. The pressures of encroachment on the indigenous lands were removed, for a time. But the water of the Río Yaqui was gone, tapped at Los Hornos for the expanse of farmland to the south. Yaquis would slowly regain their historic land, but little could be done with it.

Population Shifts and the Growth of a City

In mapping the canals to open to Valle Nuevo, Richardson's technicians fixed the economic geography of the delta. The social geography would evolve more slowly and had not crystallized by the 1920s. For much of the Porfiriato and the Revolution that followed, the center of settlement, commerce, and hostility remained along the lower river.

In his report to military superiors in 1900, Colonel Angel Garcia Peña described the major pueblos, which were under army occupation. Cocorit already had a population of 1,330 *colonos*, with only 740 *indígenas* remaining. At the nearby hacienda of La Esperanza, property of Don José María Parada, 82 *indígenas sirvientes* worked and lived as did 37 others on the ranch at Ontagota. Garcia Peña reported the following:

> Bacum is the most populous and, for this reason, has had the most influence in the destiny of the tribe, evidenced by the fact that within the limits marked by the inhabitants of Bacum two towns have been formed by the work of the Scientific Commission: Bacum and San José. The inhabitants of these towns are the rebels who now are around in the forests (Troncoso 1905:270).

Torim, the next pueblo down the river, was the center of military operations, with a population of 1,221 non-Yaquis and 416 Yaquis. Vicam had been abandoned by Yaquis. Taking their place was a colony of farmers from Chihuahua who worked the lands adjacent to a small canal. Potam had a population of 764 non-Yaqui *individuos civilizados* and 219 Yaquis:

> This town, having there a military post which at present serves as housing for the 4th and 11th Batallions and also being close to the

shore, is important as a first step for the resources which come from Guaymas. It also has a flour mill that grinds the wheat produced in this region and provides enough flour for local consumption, although this year there may not be as much wheat to grind as last year; due to the revolt, the wheat planting was scant (Troncoso 1905:272).

At the mouth of the Yaqui River, the settlement of Médano served as an unloading point for goods shipped down the coast from Guaymas. This port town, with 849 Yaquis and 177 non-Yaquis in 1900, was abandoned when railroads were constructed through the delta (Troncoso 1905:272).

By 1900 canals were beginning to draw water from the lower river, and the agricultural potential of the alluvium was unfolding. But the canals were inefficient, useful only when the river was high. It was obvious to settlers and engineers alike that the river had to be diverted further upstream (Hernandez 1902).

With the Río Yaqui in high flood, more ominous problems arose for the settlements along its course. In 1904 the equipment assembled to build the railroad through Torim was destroyed by flooding, and surveyors were dispatched to relocate the tracks on higher ground. Cocorit, Bacum, and Torim were bypassed, and a new railhead at Cajeme, in the Valle Nuevo, was established.

Faced with continued Yaqui unrest during the years of the Revolution, Cajeme grew slowly. Initially, several mills for wheat and rice were built (Dabdoub 1964:324) to handle the surpluses produced by the Richardson colonists. But little growth was possible until 1917, when the national constitution temporarily quieted the power struggles among revolutionary leaders. Confronted with a consolidation of power in the state, Yaqui raids tapered off. After 1917, Cajeme expanded, so that by the 1920s, the town itself had 450 residents (Dabdoub 1964:336), and others were spread throughout the Valle Nuevo. In 1927 Cajeme attained the status of *municipio* (Almada 1952:127)—a legal reflection of economic and political importance, both real and anticipated—and the following year was renamed Ciudad Obregón, in honor of the Sonoran revolutionary leader and Mexican president (Almada 1952:128).

General Obregón visited the valley in 1926, touching off the last rebellion by disgruntled Yaquis. The outbreak was controlled, and the Mexican army built up the garrisons in the Yaqui pueblos. This military occupation would last until the 1950s (Spicer 1961:70).

Conditions along the river finally stabilized. Cultivation around Ciudad Obregón expanded, as the town grew into the major distribution and processing center for the region's agricultural output. A new element was added to the social geography of the Valle Nuevo, outside

Table 2.2.   Land Ownership in the Yaqui Valley, 1935

Size of Holdings (hectares)	Area (hectares)	
0–100		13,915
100–150		2,752
150–200		3,890
200–400		9,079
400+		14,102
	Total	43,738

Source: Banco Nacional 1945:20.

indigenous territory: the *comunidades agrarias* or *ejidos*. The first such collective farms to receive land—in 1923—were those of "Cajeme" and "El Yaqui," followed in the early 1930s by Bacum, Cocorit, Quechehueca, and a number of others (Banco Nacional 1945:18). By the end of the 1930s, some 13,000 hectares had been awarded to 3,266 campesinos in the valley: 4 hectares of irrigated land per family head and 10 hectares of potentially arable monte (Banco Nacional 1945:20). By 1935, though, an uneasy dualism of tenure had been set. Much of the land was parceled out to small farmers or *ejidatarios* in lots of less than 100 hectares. The remainder went to a few latifundistas. An agrarian census of the region in 1935 estimated that 27,071 hectares were owned by eighty-five individuals in lots larger than 150 hectares each (Table 2.2).

Further agricultural expansion in the Valle Nuevo was stymied in the 1930s by the worldwide depression and, locally, by an aging irrigation sytem, taxed to its limits. Yaquis in the pueblos had already felt the impact of water shortage as the diversion dam at Los Hornos sent the river south to Obregón. As the valley developed, Mexican growers began to run out of water as well. Angostura Dam, built high in the sierra in the late 1930s, relieved the shortage momentarily and stimulated further growth in the 1940s. For the Yaqui, the dam simply aggravated conditions on the right bank. By 1940, the lower river was dry for much of the year (Spicer 1954:41–42).

The Presidential Decrees of the late 1930s set aside the Zona Indígena for the tribe, giving Yaquis the legal title to lands that they had contested for centuries. The Sierra de Bacatete was encircled by the new tribal boundary, and the ranges of its foothills and inter-mountain valleys would eventually be put to use by a Yaqui cattle cooperative. The coastline was also awarded to the tribe, although it would take a series of political demands in the 1970s before Yaquis were to gain exclusive access to the resources there. And, under the Cárdenas mandate, Yaquis regained control of their pueblos, but only those north of the river, on the right bank. Eventually, the massive Alvaro Obregón Dam—completed in 1952 a short way up the river

from the old diversion point at Los Hornos—would bring these pueblos the irrigation waters essential to economic viability.

The lands and towns to the south of the river were lost to the
Mexicans, but Yaquis hoped for retrieval. With a political resolve that
matched their armed struggles of the nineteenth century, Yaquis
mobilized in the 1970s to retake these lands on the left bank. The
outcome would be unsatisfying. The Valle del Yaqui was to remain in
Mexican hands.

CHAPTER 3

Ethnicity as Ascription

Few Yaquis pay attention to the details of ethnic identity. Quite simply, on first impression and through sustained observation, it appears that Yaquis know who and what they are. To the majority of Yaquis, questions of ethnic boundaries and ethnic identity are fundamentally uninteresting and open to little negotiation. But it is precisely this quality that makes such questions analytically exciting to the outside observer. The inquiry becomes: why is ethnic identity of little manifest concern?

PIVOTAL ATTRIBUTES OF YAQUI IDENTITY

Pivotal or basic attributes of Yaqui identity, attributes whose "absence or variation changes the whole identity of the role" (Nadel 1957:32), are explicitly invoked, and thus defined, by the Yaquis themselves, but in strictly limited situations. With few exceptions, an individual's group membership—his identity as a Yaqui—is founded upon genealogy. Yaqui status is ascribed to children by virtue of being born to Yaqui parents. The exceptions prove the rule. They involve, to be sure, the achievement of ethnic identity as a Yaqui. But this status is gained through the idiom of kinship, not performance. In theoretical terms, there is an element of flexibility in the "fixed-membership group." The task of this chapter is to define this interplay of fixity and flexibility.

Parentage as the criterion for discriminating Yaqui from non-Yaqui works adequately under local circumstances, where the personal biographies of most individuals and kin groups are known or easily discovered. Through observation and gossip, residents of Yaqui barrios in Potam are well informed about the genealogies of neighborhood coresidents. Kinship and coparent ties to other barrios serve to link individuals into the information networks of other barrios, so that virtually every Yaqui in Potam can classify all others according to ethnic status. In Yaqui pueblos smaller in population than Potam, the classifying task is correspondingly easier.

Such information on parentage is sought and offered only under specific circumstances, however. I will attempt to illustrate these through specific case studies, in which I have used pseudonyms. One set of circumstances involves incongruity; an individual appears out of place and his ethnic status may be called into question. In one case, a young man appeared in Potam the week before Semana Santa (Holy Week), driving a pick-up truck with Arizona license plates and wearing an army surplus jacket and long hair. My landlady, María, watched with interest as he drove through the barrio in search of a local tequila dealer. After he had passed by, I questioned her about the new arrival. She replied that he was indeed Yaqui. His father was Ramón, an old and respected Poteño, holder of several religious and political positions. Without having met the young man, María drew upon her general knowledge of family histories and recent gossip. She added that he was living in Guadalupe and had come to visit his family. The young man, as incongruous as could be in Potam, was immediately classifiable by genealogical background.

A second example involves a brief encounter on the dusty main street of Potam between a traditionally dressed Yaqui couple and several *chamacas*, teenaged girls, clothed in contemporary style of blue jeans and tight blouses. Without prompting, the couple began complaining to themselves of the "new generation," the young Poteños who evidence little respect for their elders, little interest in traditional Yaqui dress, and little desire to grasp the Yaqui dialect. Their complaints were not bitter, but simply mild, resigned observations on the state of affairs. (The couple's own son, a boy of twelve, understands Yaqui when it is spoken, but responds to his parents in Spanish, receiving no reproach.) Finally, I asked the couple whether the girls were in fact Yaqui. They responded affirmatively and briefly described the girls' parentage and residences.

A young girl, about age seven, frequently toured the house compounds of the Santiamca barrio in Potam, selling homemade donuts, tamales, and fruit. Dressed in store-bought clothes, she had an extremely fair complexion and brownish-blond hair, in marked contrast to darker haired, darker skinned Yaquis. One day María, Lorenzo, and their daughter joked with the child, pretending she was selling *lona* (canvas), not *dona* (donuts), from her bucket. They teased, calling her Mayo, then yori; the girl, unoffended, enjoyed the bantering. Afterward, I questioned María about the child's background. She assured me that the girl was Yaqui, the daughter of some close friends and neighbors.

In each of these cases, the individuals were incongruous. In the first, the young man was a stranger, unknown to most Poteños. In the second, the teenagers were conspicuous in dress and speech, not to their Yaqui or yori peers, but to older, more traditional Yaquis. And in the third, the child was phenotypically anomalous. In each instance, the parentage and the ethnic identification of the individual in question were quickly established by the observer.

Apart from incongruous situations, the issue of an individual's ethnic status or group membership arises most frequently and most importantly under jural circumstances: when an individual petitions the pueblo governors for access to resources within pueblo territory. Yaquis suggest that the permission of the governors must be sought to: (1) construct a house on pueblo territory (within the pueblo proper as well as the outlying desert, the monte); (2) cultivate crops or graze cattle in pueblo territory; and (3) utilize the wild resources of the monte. Under these circumstances, the pueblo officials must judge the petitioning individual's ethnic group membership. The criterion employed is, again, genealogical.

An occasional event, illustrative of this process, occurs when an Arizona Yaqui wants to return to the reserve, establish residence, and cultivate land. Typically, the petitioning individual will be accompanied by local relatives, who attest to family background before the pueblo governors. In such cases, ethnic status clearly overrides national citizenship. Yaqui ethnic status is acknowledged whether the individual lives in Sonora or in the United States. Sonoran Yaquis do not hesitate to comment upon the lack of facility that many of their Arizonan counterparts display with the Yaqui language, particularly the formalized procedures of greeting and leave-taking. Yet they do not question the Arizonans' ethnic status, nor do they withhold the rights and duties attendant upon that status.

Rights of Yaqui group membership consist of access to land for cultivation, house building, cattle grazing, and wild resource procurement. They also include the right to participate in Yaqui economic cooperatives—the farming and fishing *sociedades* and the cattle operation. By satisfactorily validating one's identity, an individual obtains this constellation of rights.

These rights, accorded to Yaquis by virtue of their genealogical ties, are not granted to yoris. Individuals of non-Yaqui ethnic status may not cultivate land within the Yaqui reserve, and they may not join Yaqui cooperatives. They may utilize the wild resources of the monte, but only upon payment of a fee to the pueblo governors. They are also permitted to live within the confines of a Yaqui pueblo, but are subject to threats of expulsion by the governors.

The above examples are clear-cut: genealogy serves as the pivotal attribute in defining the ethnic status and corresponding rights and duties of an individual within the Yaqui reserve. These examples, however, cover only a restricted set of circumstances. First, the classifier in each case stands as a "personal other" to the individual in question. Local residents in the preceding examples know the biography and the genealogy of other individuals. And the governors, faced with a request for land and other rights, develop—if they do not already possess—a biography of the petitioner. Second, in each of the cases discussed, the individual's biography was founded upon putative biological, not sociological, parentage.

How is an individual's ethnic identity determined when the classifier is not a "personal other," but must make a ready judgment for purposes of interaction? How is an individual's status determined when he can claim only sociological parentage? Can an individual, in practice, hide some yori skeletons in the closet? The first question implicates the area of secondary role attributes, the more-or-less adequate markers, but not definers, of ethnic group membership. This will be discussed in some detail below. The latter questions, however, address the bounds of flexibility.

Flexibility in the Fixed—Membership Group

A close friend in the field, one whom I found generally trustworthy on most topics of political and economic (but not ritual) concern, proved a poor informant when the question of his own family background arose. When not in his presence, neighbors and friends suggested, tentatively, that the man's father was yori, living in Guaymas. No one was very certain, however. The man never talked about his parents, and since early childhood had lived with his maternal grandparents in Potam. He still lives in the same compound with them, along with his maternal aunt, his wife, and his five children. He has taken the surname of his maternal grandfather, once pueblo mayor of Potam and still a most respected figure in town. Moreover, he consistently refers to and addresses his grandparents as "father" and "mother." The man's wife and children are aware of the pretense and uphold it; the man's biological father, by all accounts a rather disreputable figure, is seldom mentioned.

This genealogical fiction, hidden quite effectively from the anthropologist, but common knowledge throughout the barrio, has not prevented the man from attaining the full rights and duties of Yaqui ethnic status. Nor has it prevented him from attaining at least the trappings of respect throughout the pueblo: he was in line for one of the major political posts in Potam. He has adequately convinced present Yaqui governors of his ethnic group membership. The case at hand suggests that Yaqui status can be attained if an individual, lacking a Yaqui as biological father, has lived most of his life in a Yaqui pueblo, under the socialization of relatives who are unquestionably Yaqui.

The flexibility with which Yaqui officials interpret and apply the criterion of biological parentage is necessary for a society with an ascriptive membership rule. It allows for past demographic realities. Yaquis, at several times in the nineteenth and twentieth centuries, have been forced into close interaction and, occasionally, intermarriage with Mexicans. Recognizing the exceptions that such contact has produced, and the implication for the future of their society, the Yaquis are willing to apply some measure of laxity to their rule.

The children of Dominga Ramírez (Kelley 1978:154–96) present a more interesting and problematic study in the interplay of flexibility and fixity. Born at the turn of the century, Dominga had children by a Potam Yaqui, a Cocorit Mexican, a Yaqui descended from the leader Cajeme, and finally, a Potam Mayo. Children from the alliances with the two Yaquis present no problems of ethnic classification, but they do illustrate the complexity involved in activating Yaqui rights and duties. Guillermo Leyva (Cajeme), for example, received rights to land in Potam where his mother Dominga lived, not in the home pueblo of his father, Cocorit. Guillermo's father was deported shortly after the boy was born, and Guillermo had no subsequent contact with him.

Guillermo's half-brothers from the marriage between Dominga and the Poteño, Anselmo Romero Matus, were raised by Augustina, Dominga's mother. At the time, Augustina was living with a man who resided in Potam but worked farmland in Rahum. The boys, Anselmo Jr. and Milo, grew up helping their grandmother's consort on these Rahum plots, and now claim these lands as their own. In these cases, kinship and residence served as the key to acquiring group membership and access to resources.

The status of Dominga's sons by non-Yaquis appears to hinge on residence. Ramon Jiménez, son of the Cocorit yori, chose to live outside Yaqui territory, in the Valle Nuevo town of Pueblo Yaqui, and much of his association remained with his yori relations. While he is accepted as a member of the group by his Yaqui half-siblings, he has not been accorded access to resources within the tribal reserve.

The sons of Dominga and the Mayo, Jesús Suárez, however, did acquire Potam lands. The legitimacy of their claims could not have been fostered by the fairly contemptuous behavior of Jesús Suárez. He did, however, own Potam land, given to him as a political reward by Governor Roman Yucupicio, also a Mayo. Yucupicio bestowed similar grants upon other Mayos—close in language and culture to the Yaquis—in the 1930s, when the Yaqui Zona Indígena was in its formative stages. The rights of the Suárez offspring are largely a legacy of the governor's actions.

Some families among the original Mayo contingent have garnered respect and positions of responsibility within Yaqui society. In fact, at least one Mayo has served recently as Potam's governor (Kelley, personal communication). Here again, the sequence of events supports the argument. Acknowledgment of group membership—albeit imposed on the Yaquis by Yucupicio—preceded the ascendancy of this Mayo family to political power and social respect. Conversely, the widespread disrepute of Jesús Suárez has not invalidated his sons' claims to group membership.

With ethnic status defined by genealogical ties, there is strong, if informal, social pressure to marry within the tribe. Of the five marriages I witnessed in the field, four were between Yaquis. The nonconforming case, that between a Yaqui girl in her early twenties and an itinerant artist from Baja California, is instructive of the nature of social pressure exerted upon potential mates. Julio, a man in his mid thirties, had left his father's clothing store in Tijuana to travel Mexico in search of inspiration for his developing artistic talents. Venturing north from Mexico City and the Indian towns of Oaxaca, he took a room in Estación Vicam. Serving as an occasional interpreter (English-Spanish) for an anthropologist newly arrived in the field, Julio came into contact with a pueblo functionary, the *alawasin* of Vicam pueblo. Social visits with the alawasin and his family evolved into a close friendship between the artist and one of the daughters. After several months of association, during which Julio became increasingly interested in a quasi-ethnographic study of Yaqui *curanderas,* they broached the subject of marriage to the alawasin and his wife. The alawasin raised few objections, perhaps seeing in the marriage some financial gain for his family. Julio, without any visible means of support, was obviously not poor. However, the alawasin's wife and her mother, both traditional women, vigorously objected. The objections did not center around the rights to farming land since the alawasin controlled no land in the pueblo. Rather, the women feared that the couple would move to Tijuana. Additionally, they believed that the marriage would prove unstable due to the daughter's inexperience with the relatively sophisticated social atmosphere of the border city. Julio was unconvincing in his expressed desire to remain forever in the Yaqui Zone.

Other objections were that Julio, unable to understand or speak Yaqui, would not be able to request permission to marry from the relatives of the girl, would not have a Yaqui to vouch for his character, and would not comprehend the traditional sermon delivered to the couple by a maestro during the marriage ceremony. Moreover, Julio would have no Yaqui family to sponsor the bridegroom's household fiesta, a necessary complement to the wedding ritual being conducted concurrently at the house of the bride.

Julio and his future father-in-law obviated many of these difficulties. They enlisted the services of an elderly Poteño, who was highly respected as a *tampalero* (drummer for the pascolas) but was experiencing financial distress. The man acted as spokesman for Julio to the reluctant, traditional family, and briefed Julio on the contents of the important marriage sermon. The marriage eventually came about in modified form; a small, poorly attended household fiesta was held at the alawasin's residence in Estación Vicam.

In sum, Yaqui ethnic status, defined as the rights and duties inherent in tribal membership, is transmitted genealogically. Marriage becomes a key point at which the allocation of ethnic status can be regulated. Yaqui parents may attempt to control the marital wishes of their daughter and, accordingly, the ethnic status of subsequent grandchildren. Social pressures to ensure tribally endogamous unions exist and, if my small sampling of five observed marriage cases is any valid indication, these pressures can be effective. In the one nonendogamous case, permission to marry outside the group would most likely have been denied if both parents had objected.

SECONDARY ATTRIBUTES OF YAQUI IDENTITY

Ethnic identity consists of both pivotal and secondary attributes. The pivotal attribute is the main determinant of status. As I have suggested, the absence or variation of secondary attributes does not greatly affect status. In practice, there may be no set of unambiguous pivotal or secondary attributes. There may also be a variation of responses about the governing principles, depending upon who is asked the question, about whom the question is asked, and why the question is being asked.

The most expedient way to isolate pivotal from secondary attributes—as was done in the preceding section—is to uncover the attributes upon which rights and duties of ethnic group membership are allocated. The criterion employed by Yaquis to discriminate group membership is genealogical. This leaves a substantial set of secondary attributes commonly seen as the essence of Yaqui identity: language, dress, participation in distinctively Yaqui rituals and political organization, and shared historical experiences.

The manner in which each of these secondary attributes is practiced may be judged as more-or-less Yaqui, or more-or-less Mexican. Objectively, individual Yaquis may be placed on a scale evaluating their assimilation to Mexican society. Such a perspective, however, contradicts the data at hand, as well as my underlying claim. Specific individuals rarely display a similar degree of assimilation on each of these separate attributes. And the degree of assimilation, on single attributes or the constellation of attributes, does not contravene an individual's claim to Yaqui status, based as it is on the pivotal attribute of parentage.

Dress ⁷

In many societies, dress is an effective and visible marker of ethnic identity. Along the Río Yaqui, this is not the case. Two rather distinct styles of dress can be isolated, one a traditional Yaqui style, the other a contemporary northwest Mexican pattern. Traditional style is more easily defined for Yaqui females than for males. It generally consists of thick leather sandals with thongs wrapped around the ankle, ankle-length full dress, loose-fitting blouse, and *rebozo*, a manufactured shawl used as head covering, baby carrier, and protection against the wind and dust. The full-cut dress is most distinctive, made from brightly colored satin and ribbed with parallel bands of white lace. While the material is now store-bought, the dresses themselves are handmade. Yaqui women take great pride in their outfits, and insist on sewing a new dress to be displayed for the first time on Sabado de Gloria (Easter Saturday). Groups of industrious women spend late nights during Semana Santa at their sewing machines, finishing their dresses. Rebozos are also a source of pride. Women eagerly await shipment of new ones into town; such shipments are invariably spoken for long before they arrive from Guadalajara. And some women longingly speak of traveling to that city, where the finest Mexican rebozos are produced.

Another important part of Yaqui women's dress are large gold-plated earrings purchased from local variety stores. Earrings serve as status symbols, to be shown off to the other women, and also as pawn, held by storekeepers as collateral for small loans or credit toward food. A new rebozo every two or three years and a new dress every Easter involve Yaqui women in a sizable expense. The alternative of machine-made print dresses from large department stores in Guaymas or Obregón is cheaper, yet decidedly less attractive to Yaqui women.

Male outfits are now largely of Mexican origin and purchased in stores. Invariably a cowboy-style sombrero is worn, along with a print shirt and jeans or slacks. Most males still own sandals but more commonly wear boots. The only discriminating item, worn by some but not all Yaquis, is a brightly colored handkerchief tied around the neck, which serves as a rag, washcloth, bandage, and protection against dust. The common dress for Yaqui males is essentially the same as that of northwest Mexican cowboys and *campesinos*. Such clothing serves as an occupational rather than ethnic marker, for it clearly differentiates Yaqui and Mexican farmers and ranchers from urban white-collar professionals, service personnel, and skilled laborers.

Like women, Yaqui men use the occasion of Sabado de Gloria as an opportunity to purchase new clothing. Inability to afford a new set of clothes is often offered as an excuse for absence at the major rituals of Semana Santa.

Language

Most Yaqui adults are bilingual. In contrast, no Mexicans living in or near the Yaqui reserve (aside from missionaries) have developed any competence in the Yaqui language. Yaqui bilingualism has a long history. Incorporation of Spanish words into Yaqui lexicon has been a continuous process, beginning with early Spanish missionaries (Spicer 1943; Johnson 1943). The primary impetus to bilingualism came in the nineteenth century when Yaquis were in heavy demand as laborers in the underpopulated Sonoran frontier. Highly respected as workers, Yaquis were employed on haciendas and ranchos, and in mines, and through intimate contact with Mexican workers, many became fluent in Spanish (Spicer 1961:48–49).

In the thirty years following Cajeme's defeat by the Mexican militia in 1887, the ability to speak Spanish became a definite advantage to survival. The Mexican government, unable to peacefully settle the Yaqui Valley, adopted a policy of deportation. Captured Yaquis were sent to Yucatan and Oaxaca as plantation laborers (Turner 1969), and others emigrated to Arizona. Many, presumably, managed to escape detention by blending in with the Sonoran lower classes, speaking Spanish rather than Yaqui.

Bilingualism has continued. The overwhelming majority of Sonoran Yaquis of all ages can competently speak and understand both Spanish and Yaqui. Proficiency varies, however. The elderly understand spoken Spanish, but feel more comfortable speaking Yaqui. Most middle-aged Yaquis are comfortable with Yaqui and Spanish equally, although their spoken Spanish seldom contains the colloquialisms of northwest Mexico. Nor do they competently control the more intricate subjunctive forms of Spanish (see Thompson 1974:123–24). Yaqui teenagers and young adults, whose peer groups often include local Mexicans, and who work and live in the presence of the ubiquitous transistor radio, appear more comfortable with regional Spanish than with the Yaqui language. Virtually all of them, however, understand and speak Yaqui. The language use of young children is less easily classified. Through local schooling most are becoming literate in Spanish, but understand Yaqui as well. Many are not yet fluent in Yaqui, and choose to respond in Spanish to questions asked of them in either Spanish or Yaqui. At the same time, however, a number of Yaqui children can and do speak Yaqui.

With such variation within and between generations, it is difficult to predict the future course of bilingualism among Yaquis. Observed differences in speaking patterns seem more a function of the individual's place in the life cycle, from birth through old age, than an indication of his proclivity to assimilate into Mexican society. Elderly Yaquis, most of whom were probably quite fluent in Spanish during the turbulent first three decades of this century are now immobile, with little need or desire to interact with Mexican society. The uncomfortable feeling that these elders have with Spanish may stem simply from disuse of that language.

Fully active adults often work for Mexican patrons, shop in Mexican-owned stores, and deal recurrently with the Mexican government, economic, and health agencies. They are consequently quite comfortable with spoken Spanish. This age group is also the most active in Yaqui political and ritual institutions, which require a full command of the Yaqui language. Teenagers and young adults, recently educated in Mexican schools, are by no means immune to the prestige attached to the bantering facilities of their young Mexican peers. At the same time, many of these youths are initiating careers as Yaqui adults, for which competency in the Yaqui language is necessary.

Young children of school and preschool age acquire at least an understanding of spoken Yaqui when they are socialized in Yaqui-speaking families and barrios. Few sanctions are imposed on children who fail to speak Yaqui at this age; parents consciously recognize the need for children to develop the necessary language skills for Mexican schooling.

In sum, most Yaquis develop a working control of Spanish for instrumental purposes, for dealing directly with Sonoran society. Likewise, most develop competency in spoken Yaqui during their lifetime, through socialization within Yaqui-speaking families. The ability to speak Yaqui appears to be a significant secondary attribute of Yaqui ethnic status.

Full participation in the religious and political institutions of Yaqui society is contingent on the ability to speak Yaqui. Political deliberations by the Yaqui governors at pueblo meetings are conducted in Yaqui; any Yaqui wishing to speak up and influence the decisions must address the gathering in Yaqui. Mexican officials speak to the assembled Yaqui authorities in Spanish, but the attendant discussions among Yaquis, even in the presence of outside officials, are in Yaqui. Additionally, formal or informal petitioning to pueblo governors by Yaqui residents for access to land or other resources appears invariably to be carried out in Yaqui, by the petitioner himself or a spokesman.

Political and religious officeholding demands more than just the ability to communicate wishes and opinions in Yaqui, however. It demands a competency in what Spicer has appropriately called the "ritual of words":

> An important qualification for the office of governor, of maestro, of pueblo mayor and even of pascola dancer is the ability to speak well at public gatherings. Speaking well has to do with clarity of enunciation, deliberateness of address, and also the ability to vary the rhythm for emphasis. But such qualities are relatively unimportant, it is said, as compared with a memory of the proper phrases and the ability to combine these phrases in ways that the people are accustomed to hearing. . . . Ritual speeches are a prominent feature of every formal gathering. . . . At point after point in all the standard ceremonies there is a place for a speech, and the ceremony does not proceed until the speech has been given (Spicer 1954:160–61).

Competency in the ritual manipulation of sacred Yaqui phrases appears to vary widely among Yaquis now. Adequacy, not excellence, in the ritual of words may be sufficient for selection as governor. A close acquaintance in the field was indeed chosen to be governor of Potam despite a lack of training and aptitude for ritual speechmaking. He ultimately refused the position, relating to me that the duties would be too time consuming during a year in which he intended to begin production on a new plot of land. He also alluded to his anxiety over the ritual speeches required of the governor; he did not yet feel adequately prepared.

Facility in the ritual of words, a skill which some, but by no means all, Yaqui adults develop, comes through exposure to speeches at political and religious occasions. And it is also encouraged through actual practice, when individual family heads are called upon to sponsor household fiestas. The sponsor must deliver speeches of welcome and thanking to ritual participants:

> In these recurrent occasions a few brief words are not satisfactory. The speeches must cover the situation fully, which means mention of the supernatural sanctions operating in the case, the purpose of the ceremony, the participants and their various roles in the occasion. Speeches of this sort are made in the presence of large groups of people under highly formal conditions. A man or woman must have a command of words and be able to carry through a more or less coherent speech (Spicer 1954:163–64).

While many adult Yaquis do develop competency in the "ritual of words," some have carefully avoided the occasions that call for extended speeches. A traditional but introverted and inarticulate Yaqui man, faced with the responsibility for sponsoring his son's marriage fiesta, decided to hold the ceremony at his father's house instead of his own. The ostensible reason for the switch was that his own ranchería was too remote to attract a crowd; his father's house compound in Potam would serve better. By changing locales, the man placed the task of welcoming and thanking participants on his father, a former pueblo mayor and acknowledged expert in the ritual of words. Ritual speech, although known to most adult Yaquis, can be studiously avoided.

The numerous occasions for hearing and using the Yaqui language classify it as an important, but secondary attribute of Yaqui ethnic status. Most adult Yaquis can converse in the language, even if they never develop competency in the ritual of words, and some adults enjoy the rights and duties of Yaqui group membership with only minimal comprehension of Yaqui and little or no ability to speak it. Several of my acquaintances among Yaqui fishermen fall into this category. One shrimper of about fifty-five years of age speaks little Yaqui and seems to understand little as well. He seldom proceeds beyond the traditional and common phrases for greeting and departure. He is highly respected by other cooperative members for his boat-handling skills and fishing knowledge, gained through years of experience with Mexican shrimpers in Guaymas and Empalme. Along with his thirty-year-old son, he considers himself a Protestant. But occasionally the two attend Yaqui fiestas, maintain compadre ties in attenuated form, and live during the non-fishing season in a Yaqui barrio of Potam. While behaviorly marginal to Yaqui society, the two fishermen, father and son, are granted full rights in the Yaqui fishing co-op, signifying the acceptance of their claims to Yaqui status by co-op officials and pueblo governors.

The two fishermen undeniably represent a small minority of Yaquis—those with little or no linguistic competence in the Yaqui language, but who, by virtue of their acknowledged genealogical ties, are accorded the rights and duties of Yaqui group membership. The overwhelming majority of active adult Yaquis have enough fluency to conduct daily interactions, if not the ritual of words, in Yaqui.

Traditional Knowledge and Shared Historical Experience

Spicer (1971) and Parsons (1975:60) have stressed the importance of shared historical experience as a component of ethnic identity systems. In Spicer's view of "persistent identity systems,"

> ... the meanings of the symbols consist of beliefs about historical events in the experience of the people through generations. The belief that the experience is shared with and through ancestors is basic to such systems (1971:796).

Equally important to such an identity system is a shared understanding of the "mythological" experiences, a knowledge and interest in the charters of society. Moreover, for those professing a particular ethnic identity, we might expect a knowledge and belief in contemporary ritual symbols. In short, we might expect ethnic identity to be founded on a shared "culture," a

> . . . historically transmitted pattern of meaning embodied in sym-
> bols, a system of inherited conceptions expressed in symbolic forms
> by means of which men communicate, perpetuate, and develop
> their knowledge about and attitudes toward life (Geertz 1973:89).

One of the primary symbols of Yaqui identity is the wooden cross placed in front of houses. With some success Crumrine was able to use the house cross as a physical marker of Mayo identification (Crumrine 1964, 1977, 1981), as did Spicer for the Yaquis of Pascua in Tucson (Spicer 1940:1). For Sonoran Yaquis, the house cross may also serve as a material expression of ethnic identification, yet the meanings attached to, and the respect shown for the cross vary markedly from household to household.

Many Yaqui families maintain house crosses in their yards throughout the year, being careful to right them when knocked over by stray children, pigs, and dogs. Other families show little interest in their crosses during most of the year. Crosses are often neglected, carelessly stashed near ramadas, or leaned unceremoniously against outhouses. On occasion, during cold winter nights, house crosses may be burned as firewood. Yaquis who have done this, quite absent-mindedly, run the risk of falling to supernaturally inflicted disease; at least, any illness occurring subsequent to the burning may be directly attributed to such an act.

Less variability is evident during the two calendrical ceremonies in which the house cross plays an integral part. On All Saints' and All Souls days (Todos Santos) in early November, crosses are carefully prepared in most households for the visit of the dead Yaqui ancestors, *aniimam* (see Spicer 1954:123–24). Abutting the house cross, carefully decorated with ribbon and flowers, are tables upon which a meal is laid out for visiting ancestors. Maestros and their cantoras move from household to household during the evening of All Souls' Day, praying and singing for the aniimam. The maestros are then presented with the foods, which they eat on the spot or deposit in buckets and baskets for later consumption. Following the ceremony, the emptied table is returned to the eating ramada and the decorations of the house cross are left to deteriorate.

House crosses are readied again during Waresma (Lent). While they may indeed have many symbolic linkages to the pueblo-wide ceremonies of Waresma (see Crumrine 1964:30–34), there is a more immediate need to display the cross. Members of the Kohtumbrem make *limosna* expeditions, frequent rounds of the houses marked with crosses, collecting money to defray the costs of the ceremonies. Failing to have a cross in place, households will be bypassed by the kohtumbrem. And the result is general embarrassment for members of the household, who quickly resurrect their neglected crosses in time for the next visit. The monetary outlay is small at the limosna: a few pesos contributed, centavo by centavo, for each of the children.

However tardily, virtually all Yaqui families display a house cross during Lent. And a majority, but by no means all, participate in the ceremonies of All Saints' and All Souls' days. The symbolic associations of the house cross vary quite markedly among Yaquis, however. Less introspective and less religious Yaquis will associate the cross with protection. The cross guards the house and its inhabitants against danger, against supernaturally inflicted diseases, misfortune, and accidents. The house crosses serve a purpose similar to that of the small palm leaf crosses woven by children on Palm Sunday, which are hung on automobile dashboards and bicycle handlebars.

Less common is the knowledge of the symbolic connection of house crosses with the tomb of Christ and with the dead ancestors (Crumrine 1964:39) during All Souls' Day. When questioned about the role of the cross and table during Todos Santos, Yaquis may simply say, "that's the way we've always done it." Only a few, primarily maestros and pascolas, can articulate the association between house crosses and the Way of the Cross surrounding the church, although most Yaquis have a general, vague understanding of the symbolic acts of knocking down the crosses during the Crucifixion, then replanting them during the Resurrection.

Knowledge and interest in Yaqui myths are not prevalent throughout the Yaqui population. The origin myth, "Yomumuli and the Little Surem People" (Giddings 1959:25–27), appears to be recited only with the stimulus of inquiring anthropologists. After a brief and uninformative discussion of myths, my landlord, somewhat embarrassed in his lack of mythic knowledge, visited his grandfather. Several hours later he returned and closeted me in a room with two of his children. Proudly but with little flourish, he related the origin myth that he had just learned from his grandfather, and illustrated the tale with a drawing. Somewhat redeemed in the eyes of the children and the anthropologist, he claimed that few Yaquis know and can recite in any detail the corpus of myths.

Similarly, detailed knowledge of historical experiences is not widespread among Yaquis. There is clearly a general interest in the broad outlines of Yaqui-Mexican relations, and pride in the knowledge that Yaquis tenaciously resisted Mexican colonization attempts in the nineteenth and early twentieth centuries. Old men and women who participated in these struggles are avidly listened to by younger Yaquis. Yet such gatherings are rare, contingent upon an occasion when an

elder is feeling reminiscent or agreeable to talking with an anthropologist. Several times during my residence in the field, my landlady's aging grandfather paid her a visit, entering into rambling but
eloquent monologues on Yaqui history, particularly his role in the
construction of the massive adobe church in Potam. Clearly enraptured, María excitedly talked about how well he spoke, how clear his
mind had remained despite approaching blindness, deafness, and
physical disability. Significantly, however, the educational function of
these sessions was ignored or unrecognized; no attempt was made to
gather an audience, to call in María's children from their play.

Transmission of historical knowledge seems now to be entirely
haphazard and unstructured. I found no evidence of the persistence of
a "historical seminar" such as Spicer observed in the pueblo of Rahum,
of historical specialists actively working to preserve the main outlines of
Yaqui history (Spicer 1954:24). These native historians were once
instrumental in elaborating and transmitting the sacred myth of the
"singing of the boundary":

> There were four great men among the Yaquis who called the
> people together and led them around the boundaries of the Yaqui
> country. They started from a point called Mogonea (now covered
> with water in the sea) and went to Cabora on the Cocoraqui arroyo
> between the Yaqui and Mayo Rivers. From there they proceeded to
> Takalaim, a peak just north of Guaymas in the Gulf of California.
> As they went along the boundary the four "prophets" preached
> sermons and sang with the people. This was the establishment of
> the boundary line which was sealed by "the singing of the Holy
> Dawn" and was done in the name of the Three Gods, Father, Son,
> and Holy Spirit. The Rahum mythologists point out that it is clear
> from this that no man set up the Yaqui territory; it was done by God
> and therefore cannot be changed in any part by mere men,
> specifically not by Mexican officials (Spicer 1954:126).

Attempting to elicit a similar recounting of the charter myth, I
presented before several adult Yaqui men a copy of Spicer's 1974 map
which traces the mythical boundary from Mogonea, up the Arroyo
Cocoraqui, around the Bacatete Mountains to Takalaim, northwest of
Guaymas (Spicer 1974:3). The procedure had unexpected results.
None of my informants could articulate the myth, but they became
intensely interested in the map. Throughout the year, representatives
of all pueblos had been meeting with Mexican government officials to
discuss the zone's southern boundary from Esperanza to Lobos. The
complaint was a perennial one: encroachment by Mexican farmers and
residents onto Yaqui land. Yaquis demanded a new survey and mapping of the line, as well as expulsion of yoris from farmlands and half
the residential area of Esperanza. In the context, Spicer's map quickly
became a political tool. Yaqui governors displayed it before Mexican

officials, with the conciliatory argument that Yaquis were only asking for the return of small acreage, not the entire aboriginal domain. The ingenious argument held little weight with government officials.

Knowledge of Yaqui history and tradition has clearly diminished in recent decades. Yet this attenuation has not left contemporary Yaqui society in a "free-floating," decultured state (see Eisenstadt 1964:377). When elements of such traditional knowledge are invoked, however casually in the modern setting, they meet with immediate and interested response. At other times—indeed much of the time—traditional knowledge may remain entirely unobtrusive. But it is seldom denounced.

Ritual-Political Participation

Two of the most ostensible markers of ethnic identity are participation in ceremonial societies and assumption of political office. Yaqui institutions—political and religious—are distinctive in both contemporary and historical Sonoran society. Yet the frequency of participation has little effect on the ethnic status of the individual. Participation does not affect the allocation of rights and duties tied to Yaqui ethnic identity.

Two types of participation may be distinguished: involvement in the positions of the "realms of authority" and participation by attendance at religious performances and political gatherings. This distinction corresponds roughly to one noted by Spicer (1954:56) between active political and religious officeholders and men designated *kia pweplum*, "just pueblo."

Active participation demands sacrifice of time and money. Members of the kohtumbre ya'uram work virtually full-time for the duration of the Lenten season. Fiesteros spend less time in preparation for the pueblo saints' days, but may spend as much as $400 for food and supplies. Church officials and pascola groups must be on hand at the frequent household fiestas as well as at all major pueblo ceremonies. Governors likewise must present themselves at fiestas in addition to passing most of their days around the guardia, attending to tribal affairs. In the course of a year, upwards of 150 men and women actively fill the political and religious offices in Potam.

Opportunity for the remainder of the pueblo to participate in Yaqui institutions comes through attendance at fiestas and political meetings. Most household and pueblo fiestas run continuously for several days and nights, with performers breaking periodically for food and rest. Great admiration is accorded to non-participants who remain awake throughout the long, cold nights. Those who stay awake, comforted by companionship and tequila, are unmistakably euphoric the following morning.

Complex motives seem to underlie an individual's choice to participate in, or simply attend, political and religious functions. Yet the
degree of participation, from active role-taking to complete nonatten-
dance, has few ramifications for the allocation of basic ethnic status.
While most adult Yaquis participate to some degree in political and
religious affairs, some do not. Yaqui fishermen, for example, are noted
for their abstention (Bartell 1965:263). A small number of Guásimeños
attempted to revive the ceremonial round in the fishing village in the
1970s, but had difficulty interesting local residents in the key ritual
positions. Most performers had to be trucked in from the river pueblos.
Moreover, attendance at the Guásimas rituals was minimal: the few
staunch traditionalists living at Guásimas prefer to attend the larger
fiestas of other pueblos. I questioned a renowned Potam pascola about
the fishermen's apparent lack of interest in ceremonial participation
and attendance. He replied that they are not generally disparaged
because of this. Rather, he suggested, the fishermen "work too hard" to
have time to organize or sponsor fiestas. He remained unswayed by my
argument that the major Yaqui fiestas all occur in the slack fishing
seasons, not during the intensive shrimping months of September to
early December.

Maintenance of Secondary Attributes

Secondary attributes, with their wide range of variability within the
Yaqui population, have little bearing on Yaqui status and the rights and
duties stemming from that status. Nevertheless, these secondary attributes are employed frequently to make assessments of an individual's
ethnic identity for the purpose of interaction between individuals, not
for location of the basic rights and duties. They may serve, in the terms
of Donald Horowitz (1975:119), as the "operational *indicia* of identity,
on which ready judgments of individual membership are made." And
secondary attributes are employed frequently by "social others,"
people who have no personal knowledge of the individual being
classified. "Biographical others," classifying individuals they know, will
more likely draw upon the pivotal attribute of Yaqui ethnic status, an
individual's genealogy.

With individuals whose ethnic status is problematic, the classifier
can himself be Yaqui or Mexican. The attributes he employs in
classification—pivotal or secondary—depend not on his own ethnic
status but on his relation to, and knowledge of, the individual to be
classified. While Yaquis stand in personal other relations to many
individuals outside their own barrios and pueblos, they by no means
know, biographically, all other Yaquis in the zone. They must fre-

quently rely on indicia themselves. Mexicans, by and large, less frequently "know" individuals, and their reliance upon indicia is correspondingly greater than that of resident Yaquis.

In short, three interconnected factors determine the information to be employed in individual classification: (1) the purpose of classification, either for allocation of rights and duties or for day-to-day interaction of individuals; (2) the status of the classifier vis-à-vis the individual to be classified, as a "biographical other" or a "social other"; and (3) the ethnic group membership of the classifier.

In the Yaqui Zone the pivotal attribute of descent serves as a poor marker of ethnic group membership. Through intermarriage the range of genetic variation among Yaquis substantially overlaps that of Mexicans in Sonora. This has led to the ironic but perhaps not uncommon situation in which secondary attributes are better predictors of an individual's ethnic group membership than the pivotal attribute of descent. Thus a classifier, whether Yaqui or Mexican, has a greater chance of successfully classifying specific individuals by employing secondary but firmly entailed attributes such as language use.

This situation leads to obvious and real problems in fieldwork, in eliciting the attributes of Yaqui status from various informants. A specific question, "Is *x* a Yaqui?" may be answered in several ways. If the informant is a social other to the referent and had not been asked to definitively classify the individual for purposes of allocating tribal rights and duties, he may quickly respond with an evaluation of secondary attributes. A biographical other may respond in the same manner, drawing perhaps on his knowledge of the individual's career of ceremonial participation. In either case (and the cases are by no means hypothetical), the informant has responded with facility to the ethnographer's question by drawing upon readily available and easily observed attributes. The informant is, in effect, responding to the ethnographer as he would respond to everyday social encounters, with the most quickly available information that allows relatively accurate classification of specific individuals.

The ease of eliciting such information, of obtaining a list of secondary attributes, has led ethnographers to confound pivotal and non-pivotal markers of ethnic identity. Neither the frequency of response by informants nor the emphatic nature of such responses can serve as discriminators of pivotal attributes of ethnic status from the secondary attributes of group membership.

Summary

Viewed as a status, Yaqui ethnic identity is not something that must be or can be achieved. Contrary to Barth, ethnic identification among the Yaquis is not associated with a specific set of performance standards. Hence, there are no "circumstances where such an identity can be moderately successfully realized," and no "limits beyond which such success is precluded" (Barth 1969:25). In short, it is easy to *be* a Yaqui and be accorded full rights and duties attendant upon that status. At the same time, lacking the requisite genealogical ties, it is virtually impossible to *become* a Yaqui.

CHAPTER 4

Ethnicity as Performance

By viewing ethnic identity as a status, an all-or-nothing ascription, several important questions remained unanswered. If rights and duties are assured simply by descent, what motivates individuals to participate in the indigenous ritual and political system? What accounts for the abiding interest of Yaquis in these institutions? Rights and duties of Yaqui status are not entirely reciprocal: the awarding of land is contingent upon factors of availability and suitability, not an automatic obligation of the pueblo governors. Does greater participation and sacrifice significantly increase an individual's chances of obtaining access to land or other resources? Can prestige be exchanged for political power and wealth?

WEALTH, POWER, AND PRESTIGE

In his seminal essay on "class, status, and party," Max Weber sought to understand how power is allocated within a society. By power, Weber meant the "chance of a man or number of men to realize their own will in a communal action even against the resistance of others who are participating in the action" (1946:180). Weber saw social power as deriving singularly or in combination from three sources: economic wealth, social prestige, and political power. Acknowledging that wealth, power, and prestige may be independent avenues to an enhanced social position, Weber was primarily concerned with the empirical overlap or convertibility of these three dimensions. He suggested a variety of possibilities:

Quite generally, 'mere economic' power, and especially 'naked' money power, is by no means a recognized basis of social honor.

Nor is [political] power the only basis of social honor. Indeed, social honor, or prestige, may even be the basis of political or economic power, and very frequently has been. Power, as well as honor, may be guaranteed by the legal order, but at least normally, it is not the primary source. The legal order [authority] is rather an additional factor that enhances the chance to hold power or honor; but it cannot always secure them (Weber 1946:180−81; see Hammel 1969 for an effort to apply this scheme to Peru).

Much of the anthropological literature on Indian Middle America has dealt, directly or indirectly, with Weber's conjunction of wealth, power, and prestige. It has done so through the analysis of civil-religious hierarchies, "ladder" systems in which "adult males serve in a series of hierarchically arranged offices devoted to both political and ceremonial aspects of community life" (Cancian 1967:283). The basic features found in Indian villages throughout southern Mexico and Guatemala include

. . . ranked offices taken for one-year terms by the men of the community. The offices are ranked in two ways: first, they are arranged in levels of service, whereby a man must serve on the first level before he is eligible for service on the second level, and so on; second, authority tends to be concentrated in the top levels, making a hierarchy of authority as well as a hierarchy of service (Cancian 1967:284).

Three other aspects of the system are common to most Indian communities. First, all adult males participate. Second, service in many of the positions imposes a heavy financial burden. Third, "prestige and positions of leadership and respect are achieved through service in the hierarchy" (Cancian 1967:289).

While agreeing on these basic features of the civil-religious hierarchy, observers show less consensus regarding the functions of the system—the consequences it has for community social structure. Eric Wolf (1955), Sol Tax (1953), and Manning Nash (1958) emphasize "equalization of economic status through the operation of the hierarchy, i.e, the 'leveling' consequences" (Cancian 1967:290). Frank Cancian himself stresses the "separation into multiple social statuses, i.e., the 'stratifying' consequences" (Cancian 1967:290; see also Cancian 1965). The egalitarian interpretation rests on the fact that positions in the hierarchy are severe financial burdens on their holders. Assumption of an office thus drains the excess resources of the more wealthy families in the community, fostering socioeconomic homogeneity. The stratifying interpretation rejects this proposition of socioeconomic homogeneity. According to Cancian, there is abundant evidence for economic differentiation in Mexican Indian communities. His own work in Zinacantan, central Chiapas, led him to conclude that the rich obviously spend more than the poor, both because they take more cargos [positions in the hierarchy] and because they take more expensive individual cargos. This is leveling in some sense, but in fact the rich seem to be so rich that they do not lose their relative standing. To a statistically significant degree, sons of men who have taken expensive cargos also take expensive cargos (Cancian 1967:292).

At best, then, the civil-religious hierarchy is an ineffective equalizer, doing little to make the community economically homogeneous.

Nor, in Cancian's view, does the community necessarily become more equalized in individual status. The civil-religious hierarchy appears like a pyramid, with many positions at the bottom, few at the top. As only one man can serve in the top position each year, demographic imbalance—too many eligible men for the number of high-level positions open during their lifetimes—will result in social differentiation between those who reach top positions and those who do not. And, on the assumption that the expensive top positions can be afforded only by the rich, the inevitable differentiation in prestige will be ultimately based on wealth.

In short, the operation of leveling or stratifying effects may be primarily a function of the demographic balance between applicants and positions in the hierarchy. The two alternative interpretations, however, agree substantially on the convertibility of economic wealth into social prestige and political power deriving from occupancy of civil and religious posts. Thus, contrary to the variety of relations between wealth, power, and prestige envisioned by Weber, observers of Middle American ladder systems take wealth as the primary determinant of both political power and social prestige.

Sonoran Yaquis, while sharing many of the influences of Spanish colonial society and Catholic church organization, do not possess the civil-religious hierarchy typical of Middle American Indian groups. First, there is no well-defined ladder of social positions. Apart from the top civil and religious posts—pueblo governor, pueblo mayor, elders, church governors, and maestros—few other positions are ranked in relation to one another. There is, to be sure, an ordering of positions within the various ceremonial societies and civil government, within the five *ya'uram*. Yet members of particular ceremonial societies usually remain in that society for life and do not use high rank in a particular society as a base for further achievement in another *ya'ura*. Thus, there is no necessary alternation between religious and civil positions, nor a requirement that an individual take on higher responsibilities once he has successfully performed in lower positions.

Furthermore, not all positions involve a great expense to the holder. Sponsorship of a household or pueblo fiesta may indeed be costly.

Some performers at such fiestas may spend minor sums for costumes and instruments. But most civil and religious positions require the expenditure of time, not money. And, contrary to the pattern of civil-religious hierarchies in Middle America, Yaqui society does not demand the participation of all adults in the institutionalized positions. As discussed in the previous chapter, participation is both voluntary and variable: individuals may choose the extent of their participation and the institutions to which they devote their time and money.

Finally, the Yaqui system differs markedly from the generalized Middle American pattern in the convertibility of wealth into power and prestige. Because most of the positions do not demand heavy expenditures, it is an easy and frequent act for a poor Yaqui to achieve substantial social prestige and political power through service. It appears equally true, moreover, that a man of high prestige and respectable political power gains very little economically: power and prestige are not directly convertible into economic wealth.

These conclusions, summarily stated, may be illustrated by an examination of individual civil and ceremonial careers. Analytically, there are eight possible combinations of the three variables of economic wealth (E, wealth; $\bar{E}$, non-wealth), political power (P, $\bar{P}$), and social prestige (S, $\bar{S}$): EPS, $E\bar{P}S$, $EP\bar{S}$, $E\bar{P}\bar{S}$, $\bar{E}PS$, $\bar{E}\bar{P}S$, $\bar{E}P\bar{S}$, and $\bar{E}\bar{P}\bar{S}$. The conclusions of Cancian and others, writing on the archetypical civil-religious systems of Middle America, lead us to expect a clustering of individual cases around only two constellations of attributes: EPS and the converse, $\bar{E}\bar{P}\bar{S}$. In the first set, economic wealth is successfully converted into political power and social prestige through the mechanisms of the civil-religious office sponsorship. In the second, initial lack of economic wealth precludes the sponsorship of cargos, and in turn prevents attainment of social prestige and political power.

Within Sonoran Yaqui society, there appears to be no such clustering around these two poles. Rather, individual cases can be found to illustrate each of the eight analytical possibilities, a finding which suggests few patterned interrelations between wealth, power, and prestige. Using pseudonyms, I will describe individual cases for each of these possibilities and indicate the subjective criteria used to evaluate the relative wealth, power, and prestige of the individuals under consideration.

EPS: Mario Alvarez lives on a rancho about two kilometers outside the pueblo of Potam, near the dry bed of the Río Yaqui. Approaching sixty years of age, he resides with his wife and married sons. By no means rich, he nevertheless has substantial wealth tied up in cattle-grazing along the river bed and in an old, occasionally functioning stake truck. He lives too far from existing irrigation canals to farm, but he and his sons obtain the cash necessary to purchase food through periodic sales of cattle. And, being in the monte, he has easy access to firewood, which is an annoying expense for the towndwellers. In the past, Mario has held important ritual positions, serving as a fiestero for the pueblo fiesta of *Santisima Tiniran* as well as a member of the Kabayam. He continues to take an active interest in ceremonies, attending many household fiestas and continuously remaining on the scene during Semana Santa. He has served as pueblo governor of Potam, and frequently is sought out by leaders for advice. During the boundary negotiations of 1975, Mario was actively involved in the strategy sessions of the Yaqui officials and seldom missed a chance to attend meetings with Mexican representatives.

While Mario's social prestige and political power complement each other, his economic wealth appears to be derived independently of power and prestige. Based on cattle ranching in the sparsely populated, non-arable, and open-range monte, not on the farming of prime irrigated land, his wealth is unlikely to have been enhanced by favoritism while he served as pueblo governor. Undoubtedly, though, wealth has contributed to his relatively high social prestige and political power. It has been sufficient to allow him to serve as fiestero, where the major expense is the provision of food for ceremonial meals. And, once his year as governor had ended, Mario's wealth assured that he would be frequently asked for small donations to the governors' operational expenses, giving him the opportunity to consult and participate in political maneuverings.

$E\overline{P}S$: Pablo García, about fifty years of age, typifies a small number of adult Yaquis who are both economically well-off and socially prestigious, but who take little active interest in political affairs and make no visible effort to convert wealth or prestige into political power. His wealth is only moderate. He owns no vehicle, nor a house of adobe, yet he manages to adequately feed a large family group which includes his wife, her mother, his daughter with husband and child, and his son, also with spouse. The household gets income from several sources. Pablo is a member of a well-managed, successful agricultural sociedad, farming about 30 hectares of wheat on productive lands near Potam. All members of the sociedad appear conscientious and the group regularly harvests a good crop. In addition, Pablo farms about 5 hectares of beans and vegetables, financing this operation with his share of the sociedad's profits. The labor composition of the household contributes substantially to the success of this private venture. His grown sons and industrious wife carry out much of the farming operations, and his freedom to grow subsistence crops on his own field reduces the amount of food purchases in the market.

Encouraged by his devout wife and mother-in-law, García had recently undertaken the expensive sponsorship of the Santisima Tiniran fiesta. Prior to this sponsorship, he showed little activity in ritual roles, but was nevertheless a frequent and interested spectator at most pueblo fiestas and the household ceremonials of his friends and acquaintances in Potam. His newly activated desire to participate through fiesta sponsorship suggests that prior economic well-being may be converted into social prestige through ritual participation. He might attempt, in sequence, to convert his social prestige into political influence and civil office, but as yet he has shown little interest in Yaqui politics. He is already past the age when most Yaqui men demonstrate a desire to be involved in the political affairs of the pueblo.

$E\overline{PS}$: A fisherman from Guásimas, Felipe Choqui is both wealthy and politically powerful in the shrimp cooperative. But he has neither desired nor achieved social prestige through active ceremonial participation. Still a young man in his mid thirties, Felipe is an energetic and successful shrimper, factors which contributed substantially to his election as co-op president. He has been equally energetic as an administrator, informally controlling all phases of the co-op's operations. Employing a casual yet authoritative style, he seems to be adroit at handling finances while preserving a necessary degree of the fishermen's loyalty to the organization. And through his experience in dealing with Mexican administrators, Felipe is frequently called upon for advice by pueblo governors.

Felipe's modest wealth, evidenced in his cinderblock house in Guásimas, filled with more than an average number of electrical appliances, is undoubtedly both a cause and a consequence of his administrative position. His success as a shrimper assured him a respectable income and, as mentioned above, made him an attractive candidate for the co-op presidency. Subsequently, the perquisites of office—a good salary, access to emergency loans from the co-op treasury, use of the co-op pick-up truck (which allows him to transport groceries from the cheaper stores in Guaymas to his home in Guásimas)—have bolstered his economic position.

Felipe makes little more than *pro forma* appearances at religious occasions. He paid an official and brief visit to Potam's Semana Santa proceedings to present a small donation from the co-op to Potam governors for ceremonial expenses. Outside of his official capacity, he expresses no interest in the social prestige obtainable through religious participation, and his political influence is not diminished by his lack of ritual interest.

$E\overline{PS}$: Lucio Valdéz, like Mario Alvarez, lives with his large family outside town. He is a successful *particular* (private farmer), financing his own crops with profits from previous harvests and the occasional sale of cattle and pigs. While he lives in a traditional-style house, he has all the trappings of relative wealth: an old stake truck, a battery-operated record player (on which, when it is working, Lucio plays recorded Yaqui ritual music), and a stocked kitchen. His economic success derives from his accumulation of excellent farm land near irrigation canals and from the labor power of his household: he can draw upon the aid of his two sons and two sons-in-law living in adjacent houses. He began working his favorably situated lands before the increased demand of recent years made land acquisition difficult.

Lucio is not an active participant in either political or religious affairs. During the 1975 negotiations between pueblo governors and Mexican officials over the tribal boundaries, he attended several political gatherings but remained on the periphery, neither sought out for advice nor offering it. He attends pueblo fiestas, but to my knowledge he has not filled any ritual roles except for a brief and unsuccessful stint as pascola in his youth. At the death of a compadre, Lucio performed his funeral obligations perfunctorily and became an object of mildly disparaging gossip. He has a well-earned reputation as a drinker: on numerous occasions during my field work, he consumed heavily for three or four days at a time, spending and losing sizable portions of his harvest profits. In short, Lucio has converted his wealth into neither political power nor social prestige.

EPS: Martín Molina, in his early forties, provides an explicit contrast to Lucio Valdéz, demonstrating that economic wealth is neither necessary for, nor a direct consequence of, political power and social prestige. Martín is poor. His family in Potam seldom appears adequately fed. His teenage daughter suffered acutely from bronchial pneumonia while I was in the field, and her condition was worsened by malnutrition. Prior to obtaining a small plot of land and planting an initial *cártamo* crop in 1975, Martín had pursued an unrewarding series of odd jobs, tending livestock for others and occasionally working as a *carbonero* (charcoal maker) in the monte around Potam.

Martín's major interest, his major expenditure of energy, is in pascola dancing. He is currently the most popular and sought-after pascola in Potam. He is known by reputation throughout the Yaqui Zone as one of only two or three exceptionally talented performers. While not lucrative, his heavy schedule of ritual performances brings in some cash, and the flour, salt, sugar, coffee, and meat given to performers at the conclusion of household fiestas provide welcome additions to the family's food supplies.

Highly respected as a ritual specialist, Martín has also served well as an assistant to the Potam governor. The demands of his pascola skills seem to prevent him from taking more powerful civil positions, but he is still carefully heeded when he speaks at political meetings. Martín seems, in short, to be one of only a handful of Yaquis entirely beyond reproach, never the object of gossip.

$\overline{E}\overline{P}S$: Miguel Leyva typifies a number of Yaquis who have gained high social prestige through their active involvement in ritual, but who have little or no political influence and remain poor. Now in his seventies, Miguel has pursued a long career as a talented *tampalero* for the pascolas and deer dancers of Potam. He is highly respected for his skills and ritual knowledge, but outside of his specialty he is looked upon as somewhat of a buffoon, a constant object of entertaining gossip about his recent and unsuccessful love affairs and his parasitical living arrangements with his daughter. He has been poor throughout his life and currently, as a part-time cattle herder, he is renewing his reputation for unreliability. Miguel's low economic and political standing contrasts starkly with the rapt attention he commands when seated with his tambora and flauta.

$\overline{E}\overline{P}\overline{S}$: Adult Yaquis of this category are rare, and the one case with which I am most familiar may in fact be transitional. Lorenzo González, still in his mid thirties, has been relatively wealthy in the immediate past when he was a successful fisherman and co-op treasurer. Facing allegations of financial misdealings, he retired from fishing and spent his savings on an adobe house in Potam. Following several years of virtual unemployment, he began to farm 10 hectares of land borrowed from an inactive sociedad and financed by a patron from Estación Vicam. If the parcel becomes productive, he may again achieve some degree of wealth.

Lorenzo's relative standing in the dimensions of political power and social prestige is more easily evaluated. He was actively involved in the Yaqui boundary dispute, where his experience in dealing with Mexican officials, while working with the shrimp co-op, proved useful. Indeed, his political influence within Potam has risen steadily since he returned from the fishing villages: he has been selected as pueblo governor, an honor and burdensome duty which he initially turned down, citing his lack of experience and the time-consuming demands of his new agricultural venture.

Outside the political arena, Lorenzo has shown virtual disdain for Yaqui ceremonialism. As a young man he had made a promise to serve as a matachine for three years, but dropped out of the dance society because he felt uncomfortable, "too tall." Since then, he has not involved himself in any ritual duties of note, and has dispatched his duties as compadre at weddings and funerals with little enthusiasm.

While the relationship, in this case, between wealth and political power is somewhat ambiguous, Lorenzo clearly represents a disjunction between power and social prestige: still a relatively young man, he is one of the more influential politicos in Potam, yet gives no indication of desiring the social prestige attendant upon ritual participation.

$\overline{EPS}$: Miguel García, son-in-law of Pablo García, is marginal in all respects. In his mid twenties, he has been a shrimp fisherman for about five years, but has never been very successful. He has also worked periodically on the labor crews refurbishing the canals around Potam, but was unable to save any money. Nor has he taken any active interest in ceremonial participation. At best, he attends major fiestas only briefly. Matching his lack of interest in religious offices is his nonparticipation in political affairs. On occasion, he shows up at gatherings called to discuss business of the fishing co-op, but never voices his opinions.

Miguel's lack of political power and social prestige may reflect his youth. More likely, given his apparent disinterest in politics and religion, along with his dominating shyness in any social interaction, he will never strive to enhance his position as he grows older.

The preceding cases suggest a wide range of variability in the social positions of individual Yaquis. Some, like Mario Alvarez, have successfully achieved high social prestige, great political power, and a modest but relatively substantial income. Others, like Miguel García, have achieved none of these, but have not jeopardized their ethnic group membership. The analysis can be pursued a little farther: of the fifty-eight individuals that I was able to classify along these dimensions with some confidence, the following distribution appears in Table 4.1. The sample here is by no means random. The cases represent friends and acquaintances, drawn mostly from Potam, Lobos, Rahum, and Guásimas, but including several from the pueblos of Belem, Huirivis, Vicam, and Torim. In effect, they are individuals whom I knew biographically. Although I do not feel that my procedures for gaining acquaintances drastically skew the sample, I have no sound basis for claiming representativeness for the fifty-eight cases.

With these cautionary notes in mind, some observations may still be made. In over 35 percent of the cases ($E\overline{P}S$, $EP\overline{S}$, $\overline{EP}S$, and $\overline{EPS}$), political power and social prestige do not correspond. The remaining cases, over 64 percent, do show such correspondence between power and prestige (achieving both or lacking both). This suggests, not unambiguously, a relatively strong conjunction between power and pres-

Table 4.1 Variations in Wealth, Power, and Social Prestige

EPS	11	$EP\overline{S}$	7	$\overline{E}PS$	5	$\overline{EP}S$	3
$E\overline{P}S$	2	$E\overline{PS}$	12	$\overline{EP}S$	9	$\overline{EPS}$	9
						Total	= 58

tige. Regardless of wealth, power and prestige go hand-in-hand in the majority of cases. Furthermore, regarding the convertibility of wealth into power and prestige as suggested by Cancian, almost an equal number of Yaquis fall into two cases, EPS and $E\overline{PS}$. Contrary to Cancian's findings for southern Mexico, power and prestige appear to vary independently of economic wealth in Yaqui society.

With this separation in wealth, power, and prestige, and the resulting range of variation among individuals, it is risky to draw conclusions about underlying motivations. Such a summary must be phrased largely in negative terms: individuals are not motivated to participate in political and religious affairs by an application of strong sanctions. Nor do they participate in the hope of gaining substantial economic reward. Beyond this, it may be possible, but equally risky, to posit a driving motive of recognition or "individuation": to be marked off from the rest. But this is hardly an all-consuming drive. Miguel García would be extraordinarily uncomfortable to be singled out; Lorenzo felt a similar embarrassment to be on stage as a matachine dancer. More importantly, however, those who strive for recognition do so within separate realms: some individuals are economically successful, some are noted politicians, and others are famed ritual specialists. As distinct paths to social acknowledgment, only loosely tied to one another, the realms of wealth, political power, and prestige offer numerous outlets for individual strivings. And many Yaquis feel just as content to ignore all three routes to local esteem.

RITUAL AS PERFORMANCE

Social prestige accrues to those who participate in Yaqui ritual. But social prestige is neither a necessary cause nor consequence of economic wealth or political power. And ethnic status may be validated through ritual participation, but participation as such does not turn non-Yaquis into Yaquis. Nor does nonparticipation turn Yaquis into non-Yaquis.

These conclusions, reached in previous sections of this chapter, reflect only one way of looking at ethnic identity: as a categorization or placement of individuals into discrete ethnic groups. These conclusions reflect, as well, only one way of looking at ritual participation: as a more-or-less closely entailed attribute of individual ethnic identification. We may also examine ritual as symbolic action, carried out with an orientation "toward creating beautiful or stimulating form and expressing emotions, moral ideals, or conceptions of reality" (Peacock 1968:234). Symbolic action is analytically distinct from "technical" or "social" action, behavior designed to achieve economic, political, or social ends. Thus, as James Peacock observes of *ludruk*, the Javanese proletarian drama:

If ludruk depicts peasants sowing their seeds or a family resolving its conflicts, that is not the same as real peasants striving to sow their seeds (striving to achieve an empirical economic end) or a real family striving to resolve its conflicts (striving to achieve an empirical social end). The ludruk actors are not really struggling to make crops grow on stage or to resolve a quarrel among themselves; their main concern is to entertain (to create stimulating form), to portray a conception of reality (a conception of the nature of peasants or families or human existence), to express emotions, and perhaps to make a moral point (Peacock 1968:235).

To most anthropologists, the distinction between symbolic and technical action is only preliminary to the more interesting and important problem: tracing the reciprocal relations between symbolic and empirical acts. Max Weber pursued the connection between Calvinism and capitalism, and many social scientists since Weber have made the discovery of such linkages their primary task (see Duncan 1962; V. Turner 1969; Geertz 1973; Burke 1973; Moore and Myerhoff 1975; Cohen 1974). But proponents of a symbolic action perspective polarize around two emphases, one on the *content* of symbols, the other on the *form* of symbolic action. Peacock sees the former emphasis as stemming strongly from Edmund Leach's (1964) analysis of "Myth as a Justification for Factions and Social Change," in *Political Systems of Highland Burma*. Symbolic actions are essentially *validators*:

> When one is concerned to show that symbolic performances are statements, oral equivalents of legal documents, which validate institutional or personal claims, one naturally places emphasis on the content of the performances—what they state; thus, Leach does not deal with the form of Kachin myths, except to note briefly how each is divided into sections. He confines himself to showing how the myths are statements about genealogical relations among certain kinsmen, spirits, and ancestors, each statement being cited by a particular clan to validate its claims to superior status (Peacock 1968:245).

For Leach and others inclined toward content analysis, the connector between symbolic and social action is primarily cognitive. To effectively translate symbols into behavior, actors must reach an understanding of those symbols, of the relationships between symbols, of the interpenetration of one symbolic realm into another. These can be heavy demands, positing an articulateness, an "exegetic dimension" (V. Turner 1969:11) which may be absent among the populace of many societies. Fredrik Barth, for example, was led to the discovery that the Baktaman of New Guinea have no exegetical tradition. But the discovery came only after a carefully subdued field methodology, relying on observations of spontaneous, unelicited actions as well as "Baktaman questions and explanations to each other." Somewhat surprised at the finding, Barth comments that he was also

> . . . struck by the lack of factual comparative evidence in the anthropological literature on the presence and degree of development of native exegetical tradition and praxis; and without the careful restraint I practised, I might not have recorded its absence. As social relations in the field deepened, it would not have been difficult to obtain native help in my efforts to understand: to *make* them systematize and translate verbally in response to *my* need for system and verbal codification. My strong suspicion is that the bodies of native explanation that we find in anthropological literature are often created as an artefact of the anthropologist's activity (Barth 1975:226).

Analysis of *form* demands a different but equally precarious methodology, for the connector between symbolic form and social action is emotional, not cognitive. Thus Peacock (1968:6), in his study of proletarian plays, seeks to understand how dramatic form "seduces ludruk participants into empathy with modes of social action involved in the modernization process." He concludes, tentatively, that newer forms of the ludruk

> . . . are more action-inciting than are older forms. As the older *ludruk* performances finish, they return to a state of equilibrium that they enjoyed at their beginning. The last scene is structurally similar to the first, and is calm like the first, and when the *ludruk* is over, spectators get up and go home uttering remarks such as "Now the situation is again secure and calm." The newer performances, by contrast, having carried spectators through a two to five hour series of buildups and relatively sustained empathy with a plot, finish with an action that is unfinished . . . Hence, participants in the new *ludruk* must leave the theater before they have finished the narrative action in which they have been clutched for hours. Perhaps this pattern incites within them a drive to finish outside the theater that which they could not inside, an itch to consummate in reality what they could not in fantasy (Peacock 1969:172).

The methodological problems have yet to be resolved: "Overt audience reactions are easy enough to record, but audiences do not necessarily scream out what is going on deep inside them" (Peacock 1969:171). But the lines of research are clear and, I think, impeccable: the "dramatistic" approach, the anaysis of form,

> . . . treats behaviors as if they were organized "aesthetically" as in a play that arranges its scenes poetically and climactically to evoke appreciative and cathartic responses from an audience. The task of the investigator is to show how forms, climaxes, settings, focus around evoking such response from some audience (Peacock 1969:174).

Yaqui religious ceremony is eminently open to dramaturgical analysis. Rituals along the Río Yaqui are elaborately staged, complexly organized sequences of folk Catholic pageantry, involving a large number of differentiated ceremonial roles and performances, an expansive use of space, and a curiously shifting pattern of audience exclusion and contact, even integration, with performers. Yaqui rituals are, likewise, well suited to the maintenance and frequent communication of strict ethnic boundaries between Yaqui and Mexican. They are staged on Yaqui land, conducted by Yaqui specialists, infused with Yaqui meanings.

Yet this potential is underutilized. Yaqui rituals, so culturally distinctive, are predominantly "front regions" in the terms of Erving Goffman (1959:106ff), settings and events for the open intermingling of Yaqui and Mexican. It is this paradox—Yaqui rituals are staunchly Yaqui, yet unabashedly public, noncompartmentalized—which a dramatistic outlook on Yaqui ritual form can illuminate.

Audience, Space, and Time

On several ceremonial occasions, I heard variations of an insightful but unexplained claim, "the fiestas in Potam are carried out well, aren't they?" The Yaqui religious fiestas in Potam are indeed recognized as standards for the rest of the zone, the most elaborate, exciting, and reverent rituals. On the surface, the claim is not surprising. Potam is the largest of the river towns, and has a larger pool of ritual performers to draw upon. The expense and time of ritual sponsorship and performance can be spread around, easing the burden on each individual. Potentially, too, more individuals can take up roles in the expandable ritual segments. More *chapayekam* can "come out" during the successive Fridays of Lent, increasing their numbers week by week until the climactic events of Semana Santa.

Yet Potam dresses fewer chapayekam in proportion to its size than the other pueblos. And the individual burdens in smaller towns are relieved by corporeal loans from Potam. Poteños frequently assume ceremonial roles in other pueblos where they maintain kinship, compadre, and residential ties. Specialists outside Potam are just as likely to be found hosting fiestas in Potam. The success of Potam fiestas, then, does not seem to be a simple reflection of the town's size, nor of the town's possession of skilled and popular performers.

Nor is Potam the most "traditional," the most restricted or closed of Yaqui settlements. It is, in fact, the most infiltrated by Mexicans, save for the railroad service center of Estación Vicam. Potam possesses the trappings of modern Mexico: electricity and street lighting, a clinic, a private doctor, an office of the Mexican police, a federal agricultural school, many stores and, until recently, cantinas and a decrepit pool hall—objects of attack by the locally run, poorly attended chapter of Alcoholics Anonymous. Finally, Potam has a large resident population of Mexicans. Few of the other river towns boast all or any of these penetrations of national society.

Yaqui ritual is public, and Potam is infiltrated by Mexicans and Mexicanisms. But ritual in Potam is "put on well," as the Yaquis claim. It is a standard against which the rituals of other towns frequently do not match up. To understand this, we need to comprehend the nature of the audience, space, and time in Yaqui ceremony.

Fusing indigenous elements and Catholicism (Spicer 1954, 1958), Yaqui religion is nevertheless explicitly "universalistic." It concerns itself, in Robert Bellah's terms, with the fact that "man is no longer defined chiefly in terms of what tribe or clan he comes from or what particular god he serves but rather as a being capable of salvation" (1964:366). But its universalism is slightly different from that envisioned by Bellah. Yaquis have altered and localized the standard Catholic beliefs. As Spicer recounts, the Lord

> . . . came into the Yaqui country long before the Spaniards arrived, coming from the west out of the country of salt flats and desert beyond Belem. He began to go from village to village, and wherever He went he cured people. Because He was so successful in this people call him Salvador Maestro [The Savior Teacher] (1954:118).

The Lord is more a healer than an ultimate adjudicator of individual salvation. As a healer, He was apparently indiscriminate: informants now say that He takes care of Mexicans as well as Yaquis. Hence, Mexicans—and all non-Yaquis—can benefit from the penance displayed by Yaquis in ceremonial efforts.

There are reciprocal benefits to be derived from a large audience. Observers validate the pious efforts of the ceremonial sponsors and hosts:

> The human beings without vows to ceremonial labor who come to the event are important because the fulfillment of obligations should be publicly witnessed and hence the bigger the crowd the bigger the fiesta. It is a focus of Yaqui interest to make the event attractive and to provide for those who are attracted (Spicer 1954:182).

This belief underlies claims in the previous chapter that mere attendance at Yaqui fiestas is a respectable mode of demonstrating adherence to Yaqui custom (see Spicer 1954:177, 178). There is frequent and meaningful use of the verb *amanecer* in connection with prolonged Yaqui ceremonies. The word has the connotation of staying for the duration of the fiesta, throughout long, cold nights of often repetitiously uneventful ritual acts. Night-long attenders are invariably exhausted the following morning, frequently drunk or hungover, but unmistakably euphoric. Conversely, those who habitually put in nothing but a brief appearance (and many, both Mexican and Yaqui, do just this), a token demonstration of their interest, are somewhat suspect.

Yaqui rituals are expressly designed to attract an audience. Pascolas act as ceremonial hosts and ribald entertainers at most household and pueblo fiestas. Their role as crowd-pleasers has long been recognized by anthropologists (Spicer 1940:184–87; 1954:76). Upcoming fiestas are the subject of much conversation and anticipation, and the merits of individual pascola performers are in many cases central to the decision to attend or ignore the fiesta. A good pascola team, glib in speech and quick and skilled in movement, can easily enthrall an audience.

In its universalism, its explicit promise of sacred benefit to performer and viewer, and its orientation around the pascola as host, Yaqui ritual demands and recruits an audience. This audience is biethnic; Mexicans from Potam, from other pueblos and communities on the Río Yaqui, and from major Sonoran cities come to Yaqui fiestas as interested observers. The dates of calendrical Catholic fiestas are well known and the times of movable celebrations are easily obtained. To the Mexican residents of the Yaqui pueblos, the times and locations of household fiestas are likewise common knowledge, picked up from storekeepers who sell ritual goods to ceremonial sponsors. While Yaquis make no effort to advertise upcoming rituals across ethnic lines, neither do they attempt to disguise the occurrence, to "compartmentalize" ceremonies.

Even when Mexican neighbors have no desire to attend Yaqui fiestas, they cannot avoid them. Yaqui ritual is expansive, intruding noisily and forcefully into main pueblo streets and paths, into whole neighborhoods. Residentially, Potam is incompletely segregated, with the majority of Mexicans living within a couple of blocks of the central street and the remainder interspersed with Yaquis in modified grid pattern around the center. With fireworks, dancing, and the continuous droning of musicians, Yaqui household fiestas inevitably announce themselves to neighboring Yaquis and Mexicans. Household fiestas also tend to fill and encompass available space: there appear to be no regularized restrictions on the distance between the pascola-santo ramada and the cross to which processions travel throughout the ceremonies. If unobstructed by houses, brush, or canals, the procession grounds may extend several hundred feet, monopolizing streets, adjacent house compound yards, and open spaces.

Expansiveness is even more evident in Estación Vicam, the service town dominated by Mexicans, but also the residence of many ritual specialists and politicians of Vicam pueblo. Rituals in enclaved Yaqui households intrude into surrounding Mexican residential clusters, communicating to Mexican residents the intensity and persistence of Yaqui ritual as well as a certain arrogance. Yaquis have no qualms about using Mexican space in a Mexican town for their own ceremonial displays.

Temporal dimensions of Yaqui ritual have equally important implications for the symbolic communication of ethnicity. Public performances at household fiestas—of pascolas, *venados* (deer dancers), matachines, maestros, cantoras, and the santos—run throughout the night. In the culminating days of Semana Santa, the ritual manipulations of santos, the *kontis* (processions), and chapayekam activities likewise are continuous. But audiences rapidly dwindle late at night and into the cold hours before dawn. Hardened Yaqui celebrants may remain, but virtually no Mexicans do. During these hours, the public nature of the ritual is fortuitously altered; the opportunity exists, by virtue of the absence of Mexican observers, to present private, compartmentalized ceremony.

At a memorial service (*cumpleaño*) for a deceased Yaqui resistance leader, the Coyote dance was conducted during these hours, without Mexican onlookers. While I heard no comment by Yaqui officials that the Coyote dance is properly a nonpublic, "back-region" display, the dance itself is surprisingly incongruous to the staid and stoic appearance of the sponsoring military society in its other ritual functions. The Coyote dance is, seemingly, a licensed frivolity by an otherwise humorless ya'ura.

Performed first by two groups of novices, in their teens and unskilled, the dance was nevertheless the center of attraction. As dawn broke, another group of three, ranging in age from the mid twenties to around fifty, began to perform. Accompanied by a drummer seated on a hide blanket, the three lined up facing an earthen bowl of dried meat. Shuffling back and forth between the bowl and the drummer, each dancer continuously rapped a short beater against a bow with arrows, held at the crotch between the legs. Imitating coyote movements with his head, the center dancer stooped to pick up the meat in his mouth. He then deposited it on the drummer's blanket, pantomiming excretion on the drummer. He then tidied up his work—drummer, meat, excrement—with sand, in canine fashion. This sequence was then repeated by the remaining two dancers.

Throughout the dances of the experienced group at dawn, and that of the novices earlier, the reaction of the audience was one of restrained, somewhat embarrassed laughter, different from the generally unabashed enjoyment of the pascola antics. I found myself, as an outsider, being eyed a little nervously by the Vicam governors, and I was at several points asked for my reactions to the dance. The questioning was unlike what I was exposed to at other rituals. It was not rhetorical, not the usual inquiry that allows only one answer—sincere agreement about the profundity and impressiveness of the ceremonies. Rather, the questions surrounding the Coyote dance were fact-finding probes, attempts to test out my real reactions on this exposure of private ritual.

If the temporal progression of Yaqui ritual generates fortuitous "back regions"—where "the suppressed facts make an appearance" (Goffman 1959:112)—it also allows for covert participation by professed nonparticipants, by conspicuously marginal Yaquis. *Chamacos* as a group are marginal to mainstream Yaqui interests. As teenagers, they have not yet reached the age of choosing a working career in Yaqui farming, fishing, cattle-raising, or as wage workers in Mexican towns. They have not reached a stage of ceremonial or political responsibility. And, through schooling, they have come into close association with a peer group of modernizing, fad-oriented Mexican youths. To many Yaqui teenagers, ostentatious ritual participation is an embarrassment, even negatively sanctioned by their Mexican and Yaqui peers.

Darkness offers a cover for these marginal youths. This is evident at household fiestas, where chamacos often form the core of all-night vigils. The accepted drinking, the pascola entertainment, and the camaraderie all provide attractions to teenagers, more compelling than the religiosity of the maestros and cantoras. But these irreligious motivations for attendance are accepted. The judgment is not of one's devotion, but of one's willingness to stay all night.

Chamaco participation is also manifest in the pueblo fiestas of Semana Santa. Throughout the day of Good Friday, ceremonies steadily build to the climax of Sabado de Gloria. The Crucifixion is portrayed on Friday morning by a konti or procession around the Way of the Cross. Subsequently, during the day, additional kontis move around the church, marking other events of the Passion. From roughly 9:30 on Friday night to 3:00 in the morning on Saturday, a series of poorly heralded, hastily assembled kontis takes place, representing the Resurrection. While most families have stationed themselves inside the church for the night, chamacos remain actively interested in the chapayekam burlesque outside. Ostensibly just loitering, chamacos mobilize at a moment's notice for the kontis, with little urging from the chapayekam. On the "Way," these teenagers perform the devout ceremonial labor of bearing the santos. The situation is striking, in its complete inversion of the usual chamaco behavior. The teenagers eagerly bear the images, unselfishly trading off with one another so that all may participate.

Audience, space, and time in Yaqui ritual are key dramatic elements. Ceremony is public, and the entertainment of the pascolas draws the requisite crowds of Yaquis and Mexicans for a successful fiesta. At the same time, though, the temporal dimension of rituals provides a fortuitous compartmentalization, allowing individuals to perform and participate without the apparent embarrassment of being in full public view.

Sanctions and Incitement: Boundary Maintenance and Stereotypy

Captivating a biethnic audience, Yaqui ritual would seem a very effective vehicle for the communication of ethnic identity and the forceful demonstration of tribal cohesiveness and distinctiveness. Indeed, ethnic boundaries are maintained and fostered through ritual. But these boundaries are drawn in somewhat devious ways.

Peacock speaks of the Javanese ludruk as limited in its direct organizing power:

> Ludruk, unlike speeches in a party cell or sermons in a sect, is not tightly bound to an organization with sanctioning powers: that is, commercial ludruk performers and their audiences do not form a corporate group such that ludruk can apply sanctions if its audiences do not act as ludruk tells them to act (Peacock 1968:243).

Yaqui ritual, in this regard, has something in common with the party cell and the sermons of the sect. Yaqui ceremonial sponsors, performers, and the Yaqui audiences do form a corporate body. Performers do tell their Yaqui audiences how to act and how not to. And there are sanctions for those who transgress the accepted limits of behavior during rituals and during ceremonial seasons. This is most evident in Semana Santa, at the close of the long Lenten season. Waresma, as Spicer has succinctly observed,

> . . . is a sad time, a hard time, a time of penance for everyone. There is a definite effort on the part of the *Kohtumbrem* leaders to create among not only their own numbers but also among the people at large a sense of oppression. They give the impression in their ritual activities of disciplined, purposeful and unrelenting devotion to duty. Young men frequently express fear of what will be done to them if they do not follow a request of the Kohtumbrem or if they neglect ceremonial duties or proper behavior during the period (Spicer 1954:145).

The limits of proper behavior are well defined during the ritual climaxes of Holy Week. Men must not drink or work in their fields. Women must not wash clothes or sew. And families cannot eat meat. Recently, too, baseball has been prohibited on the *llano*, the great open space in front of the church in Potam. The *konti bo'o*, Way of the Cross, cuts through center field.

Infractions are handled by the chapayekam who, at irregular intervals, in small groups, unmasked but with silk kerchiefs tied over their heads and eyes, proceed through the village streets searching for transgressors. They no longer use the stocks and whipping post; they place violators in the carcel attached to the guardia. The most serious taboo seems to be against drinking. And the most frequent violators of Lenten restrictions are the inveterate drunks. Escorted to the jail by chapayekam, the inebriated must spend the night and pay a fine of 50 pesos. Throughout the evenings of Semana Santa, the rituals on the llano are punctuated by the falsetto choruses of prisoners from the jail, a hundred yards away.

Yaqui reactions to drinking and its taboo are varied. A former chapayeka and matachine, himself a frequent drinker but entirely sober prior to Sabado de Gloria, remarked that the violators have no respect for religion. Others seemed to enjoy the comic humor in the juxtaposition of jailhouse chorus and church ritual. And my landlady, not publicly reverent and somewhat of a jokester, suggested that drinking during Semana Santa was not bad: you got a front-row seat for the kontis as they passed by the guardia.

Apart from drinking and baseball, the taboos of Lent appear now to be honored mainly in the breech. Transgressions observed by others or performed by oneself will elicit comment, but little penance. My landlady, again, got up very early one morning of Semana Santa to do her wash—she had failed to do it earlier in the week because she was busy trying to finish her new clothes, sewing late into the night. She explained her industrious and uncharacteristic washing behavior at dawn as an attempt to avoid the prowling chapayekam. The explanation was not very satisfactory, either to her or myself. She knew that chapayekam do not wait until midmorning to walk through the pueblo. And she was fully aware that a week's wash hung to dry on the mesquite tree in her yard would quickly expose her subterfuge to the chapayekam.

That the application of sanctions is in many cases haphazard does not diminish the saliency of the taboos. Most Yaquis recognize the existence of the restrictions. They simply choose to ignore them if they have good reason to do so: dirty laundry, unfinished Easter dresses, weeds to be pulled. More importantly, though, lack of enforcement does little to reduce the *appearance* of corporateness to outsiders, Mexican residents of the Yaqui towns. Yoris in Potam view the incarcerations of drunks as strict enforcement of religious prohibitions. They view the policing rounds of the Kohtumbrem as evidence of the oppression and discipline of Waresma. Occasionally I heard explicit statements about the seeming unity of the pueblo during Semana Santa and of the submission of all Yaquis to the ceremonial rule of the chapayekam, pilatos, and cabos.

Edmund Leach provides an instructive counterpoint to Peacock's position on dramaturgy. Myth and ritual are, Leach claims, charters for society. But they are not necessarily reflections of long-term solidarity and integration of social groups:

> If then we accept the Durkheimian view that religious rituals are representations of the solidarity of the participating group, we need clearly to understand that the solidarity need exist only at the moment at which the ritual takes place; we cannot infer a continuing latent solidarity after the ritual celebrations are over (Leach 1964:281).

The tribal solidarity that seems manifest in Yaqui ritual may, like that in highland Burma, be only temporary. And even then solidarity may only be apparent to the Mexican audience which, overestimating the enforcement of Lenten taboos, sees a drama of the trappings, not the substance of corporate strength.

This inference highlights the crucial question of cultural performances, what Peacock calls the incitement to action. In contrast to the suggested action inducement of Javanese ludruk, James Boon raises the other possibility:

> . . . often, perhaps usually, the effects of performances, while intense at the time and place of their production, fade with disconcerting celerity as soon as the participants leave the "theatre." The forms seem of little direct consequence in subsequent general action (Boon 1973:20).

The issue can be phrased in local terms. To what extent is the image of corporateness carried over into encounters between Mexican and Yaqui? To what extent is the Mexican stereotype of the Yaqui-as-religious-fanatic (Spicer 1954:175) implicated in social, political, and economic interaction across ethnic lines? These questions form the basis for the next three chapters.

CHAPTER 5

San Ignacio, Río Muerto: The Politics of Land

At dawn on Thursday, 23 October 1975, Sonora's judicial police moved out onto the irrigated fields of Block 717, a few kilometers from the small town of San Ignacio, Río Muerto. Accompanying Lieutenant Colonel Francisco Arellano Noblecía's *judiciales* were contingents of police from Guaymas, Obregón, and Empalme, supported by the automatic rifles and well-disciplined forces of the Eighteenth Regimiento de Caballería, the Mexican army. Unarmed, Arellano Noblecía bore two court orders issued the night before by a judge in Guaymas at the request of Dengel Kuel, one of the proprietors of the 400 hectares of Block 717. One order demanded the peaceful evacuation of the three hundred campesinos who had invaded the land and set up a camp early Monday morning under cover of darkness. The second order called for the detention of the principal leaders of the squatters: Juan de Dios Terán, Jose Alatorre, Juan Alberto García, and Heriberto García.

A reporter for Ciudad Obregón's daily *Tribuna del Yaqui* (24 October 1975) reconstructed the subsequent confusion from eyewitness accounts:

> "He told them if they didn't get out willingly, he had orders to take them out by force," the young man continued, "and when he repeated it to Heriberto García, the latter replied: 'They will only take us from here dead.'"
>
> "Given this answer, Lt. Col. Arellano Noblecía," narrates a Guaymas urban policeman, "ordered us to get down from the trucks, and together with the judiciales, we started forming a semi-circle, in order to surround the *invasores* [invaders] to move them toward the trucks in which we were going to move them out ... The soldiers, meanwhile, took positions near the canal in order

to guard access." And a young reporter from *Periodicos Sonorenses* continued: "Then the police began to advance, in a very large arch, more or less from here to there," he motions to an area about 700 meters in length, "and some of the *paracaidistas* [squatters] began to move peacefully toward the trucks . . . A little while before, the chief of the *judiciales* had managed to get them [los invasores] to willingly remove a disk plow and some of those large tubes (of concrete, used for irrigation or drainage) that were in the entrance to the field . . . and they were doing that when the mess began."

An agent of the Policía Judicial del Estado adds to the story: "We were closing in little by little, and we had already made contact with a few, from whom we removed, without violence, their garrotes or machetes, and Lt. Col. Arellano Noblecía along with Guillermo Olivas, the head of the Guaymas *judiciales*, was standing to one side, but in front of leader Heriberto García when suddenly the latter shouted 'Everyone to his place . . . to arms!' And all hell broke loose; they began to run to a shed where there are pieces of metal sheeting and machinery and shots began to rain from there. Chief Arellano remained standing, yelling to us 'Don't shoot, don't respond, don't shoot!' . . . but already some of the Guaymas police had taken out their pistols and some of us, too . . . Then I saw Olivas make the chief throw himself on the ground and Olivas flung himself at the chief's side."

Later Guillermo Olivas told me that he had made Arellano Noblecía throw himself on the ground "when the bullets were already around our feet" and that then the chief had ordered tear gas bombs to be thrown at the ones shooting. Until then, he assured me the police had not opened fire.

"They threw gas on them," says a young girl who saw the battleground from her house, one-half kilometer away, "and the shooting was stilled, but it began again a little while later."

Another campesino tells me they began to come out of the shed with their hands up, when suddenly again there were shots, and then, indeed, the police were also shooting.

"The whole thing was very hard," says a Guaymas agent, they were even throwing the gas grenades back at us by catching them with handkerchiefs and the bullets came very close to us . . . And they shouldn't blame us solely; the soldiers were shooting too." In the shed one could see the marks left by large caliber bullets. An agent told me they are 30–40 caliber, "from some crazy man who didn't even lift his head to aim and shot without rhyme or reason."

Later in the Municipal Hospital in Ciudad Obregón, a doctor stated that one of the wounded had a bullet cross from one side to the other. "That was Fal," he said, referring to the automatic weapons of the army.

All the witnesses agreed that the shooting lasted for more than 10 minutes, and then gas grenades rained until the paracaidistas surrendered.

Lt. Col. Arellano Noblecía refused to make any statements. He said that the press would be given the facts through official channels. But one of his subordinates explained that more gas had been ordered so that the situation "would not be a slaughter."

Juan de Dios Terán, a twenty-seven-year-old teacher in a rural school in the valley, was buried twelve hours later at San Ignacio. At least five campesinos, perhaps as many as nine (Sanderson 1981a:187), died with Dios Terán in the confrontation: Gildardo Gil Ochoa, twenty years old, of Block 621 in the Yaqui Valley; Rogelio, twenty-seven, and Benjamín Robles Ruiz, thirty-one, of San Ignacio Río Muerto; Enrique Félix, also of San Ignacio; and Rafael López Vizcarra, thirty-eight, of Block 221. Thirteen of the *invasores* were wounded: three from San Ignacio; three from Colonia Militar on the outskirts of San Ignacio; two from El Polvorán along the dried bed of the Río Muerto; two from Obregón; one from Navojoa in the Mayo irrigation district; and two with unknown residences.

The survivors vacated Block 717 the same morning. But the battle provided no conclusion to the long and violent struggle for land in the Yaqui Valley. It proved, rather, to be only the first step in a bitter exercise in politics. Over the course of three years, every domain of power in the state of Sonora, in the Partido Revolucionario Institucional (PRI), and in the presidency came to be tested. The Yaquis mustered their power too, but were inevitably outmaneuvered as the events of San Ignacio quickly took on national and international importance.

News of the dawn battle spread immediately throughout the Yaqui pueblos, broadcast by a loudspeaker truck from Obregón. There were quick and sincere reactions to the loss of life at San Ignacio, but little sympathy for the cause of the invasores and few of the heated political discussions and commentaries which Yaqui men, usually aloof and introverted, sometimes carry on. Yaquis realized immediately that their own political and economic demands—for more farmland and more economic aid—would be pushed aside until the pressing, volatile issues raised at San Ignacio were settled. Indeed, much of the political maneuverings to follow San Ignacio had little to do with the tribe. Rather, these events involved Mexican campesinos, Mexican *latifundistas,* and the Mexican government. Yet the Yaquis did become involved, deeply, on the basis of a largely fortuitous circumstance: they had laid claim to the same lands that the campesinos had just invaded (see map).

THE PEQUEÑOS PROPIETARIOS AND THE CCI

Violence for the most part ended on October 23. The battle of rhetoric commenced immediately. Government agrarian officials and national peasant leaders began arriving in Obregón with the initial occupation of Block 717 early Monday morning, contributing to the

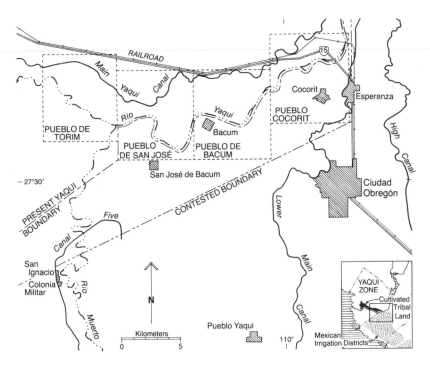

San Ignacio and the Disputed Boundary, 1975–1976

atmosphere of ominous expectancy. One of the last to come, on a presidential jet from Mexico City the night after the shooting, was Alfonso Garzón, national leader of the Central Campesina Independiente (CCI). The victims were members of CCI and Garzón had come to investigate. In what was to become the dominant theme in subsequent months, he bemoaned the deaths but urged a halt to violence: "We regret what has happened and hope there will be no more bloodshed" (*Diario del Yaqui,* 24 October 1975). Jaime Miranda of the Confederación Nacional de Pequeña Propiedad—the "small landholders" association, main protagonist to Garzón and the campesinos—likewise decried the violence, urging a return to negotiations: "Farmers and representatives of the governor of the state had been talking peacefully with the campesinos and their leaders for two consecutive nights. Those talks were coming along nicely. They had been productive to the point that they (campesinos) had agreed to vacate Mr. Dengel's land the next day. Nevertheless . . ." (*Tribuna del Yaqui,* 24 October 1975). Miranda perhaps sought to avoid the ramifications of peasant martyrdom. He was unsuccessful, and the killings at San Ignacio initiated an intense period of public and governmental scrutiny of the *pequeña propiedad,* of the alleged discrepancies between the lands of "small holders" and Mexican agrarian law.

To be put to the test, in the aftermath of San Ignacio, would be two significant changes in federal statutes. One, encoded in the new Agrarian Reform Law of 1971,

> ... outlawed the common practice of 'concentration of advantage' (*concentración de provecho*), by which the use of more than one plot fell to one owner through registering small children as farmers, obtaining *prestanombres,* and other shady mechanisms for avoiding the intent of the reform (Sanderson 1981a:173).

The second, contained in the Federal Water Law of the same year, restricted new water allocations to parcels of land 20 hectares or less in size, and similarly limited the size of holdings in newly created irrigation districts to 20 hectares or less (Sanderson 1981a:174). Together, these legislative reforms of President Luis Echeverría Álvarez sought to give hope, once again, to the nation's peasantry.

The history of the CCI under Alfonso Garzón exemplifies the uneasy and ambiguous role of the peasant sectors in Mexican national politics. It displays a recurrent pattern of dissent and co-optation (Anderson and Cockcroft 1969:384). Initially a splinter group formed by peasant leaders unhappy with the efforts of the official peasant organization, the Confederación Nacional Campesina (CNC), Garzón's CCI has "returned to the fold," to become a loyal element of the umbrella CNC.

The CNC was organized during the Cárdenas administration of the late 1930s for several official and unofficial purposes. By giving the affiliated local agrarian committees and state peasant leagues a responsive voice at the national level, it was to be the primary framework for carrying out Cárdenas's extensive program of land distribution. And it was designed to give presidential sanction to local efforts at overruling obstructionist officials. Finally, CNC was to be the vehicle for tying peasant interests directly to the presidency, bypassing the independent organizing attempts by the Mexican Communist Party.

Under Cárdenas, CNC did indeed effectively streamline agrarian reform. But with subsequent administrations and less radical agrarian policies, CNC came increasingly to respond to presidential directives at the expense of peasant interests. Gerrit Huizer has summarized the role of the organization under the Alemán regime, 1947–52:

> Peasants were not given the opportunity to discuss the changes in the agrarian laws that undoubtedly have been of great importance in the process of change in the structure of land tenure from that time on. The changes in the legislation were submitted to the official party and the national Congress. Some legislators and some

officials of the CNC openly said many times that it was not con-
venient that the peasants know the details of the new legislation,
even if these were harmful, so as to avoid any agitation in the
countryside, which would be harmful to the entire economy of
Mexico . . . (Huizer 1970b, translated and quoted in Montes de
Oca 1977:53–54).

Amendments to the Agrarian Code gave renewed support to the
pequeños propietarios against the demands of effective land redistribution. And CNC's failure to block the amendments gave new impetus for dissent within the national peasant organization, enhancing
the attractiveness of independent peasant unions. One such group, the
Unión General de Obreros y Campesinos de México (UGOCM), was
founded in 1949 under the wing of the Partido Popular Socialista. With
an original membership of some 300,000, the UGOCM quickly suffered attrition through political repression. "The Secretary of Labor's
refusal to register the UGOCM, thus denying it the capacity to act in
legal matters for workers affiliated with it, caused many of the unions
that had joined it to leave. Only the peasants remained" (Montes de Oca
1977:55).

This peasant strength was most evident in the northwest. Under
the leadership of Jacinto López and regional Communist head Rámon
Danzós Palomino, peasants in 1958 threatened seizure of 400,000
hectares belonging to the Cananea Cattle Company. Stymied by federal troops and judiciales, López shifted his front quickly to the
Culiacán Valley of Sinaloa. He was jailed for the remainder of the year
and his peasants were removed. The following January, though,
Jacinto López renewed his agitation for land reform by leading three
thousand squatters onto land around Obregón. No immediate gains
resulted: López received a governmental promise of "a solution of the
land problem within the law" (Huizer 1970a:494).

Coinciding with UGOCM's activity in Sonora, disaffection with
CNC arose among the peasants of Baja California. The initial confrontation centered on the Colorado River, where the CNC and PRI
had failed to meet demands of the peasants for a stop to the saline
runoffs of upstream, United States agriculture. And Alfonso Garzón
led the unrest. Prominent as a state leader of the CNC in the late 1950s,
he broke with the national organization to form the Confederación
Campesina Independiente (CCI) in January 1963 (Anderson and
Cockcroft 1969:385; Montes de Oca 1977:55–56).

The autonomy of the CCI was tested from the start. Pressure from
the PRI intensified in 1964 as Communist-oriented members of CCI
supported the presidential candidacy of the Frente Electoral del
Pueblo. Garzón, as Anderson and Cockcroft report,

. . . had vainly essayed the tactic of political candidacy against the
PRI in 1962, when he ran for mayor of Mexicali but was refused

recognition as a candidate. The failure of FEP candidate Ramón Danzós Palomino, himself a peasant leader from the north (the impoverished La Laguna area), in the 1964 presidential elections, may have further disillusioned Garzón with the efficacy of political dissent. In any case, repression of CCI demonstrations continued apace, and by 1964, Garzón seemed willing to reconsider his relationship with the PRI &1969:384–85).

Garzón did indeed restructure his ties to PRI. In September 1964, he expelled Communist members from CCI. They immediately organized a second CCI under Ramón Danzós. The subsequent fate of the two leaders is instructive. Danzós's CCI remained independent, but the leader himself was "constantly in and out of jail" (Montes de Oca 1977:56). By contrast, Garzón quickly achieved the initial goal. In March 1965, Mexican President Díaz Ordaz reached an agreement with the United States to end the dumping of saline water into the Colorado River. The president additionally promised large sums of money for the rehabilitation of the Mexicali Valley. By the time of the gubernatorial elections in August 1965, Garzón and his associates were firmly within the PRI: "Garzón was photographed frequently with the PRI candidate, and at least according to the PAN, Garzón openly campaigned for the PRI among the peasantry . . . (Anderson and Cockcroft" (1969:386).

By the 1970s, the PRI had succeeded in incorporating the peasant splinter groups into the unified Pacto de Ocampo (Fig. 5.1). In October 1973, the CNC, Garzón's CCI, the Congreso Agrario Mexicano (CAM), and the "Jacinto López" UGOCM together supported a joint declaration to "back firmly the internal and external policies of the President of the Republic" (Montes de Oca 1977:60).

In the battle for the Yaqui Valley, the CCI found itself ideologically opposed to the Confederación Nacional de la Pequeña Propiedad (CNPP). The CNPP is the largest interest group within the party's Confederación Nacional de Organizaciones Populares (CNOP), thus replicating structurally the CCI's position within the CNC. Founded in the early 1940s, CNOP gave political representation to the growing middle class, and effectively gained the support of that class for the government party rather than the conservative Partido Acción Nacional (PAN). CNOP is a residual organization, encompassing diverse groups which do not fit easily into the party's other sectors: "small agriculturalists, small merchants, artisans, members of cooperative enterprises, professional men and intellectuals, youth groups, women's clubs" (Huizer 1970a:477). However diverse in origin and composition, the CNOP has a coherent ideology. As Padgett summarizes,

. . . it is necessary to keep in mind that the CNOP is dominated by professional people who are often also propertied people. Thus the CNOP tends to stand against any raise in property and income

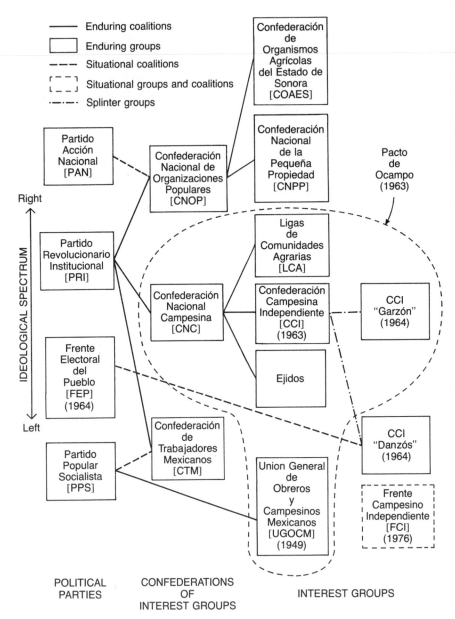

Fig. 5.1 Primary Actors and Coalitions in the Struggle for Sonora, 1975–1976

taxes. It also promotes the cause of the rural property owner in relation to demands for expropriation on the part of landless peasants, and it stands for increased emphasis upon urban improvements and investments, and investments in the industrialization process as opposed to larger allotments of government money for credit to those on the ejidos (Padgett 1966, in Huizer 1970a:477).

The Pequeños Propietarios have been rewarded for their loyal support of CNOP and the ruling party. During the last years of the Cárdenas administration, while land was being distributed to peasants throughout the country, legislation was passed to favor private commercial farmers and ranchers. The Ley de Fomento Ganadero reassured cattlemen that lands sufficient to breed 500 head would not be expropriated. According to Huizer, the decree ". . . led to hidden persistence of many latifundios in the hands of those who simulated cattle-breeding on a large scale, but who in reality did not use a large part of the protected lands or who dedicated them to agriculture" (Huizer 1970a:475).

Subsequently, the government and agriculturalists worked out a new agrarian code. Approved in 1942, the code declared as nonexpropriatable up to 100 hectares of irrigated lands. Additionally, it legalized tracts of 300 irrigated hectares planted with specific cash crops—bananas, sugarcane, coffee, henequen, grapes, olives, rubber, vanilla, and coconuts (Huizer 1970a:475; Erasmus 1970:320). Further revisions under the Alemán regime increased the maximum size of farms planted in cotton to 150 hectares (Montes de Oca 1977:53). Finally, small proprietors were given the right to request a court injunction (*derecho de amparo*) against expropriation (Huizer 1970a:485).

Most of these changes met with vocal opposition from representatives of the CNC, but the opposition was tempered with begrudging allegiance to the presidency (Huizer 1970a:486). Loyalty within the CNOP and the CNPP was enhanced, however. The new agrarian code assured the legal underpinnings for "small property" and increased confidence and the investments of private commercial farmers. Inevitably, too, the code laid the foundations for confrontation in the Yaqui Valley.

YAQUI POLITICIANS AND THE ISSUES

In the recurrent irony of Mexico's political system, both the "small-holders" of northwest Mexico and the peasants of the CCI became expectant beneficiaries of the PRI's Agrarian Code. The Yaqui tribe owes no allegiance to the PRI, and thus expected no political reciprocities from the ruling party. Yet they were inexorably drawn into the confrontation at San Ignacio, as perennial claimants to a disputed tribal boundary.

Lázaro Cárdenas had sown the seeds for confrontation between campesinos and landed farmers by seeking the loyalty of both. He also endowed the Yaquis with an ambiguous boundary—much firmer than it had been in the past, but still imprecisely demarcated and imperfectly understood. Alfonso Fabila, sent to examine conditions of the Yaqui reserve, notes that the presidential decree laid the southern boundary ". . . from the southern edge of Isla de Lobos to the southern and eastern limits of the property of the pueblo of Torim; from this point, following the course of the river upstream, to the property of Buena-vista" (Fabila 1940:28).

The text of the Cárdenas decree, contained in Fabila's report (translated in Bartell 1965) shows no such precise marking, however. Leaving the boundary unspecific, the 1937 decree may have been purposely designed to avoid direct confrontation between Mexican and Yaqui in the Valle Nuevo. By the late 1930s, both parties claimed *de jure* as well as *de facto* possession of the territories which ultimately came under dispute in the 1970s. On the basis of these rights of possession, both sides may have been waiting expectantly for a settlement favorable to their interests. A final soution was postponed by the vagueness of the Cárdenas line, but by the 1970s Yaquis felt politically and economically confident to push for a favorable conclusion to the dispute.

In addition to this emerging confidence, the face of the land along the tribe's indefinite southern boundary had changed dramatically. In 1940, much of the land was still monte. Thirty-five years later, with a new water supply, it had become prime irrigated farmland.

These two factors, the land rights which Yaquis felt they had won from Cárdenas, and the immense value of the land under present conditions, motivated Yaqui political activity in the 1970s.

Gradually through the fall of 1975, a period of intense discussions within the tribe and frequent negotiations with national agrarian officials, the Yaquis decided on their demands. They claimed a new boundary line running from the southern tip of Isla de Lobos to a point on the highway roughly midway between the Mexican cities of Esperanza and Obregón, and from there northeast into the Bacatetes. The line neatly encompasses within Yaqui territory the massive Oviachi Dam and reservoir, primary water source for all the irrigated lands of the Valle Nuevo and Zona Indígena.

It was a bold stroke. Not only would the tribe control anew a healthy expanse of farmland, it would also possess the heart and artery of the arid delta. And Yaquis would again own the ground under three major Mexican population centers in the valley: Bacum, Cocorit, and the military garrison and railhead town of Esperanza. The demand was entirely reasonable, according to astute Yaqui politicians. For they were not requesting restitution of all original territory, which by legend and by validation in a map published by the anthropologist Spicer (1974; see discussion in chapter 3), extended southward to the Arroyo Cocoraqui at the present division between the Yaqui and Mayo irrigation districts. The Yaquis did not seek the entire irrigated valley, simply a thin wedge.

With its demands set, the tribe mustered considerable political power for the confrontation late in 1975. Yaqui power rested upon organization (the corporate structure of the tribe) and upon a fleeting display of unitary interests. The battle for San Ignacio would be won, provisionally, by a different type of power—the force of numbers.

"EL CAMINO DE LA LEY"

Through the winter of 1975–76, most Yaquis were only vaguely worried about the outcome of interminable boundary disputes. Their governors and representatives were, after all, doing as best they could to further tribal interests in the valley. Of more immediate concern to pueblo residents was an almost epidemic level of bronchial pneumonia, and their anticipations were directed to the upcoming Waresma, signaling the end of a hard winter.

Outside the zone, an uneasy truce had been drawn between campesinos and neolatifundistas. As more-or-less loyal contingents in the PRI, both groups were awaiting a presidential settlement to the tensions that surfaced in San Ignacio.

In January 1976, however, responsibility for a solution was delegated to the new Sonoran governor, Alejandro Carrillo Marcor. Former state governor Carlos Armando Biébrich, a dynamic young party loyalist with a bright political future, had been deposed by Echeverría shortly after the shootout at San Ignacio. Biébrich was accused of letting the situation get out of control, necessitating the massive deployment of force to Block 717. Subsequently, he was also accused of absconding to Tucson with 2 million pesos from the state's treasury. Biébrich's name was immediately whitewashed from the ubiquitous tricolor campaign slogans painted on walls throughout the state. Symbolic, perhaps, of the imposing power of the official party, the slogans were not quickly retouched with the new governor's name. For much of Carrillo Marcor's tenure in office, the signs read simply and ominously, "PRI with. . . ."

Carrillo Marcor attempted to solve the conflict by setting up a Comité Tripartita Agrario Estadal. Jaime Miranda Peláez continued to represent his Confederación de la Pequeña Propiedad on the Comité. The Secretariat of Agrarian Reform sent a delegate, as did the state's

Unión Ganadera Regional de Sonora. Carrillo Marcor was represented through the Director Ejecutivo de Asuntos Rurales, the state's rural ombudsman. The CCI had no official voice, but the interests of CNC were represented by the state leader of the Liga de Comunidades Agrarias, Ignacio Martínez Tadeo. Young and charismatic, "Nacho" Tadeo had a bright political future under Biébrich. His retention of control over CNC's state Liga signified the continued confidence placed in him by Carrillo Marcor and the PRI. Tadeo is a Yaqui, and frequently portrayed in newspapers as the spokesman for Yaqui interests in Hermosillo. In the Yaqui Zone, however, his position seems to be that of a translator, not a spokesman. Infrequently, he is called upon by Yaqui governors to report the proceedings of juntas to Mexican officials and interested bystanders. Indeed, many Yaquis scoff at Tadeo's presumed influence in Hermosillo, and there was little doubt that Tadeo was representing the interests of the CNC, not those of the tribe, in the struggle for land around Ciudad Obregón.

Local newspapers gave little attention to the work of the Comité Tripartita in the early months of 1976. Designed to mediate the dispute, the Comité seems, more importantly, to have simply moderated tensions, diffusing the potential for further violence. The shroud of silence around the Comité's work is significant, though. Conflict was temporarily but effectively removed from the volatile arena of national politics, an arena which demands public commitment to revolutionary ideals, effusive rhetorical homage to past agrarian fighters and national heroes. Quietly, in the closed arena of the state, negotiations could be carried on with less inflammation. It is most likely that the embattled pequeños propietarios saw more chance of success once the dispute was localized to the region. Their political and economic power could be more readily marshalled against the governor of a state heavily dependent on commercial agriculture, and equally against a state peasant organization bereft of the organizing power and front line experience of the national campesino leaders.

The potential for local compromise ended precipitously in early April 1976. Members of the Frente Campesina Independiente invaded Block 407 in the Yaqui Valley. The situation was more pressing than in October because 400 hectares of wheat were ready to be harvested.

Echoing the determination of the San Ignacio campesinos—"Only the dead will leave this land and we are ready to die fighting" (*Diario del Yaqui*, 10 April 1976)—the invaders of Block 407 were less naive to the exercise of political power. They came in great numbers—about one thousand campesinos—and they were armed. They took, as well, an extraordinarily bold precaution against retaliation by the police and the army. They seized as hostages a delegate from the Secretaría de Reforma Agraria and a field inspector from the Unión de Credito Agrícola, accused of spying on the activities of the invaders.

On April 6, hostages in hand, the FCI made its demands. The army and judicial police were to retreat from the immediate area. The Secretary of Agrarian Reform and national peasant leaders must come to Obregón to initiate a dialogue. And finally, talk had to center around a specific issue: "to reduce the small property holdings and irrigation rights presently at 100 hectares to only 20 hectares per user" (*El Imparcial*, 19 April 1976).

The first two demands were met. The army drew back as the prisoners were released, and a host of state and national agrarian leaders and politicians arrived in Obregón. Debate over the third demand—substantive land reform—began immediately in an idiom more explicitly economic than political. Massive financial incentives were announced for farmers who would willingly give up their land and turn to industrial investment. The precise nature of the incentives was not clearly spelled out, but the course of economic development was clear: to buttress the processing activities for agricultural products. Proclaiming that "industry is the only path for the state," Governor Carrillo Marcor promised to invest 450,000 pesos of state and federal money for infrastructural development, including a sesame-seed hulling plant, a meat-packing operation, a gypsum plant, mills, and dairies for Ciudad Obregón (*Diario del Yaqui*, 13 April 1976).

The purpose of the investments was explicit. "The facilities that President Echeverría's regime was providing to regional farmers were to divert their activities toward industrialization" (*Diario del Yaqui*, 13 April 1976). Large landowners were to be attracted into industry and off of the land. Spokesmen for the pequeños propietarios responded to the government promise quickly and suspiciously. "They won't do it if they are obligated, and even less if they are deprived of their lands which would, in any case, be the collateral needed to obtain the credit to participate in the activity [of industrialization]" (*Diario del Yaqui*, 13 April 1976). Moreover, the agriculturalists seemed wary of industrial investment and stuck persistently to their self-image as small farmers, virtual "country bumpkins." Hector Aguilar Parada, president of the Confederación de Asociaciones Agrícolas del Estado de Sonora (CAAES), communicated this image eloquently:

> They are already familiar with agricultural activities and therefore act with confidence in this medium; but to go look for new experiences in areas they haven't practiced would be running the risk of making an industry into a mediocre business (*Diario del Yaqui*, 13 April 1976).

While Mexican officials proposed economic incentives to the landowners, they dealt political rhetoric to the campesinos. A massive meeting was called for the Cine Cajeme in Obregón on April 10. Alfonso Garzón of the CCI returned to the city along with the national leaders of other agrarian organizations. Unanimously echoing the demands of the invaders of Block 407, the leaders spoke for a reduction of the maximum extent of pequeña propiedad to 20 hectares. A local newspaper gave prominent headlines to the triumphant words of Professor Humberto Serrano, leader of the Consejo Agraristo Mexicano (CAM): "We will strip the arrogance from the latifundistas" (*Diario del Yaqui*, 13 April 1976).

The same edition of the *Diario del Yaqui* carried a short report on the progress of the Yaqui boundary claims. Yaqui governors and several pueblo secretarios had gone to the Obregón hotel the previous night, April 9, to meet with incoming officials and, it was hoped, to obtain an audience with the Sonoran governor. When they arrived, the motel courtyard was already filled with pequeños propietarios and campesinos, loitering around the eucalyptus-lined swimming pool awaiting the official entourages. The officials arrived, and the mass of farmers—owners and landless peasants—theatrically divided themselves. Groups of campesinos and latifundistas moved to separate doorways of the motel rooms, listening to the statements of one official after another. Sensing an end to the interviews or refusing to accept the propositions, each group then moved hurriedly to the next doorway, the next governmental spokesman, and a new group filled the vacated spot.

An unmistakable differentiation of political styles developed in the motel courtyard and adjoining parking lot. Mexicans, campesinos as well as pequeños propietarios, frequently interrupted the governmental spokesmen with the embellished curses of northern Mexican Spanish. They moved from one speaker to the next at the threatening cue of "¡Vámonos!" from their own leaders. Watching the spectacle, Yaquis sat quietly and nervously along the curbstones, awaiting their opportunity for discussion but not forcing their presence on the assembled officials.

I had driven the officers of Rahum pueblo to Obregón. In the car, the governor spoke, vitriolically but with reason, against the Mexican government, against the lack of financial aid for development, for education, for health. The government, he said, was very hard in its bargaining position, very unresponsive to Yaqui petitions.

At the motel Yaqui governors finally got the opportunity to talk, or rather to listen. Carrillo Marcor gathered the Yaquis about him at one end of the parking lot. Nacho Tadeo sought to orchestrate the confrontation. There was no confrontation, and Tadeo was ignored. The introductions were prolonged and patterned, though. Each pueblo governor moved to the center and shook hands with the state governor and with Félix Barra García, Secretary of Agrarian Reform (SRA). Sombreros were raised, politely and deferentially, by each Yaqui official in his turn. The Rahum governor, who hours before had confidently attacked the state and the nation, now sheepishly met the leaders. His own pueblo secretary, young and suave, almost refused the introduction altogether, but from shyness rather than defiance.

Yaqui governors expressed their demands concisely: a definitive settlement of the boundary question and a step-up to the rehabilitation of the Porfirio Díaz Canal through the Yaqui Zone. Carrillo Marcor and Félix Barra were evasive in their responses. The head of SRA agreed to further meetings with Yaqui governors and to further study of the issues in the line dispute.

Returning to Rahum that night, the pueblo officials were ambivalent, neither encouraged nor especially discouraged by the deflecting replies they had witnessed. They agreed, though, to return en masse to the Cine Obregón in the morning.

Arriving late, the Yaqui contingent found space only in the back rows of the balcony. Campesinos packed the spacious theater as local, state, and national agrarian leaders crowded the stage. For the Yaquis, there was to be an unfortunate continuity to the proceedings of the night before in the motel, in political style and government unresponsiveness. Throughout the long morning and afternoon of impassioned and embellished speeches, Yaqui requests for land were never addressed. Perhaps to counteract this studied neglect of their demands by government officials, the Yaqui observers maintained quiet aloofness in the balcony. As on the previous night, the contrasting political styles of Mexican campesinos and Yaqui officials were stark. Four thousand assembled campesinos responded boisterously and approvingly to the speakers on stage and unanimously cheered the continuous invocation of the names of Jacinto López, Emiliano Zapata, and of Lázaro Cárdenas. They applauded the frequent rhetorical condemnations of latifundistas and *norteamericanos*. And they quickly responded to the rallying beat of a Mayo drum, reported erroneously by the newspapers as Yaqui. Yaqui and Mayo drums are identical, but the Yaquis in the balcony were quick to disassociate themselves from such secular use of the integral ritual instrument. The balcony and the main floor of the Cine Obregón stood in marked contrast to each other. From the balcony, the Yaqui presence exuded corporateness. On the main floor, the Mexican show of force communicated disorganized boisterousness.

The campesino mass received what they had come for: a public, if still tentative, government commitment to the 20-hectare limit. But Félix Barra, the final speaker (later indicted by the regime of President López Portillo for embezzlement), urged an immediate return to *el camino de la ley,* the legal road, an explicit condemnation of the unauthorized invasion of Block 407 several days before:

> . . . we have investigated the present situation of the people who now hold the land and the misery and desperation which you

combat. I will convey it to him [Echeverría] like this and also tell him of this great mass of campesinos who have attended this meeting, ready to follow *el camino de la ley.* I am going to tell him that, in an organized manner, as has been expressed here, the reform of the Constitution is indispensable to assure the transfer of land and to confer the necessary water (*Diario del Yaqui,* 11 April 1976).

In his turn, Governor Carrillo Marcor expressed his allegiance to the Revolution, and equally to the law:

We are not asking Echeverría to disregard the legitimate rights of those men who really do have a small property holding and who are as much victims of the present situation as are our landless brothers and ejido owners, because the Revolution created distinct property classifications: the ejido, the collective farm, and the authentic small property holding [*la pequeña auténtica propiedad*] (*Diario del Yaqui,* 11 April 1976).

Carrillo Marcor's comments were pregnant. The conflict was ultimately to turn on discrepant notions of "la pequeña auténtica propiedad." And the ironic casuistry of el camino de la ley was to become increasingly apparent in the months following the cine meeting.

The immediate result of the meeting was a call for President Echeverría to come to Sonora, survey the tensions, and pronounce a solution. Echeverría arrived on April 19 with a score of state governors, top-level party and agrarian leaders, and official party candidates for the national elections of July. Before an estimated fifty thousand campesinos—the CNOP was officially excluded from the rally—in the spacious, immaculate plaza of Ciudad Obregón the candidates were displayed, governors and party leaders spoke in unending succession, and Echeverría gave a remarkably passionate but evasive summation of presidential agrarian policy. He adroitly avoided reference to the proposed 20-hectare limit, a tacit but unmistakable signal that the demand was premature. His theme was conciliatory: through land invasions and armed retaliation, both sides in the struggle had departed from the law. Campesinos and latifundistas shared equally in the blame and both must work together for a peaceful and constitutional solution:

Fellow campesinos: I have not come to just another political meeting. I have come to personally feel this experience, this dramatic and in many aspects, tragic situation of the agrarian south of Sonora. And I have come to tell you that the *camino de la ley* is still good . . . I have come to tell you that neither the violence of the latifundistas nor some isolated policemen, who in reality were in the service of the latifundistas, nor the violence of the invaders is a good way for Mexico to resolve its problems . . .

I want to ask all sectors of southern Sonora to make an effort to understand what is happening here: some are not bad and others good; we are all Mexicans who want the unity and progress of our country. When Mexico was divided in the last century, it lost half of its territory, and when Mexico is deeply divided violence and bitterness reign over us. We have to make a solid and optimistic, a vigorous and united country for our children. This is the wish of all Mexicans of good faith. With all intensity, let us work within the bounds of the present Constitution and the law (*El Imparcial,* 20 April 1976).

Outraged initially by their exclusion from the mass rally, the pequeños propietarios soon expressed support and confidence in Echeverría and the law. Jaime Miranda Peláez offered his sentiments to a reporter for *El Imparcial*: "I was pleased when the President said he will act with the law in his hand. That is all we, the pequeños propietarios, are asking" (*El Imparcial,* 20 April 1976). Assembled campesinos, through their spokesmen in the CCI, CNC, and CAM, were also officially satisfied with the presidential address.

I accompanied several young Yaqui men to the mass rally. Their reactions to the interminable speeches were markedly different from the attitudes of seasoned Yaqui politicans. The young men seemed to be enraptured by the revolutionary rhetoric and symbolic resort to the memory of dead agrarian heroes. They felt, I suspect, a strong if only situational solidarity with the Mexican lower classes assembled in the plaza.

The official and organized Yaqui presence at the gathering was disappointing, though. In the morning, a dozen buses had been mustered on the llano in Potam to carry a Yaqui contingent to Obregón. Governors and pueblo officials dutifully went, but more than half of the buses departed empty. The marginality of their demands was, by now, patently obvious to astute Yaqui politicians. And this marginality was reproduced, spatially, when the Yaqui contingent arrived in the city. Gathering disinterestedly in a peripheral square well down the street from the main plaza, the Yaqui representatives were barely within hearing distance of the speaker's platform. Tribal boundaries and questions of Yaqui development were ignored by the succession of orators. By late April, the wheat had been harvested and Yaquis had already turned their concerted efforts to the ritual of Semana Santa.

Progress of the conflict to this point can now be assessed. Instability in southern Sonora has a long history, and the wave of invasions and violent repression at San Ignacio in October again brought the region to national attention. Swift occupation of the Río Muerto, apparently unauthorized and unexpected, caught Alfonso Garzón and the CCI off their guard. Garzón came immediately to Obregón to act as the official conduit for the demands of the campesinos and to attempt a quieting, if not a settlement, of the explosive situation at San Ignacio.

Invasions and further violence were avoided for the remainder of the fall, but the expectations of campesinos in the Yaqui Valley and south along the Mayo River had been raised by the official presence of Garzón and the CCI in the region. Quick and acceptable solutions to the conflict proved intractable, though, even after January when the negotiations were turned over to the Sonoran governor's Comité Tripartita Agrario. Briefly, the dispute was removed from the arena of national politics.

The dialogue of the Comité was abruptly superceded when, in early April, the unco-opted and unyielding Frente Campesino Independiente invaded Block 407 near San Pedro. Autonomous from the PRI, the FCI undoubtedly felt that government attempts to negotiate a settlement were moving too slowly, if at all. Strategically timed to disrupt the wheat harvest, the FCI's invasion forced the government's hand: president and party again were drawn publicly into the politics of southern Sonora. They entered, though, in a curiously uncoordinated fashion. Leaders of the Pacto de Ocampo, the agrarian truce of the 1970s which brought the CCI, CNC, and CAM together under the tutelage of the PRI, immediately supported the demands of the autonomous FCI for a 20-hectare limit to irrigated parcels. A week later, however, when Echeverría convened his massive rally of campesinos, politicians, and party hopefuls, the official backing for the 20-hectare limit was conspicuously absent. Faced with the potential for massive economic counterrevolution, should the limit be imposed on wealthy landowners and investors of Sonora, Echeverría was conciliatory. He gave every indication, publicly, that the camino de la ley would be followed for campesinos and pequeños propietarios alike. Perhaps fortuitously, too, the president's stance of appeasement bought some time, sufficient to harvest the wheat on disputed parcels around Obregón.

Coincident with these explosive events in the valley, the Yaquis had chosen to press their perennial demand for a definition of the southern tribal boundary, as well as for increased financial and technical aid. The demands received token responses: periodic visits by government bureaucrats, occasional audiences with high-level state and national politicians, and temporary uneasiness among the established Mexican residents of the towns abutting the Yaqui reserve.

Yaquis found themselves ironically constrained by the very strength of their corporate political organization. They chose, in their petitions and their disciplined discussions with Mexican officials, to follow strictly el camino de la ley. In consequence, their demands were easily ignored by a government more directly confronted with the explosive portent of landless campesino masses.

By April the tribe had played its political hand, with no apparent recompense by the Mexican government. And the strains of the political contest began to show in the pueblos. January's Dia de los Reyes, traditionally the day new pueblo officials are installed, had passed without a turnover of leaders in most of the town. With some pueblo support, the governors had decided to remain in office while the boundary negotiations proceeded. But by April the governors had little to show for their efforts. Increasingly there were demands that the canes of office be turned over to new men. A "shadow" government had in fact been organized in the pueblo of Huirivis and throughout Waresma the village was tensely divided. Residents of Rahum and Potam seemed equally discontent over the failure of their leaders.

Through April 1976, then, the best efforts of the Yaqui corporate polity had achieved little. Ironically, as subsequent events in the Valle Nuevo would show, neither the campesinos nor the pequeños propietarios had even begun to marshal their full power. After Semana Santa and the harvest of wheat the character of the dispute changed dramatically.

END OF THE SEXENIO

Events through April 1976 were not extraordinary. Peasant demands, initial violent repression, small government concessions, attempts to mollify all competing interests through promises—this pattern had occurred elsewhere in Mexico before. Little had happened to signal a drastic departure from the well-studied cycle of repression, co-optation, and subsequent normality.

A brief story in the Hermosillo newspaper, *El Imparcial,* of 21 April 1976, however, presaged change. José López Portillo, the PRI's presidential candidate for the July elections, offered his tentative reactions to the 20-hectare limit and to the growing agrarian upheaval:

We must step ahead. We must avoid reaching the absurdity of continuous divisions in landholding. Otherwise we will reach the severe restrictions of the *minifundio,* which are not only limitations on land, but also on the imagination and even on the will to work.

The individual and isolated small holding impedes great advances in agricultural production. To leave the *minifundio* to chance is a risk taken by the revolution and paid by the Mexican people.

It is absolutely necessary that the unit of production remains intact, that it not be divided. This is of basic and fundamental importance to the country. What we have to do is to create and recreate units of production which permit economies of scale sufficient to augment productivity.

Our main concern is that the land be sufficient to feed the people of Mexico. In no way will we take the step backwards to recreate the

minifundio. This is not the solution to the country's basic problem:
self-sufficiency in the production of food.

We cannot leave the *minifundio* isolated, nor let it reproduce as a
general system of production. We have to organize it to create
productive units; otherwise, the campesinos and the Mexican
people are going to suffer even more. This is the fundamental
effort we should accomplish in the next six years (*El Imparcial,* 21
April 1976).

López Portillo obliquely revived an issue that had been studiously
avoided in the official rhetoric of Echeverría and the national agrarian
leaders: the growing crisis in Mexican agriculture—the failure of
production to keep pace with the country's explosive population
growth. Explicitly, López Portillo was only decrying the presumed
effects of minifundismo: low productivity and inefficiency. Implicitly,
he seemed to be expressing guarded support of the large and productive agricultural enterprises, the pequeñas propiedades of the rich,
irrigated northwest coast. And tacitly, his position could be interpreted
as an attack on the underproduction of ejidos. In the uneasy tension
between agrarian reform and economic development, López Portillo
appeared in April to be throwing his weight, his imminent presidential
power, behind development, not reform.

Officially, however, López Portillo's brief statement of policy in
April did not depart radically from Echeverría's proclamations. The
outgoing president had not enthusiastically supported the 20-hectare
limit in Sonora, nor had he publicly threatened mass expropriations of
land. He had simply called for a strict and conscientious application of
the Constitution.

By the end of his term in November, though, Echeverría had
expropriated tens of thousands of hectares in the Yaqui valley, turned
irrigated farms over to campesinos, and used the power of his office to
nullify the legal redress of the pequeños propietarios.

The course of action unfolded slowly after tempers quieted in
April. Immediately following the public drama of Echeverría's appearance in Obregón, government agrarian officials began a protracted
series of private negotiations with local landowners. As reported later
by a North American newspaper (*Washington Post,* 27 November
1976), the secrecy of the bargaining was designed to "save the face" of
both government and pequeños propietarios, presumably because the
landowners had been adamant in their public stance against losing or
even selling their lands, while the government had, perhaps, been
embarrassed when its belated attempts to buy off landowners through
favorable incentives to industrialization had been quickly rejected.
Quietly, throughout the summer of 1976, the issue debated was one of
just compensation should the lands be expropriated.

The negotiations were unsuccessful. Some landowners, evidently, were prepared to sell, but at double the price offered by the government. Stalemated, the bargaining broke off in mid-November (*Washington Post*, 27 November 1976). In late summer, during the course of the secret talks, Echeverría announced that he would not leave office without distributing land to the campesinos.

Despite the president's warning, though, few people outside the highest levels of government and party were prepared for the massive and swift campesino invasion of thousands of hectares of Sonoran and Sinaloan farmland in mid-November 1976. Within a week of this squatter movement, Echeverría ordered the expropriation of 100,000 hectares around Obregón for distribution to eight thousand campesino families (*Los Angeles Times*, 22 November 1976). This series of invasions differed dramatically from the isolated actions at San Ignacio and Block 407, San Pedro. Organized and initiated by the government, they undoubtedly had the full knowledge and support of the outgoing president. As a North American reporter wrote:

In a visit to the region, I found that shabby peasants who had suddenly received stretches of the perfectly plowed and fully irrigated fields still seemed dumbfounded.

After hearing 20, even 30, years of promises, they said they were suddenly told two weeks ago by pro-government peasant leaders to set up camp on paths and irrigation dikes and ditches beside the disputed fields. Eight days later, on Friday, the word came that they were to plant their flags on the land that was not theirs. When dawn broke and 25,000 people had taken possession, it was too late for the former owners to seek a restraining order from the local court (*Washington Post*, 27 November 1976).

In the days following the expropriations, a bitter contest of words ensued. Pequeños propietarios sought recourse in the Constitution, but they were adroitly outmaneuvered by the president and his agrarian advisors. Dispossessed farmers argued that Echeverría had violated the law in bypassing the courts which have, in theory, the right to decide on the legality of landholdings. They also claimed that the president had misinterpreted the argarian statutes which allowed farmers to hold tracts of up to 100 hectares: nothing in the law, pequeños propietarios maintained, prevented members of the same family from possessing 100 hectares each (*Los Angeles Times*, 22 November 1976).

The Echeverría response was terse: his officials had made a careful study of land tenure in the Yaqui Valley and discovered that seventy-two families were illegally holding vast tracts of irrigated lands. Moreover, his presidential decree of expropriation overruled any court injunctions and judicial appeals of farm owners (*Los Angeles Times*, 22 November 1976).

Peasant leaders quickly marshalled another defense and revealed the ultimate strategy of the well-timed invasions. If farmers refused to plant winter crops, then "we the peasants will do it. And we will take their farms in any way needed, because the constitution says that the land shouldn't stay idle but belongs to those who work it" (Celestino Salcedo Monteón, quoted in *The Miami Herald*, 16 November 1976).

Stymied by presidential invocation of land tenure statutes, faced with further expropriations should they fail to plant winter wheat, unwilling to invest in cultivation under these uncertain conditions, the pequeños propietarios had been effectively defeated by the well-orchestrated governmental attack. They responded with a nationwide call for sympathy in the form of a massive show of economic power, a strike, during the final week of November. The president of Sonora's Chamber of Commerce predicted ". . . a complete halt of commerce and industry in western Mexico and some other cities of Mexico as a protest for what has happened to these farmers, to private property and to freedom" (*Los Angeles Times*, 22 November 1976).

When the strike came eleven states were paralyzed for a day. Strike leaders estimated that 90 million pesos of industrial output and trade were lost. Candidly realizing that their action would have little effect on Echeverría, protest leaders were looking ahead to the new administration:

> It is important to show Mexico and the world that such illegal actions cannot be taken without strong protest in Mexico. . . . And it is essential that we urge the incoming government to take strong legal measures to rectify the situation quickly. If we do not, who will invest here? Who will know where they stand? (*Los Angeles Times*, 25 November 1976).

As expected, the strike did nothing to alter the outgoing president's resolve. He proceeded with the expropriation of 100,000 hectares in the Yaqui Valley: 37,500 of prime irrigated farms, and the remainder, unwatered grazing land (*Los Angeles Times*, 2 May 1977; Sanderson 1981a:198).

Under the new president an unstable peace was restored to the valley, with dispossessed farmers expecting redress from the government. Campesinos were equally determined to remain in possession of their lands. Jaime Miranda, again representing the pequeños propietarios, was quoted in February 1977: "Things are somewhat more peaceful, but we're pressuring the government for more assurances before we reinvest in our farms or equipment" (*Wall Street Journal*, 24 February 1977). And some of the plots in contention were returned to the courts for settlement, an arena which Echeverría had successfully bypassed in the closing days of his administration. Many observers predicted, early in López Portillo's control, a return of the land to its former owners. One unnamed commentator suggested: "The party doesn't need the campesinos' votes for another five years. Mexico needs these big landowners' investments right now" (*Wall Street Journal*, 24 February 1977).

President López Portillo waited until May, after the harvest of winter wheat, to make his position clear. His government investigators had discovered that 17,500 hectares of the 37,500 irrigated hectares expropriated by Echeverría were in fact held legally by their former owners, within the 100 hectares allowed by law. Now, however, it would be politically impossible to take the lands away from the campesinos with another presidential decree. Such a move would "set the country ablaze." Instead, López Portillo offered to compensate the dispossessed landowners at a rate of 30,000 to 40,000 pesos per hectare. He bolstered his offer of compensation with a threat: "The president said he was aware that farmers might reject the offer and go ahead with their court action. But he warned them that if they did, the government would use all its power to ensure that the campesinos who now occupy the land keep it" (*Los Angeles Times*, 6 May 1977). Germán Pablos, landowner and member of an agricultural credit union in Obregón, responded for the pequeños propietarios, "I think most of the farmers will accept, not because it is an especially good offer, but because the way the president put it doesn't give them much choice" (*Los Angeles Times*, 6 May 1977).

In August of 1977 the final settlement was announced. The government would pay, within thirty days, for 17,900 hectares. By December 1977, newspapers reported that 80 of the 750 affected agriculturalists had been compensated; the remainder were waiting expectantly. In the final calculation, latifundistas were awarded payments for 17,000 hectares of irrigated land taken by Luis Echeverría. The remaining 20,000 hectares remained uncompensated (Sanderson 1981a:200).

Some former landowners survived economically by contracting their machinery out to ejidos and private farmers; others were less fluid in their adaptations to the expropriations. The president of Obregón's Chamber of Commerce summarized the position of the formerly landed elite of the valley:

Some of them had money or other business interests, but the majority had nothing but their land. They had debts, loans outstanding. Everyone in the community has tried to help them, especially the credit unions and private banks. But some of them are in a very bad way economically (*Los Angeles Times*, 4 December 1977).

MASS, ORGANIZATION, AND RESOURCES:
AN ANALYSIS

When Juan de Dios Terán and Heriberto García led their small group of campesinos onto the irrigated fields of San Ignacio, they were reviving a long-standing tension in the Yaqui Valley. In the ensuing months of public rhetoric and private political dealings, three protagonists battled persistently to gain and to retain lands: the Yaqui tribe, the campesinos loosely organized into PRI-sponsored agrarian unions, and the wealthy landed elite of Ciudad Obregón. To analyze the temporary outcome of the confrontation—an outcome which even a cursory reading of the history of Mexican land reform would show to be mutable—three questions must be raised. First, why did the Yaqui tribe, with a corporate structure effective in articulating and communicating the interests of the Eight Pueblos, fare so poorly in the conflict? Second, why did the campesinos ostensibly gain the victory? Why did outgoing President Echeverría, in the face of a crumbling national economy, throw his weight behind the ejidatarios and expropriate the presumably more productive and efficient latifundios? Third, in spite of their demonstrated ability to mobilize a great deal of economic power, why did the pequeños propietarios, the latifundistas, ultimately concede to the campesinos and the government?

These questions seek to uncover the bases of power of the three protagonists. They seek to return the analysis to the issue raised in chapter 1, the notion of "composite interference" proposed by F. G. Bailey. Looking again at the course of events in the valley, we can evaluate the Mexican government's *capability,* as well as its *determination,* to intercede in the land dispute, to direct the outcome.

Capability is simply power. Determination is the willingness of an entity—the national government or the local protagonists—to exercise that power. In a well-known formulation that addresses more directly the issue of power among social groups than does the scheme of Max Weber employed in chapter 4, Robert Bierstedt speaks of three major sources of power: numbers, social organization, and resources. Of the masses, Bierstedt observes that, "Given the same social organization and the same resources, the larger number can always control the smaller and secure its compliance" But numbers are not always sufficient: "A well organized and disciplined body of marines or of police can control a much larger number of unorganized individuals. An organized minority can control an unorganized majority." Finally,

> of two groups, equal or nearly equal in numbers and comparable in organization, the one with access to the greater resources will have the superior power. And so resources constitute the third source of social power. Resources may be of many kinds—money, property, prestige, knowledge, competence, deceit, fraud, secrecy, and, of

course, all of the things usually included under the term "natural resources" (Bierstedt 1950:737).

While all levels of society may draw some power from each of these three sources, there is an obvious if inexact relationship between source of power and social class. Bierstedt sketches this relationship in a subsequent discussion. The lower class, generally propertyless and unorganized, retains the residual power of *numbers*:

> They have so much latent force in their numbers alone that every innovator must solicit their support, every demagogue must appeal to their emotions, every leader must treat them with care lest they turn against him and nullify even the efforts he might expend on their behalf (Bierstedt 1967:80).

And the middle class, frequently smaller in size than the lower, poorer in resources than the upper, characteristically resorts to *organization*:

> For the middle class is the class of the voluntary association; its people form organized groups with others of similar interest and intent, and they pursue these interests sometimes in harmony with and sometimes in opposition to the *status quo* (Bierstedt 1967:90).

Finally, the upper class "has access to the resources of society, makes the big decisions, and is the pre-eminent manipulator of power" (Bierstedt 1967:90).

Thus classes have their characteristic sources of power. What Bierstedt does not sufficiently acknowledge—although he certainly anticipates it—is that the power of one class may be put to the service of another. Here Richard N. Adams's concept of *derivative power* proves useful. Groups may hold independent power, a "direct control over some source of power (land, weapons, mass of people)," or they may derive or receive power from another group. They may "call upon other power holder to use his power on their behalf" (Adams 1970:57). Adding this concept of derivative power to Bierstedt's hierarchy of power sources, it is clear, in theory, that the masses may gain the power of resources or organization from superordinate classes. Or, as ultimately happened in the Yaqui Valley, the government may derive the power of numbers from the masses, and the masses in turn may derive the power of resources and organization from the government, all to confront a rich and organized landed elite.

With these concepts of power in hand, the initial question can now be examined: why did Yaqui petitions and demands go unheeded through 1975 and 1976? The tribe was, in a real sense, simply overpowered. It was, as well, constrained by its own autonomy. Political power for the Yaqui stems primarily from organization—the Yaqui corporate polity—and more diffusely from the resources of their land.

At least around the issue of the tribal boundary, the pueblo governors were able to transmit a unitary opinion to government and state officials. And as sole representatives for the tribe, the assembled governors were able to meet officially and directly with agrarian spokesmen and the state governor. Moreover, the pueblo governors had at hand the established procedures—the traditional Sunday meetings in each pueblo and the capacity to mobilize all pueblo governors and officials for extraordinary meetings in the primera cabecera of Vicam pueblo—for gathering opinions and obtaining legitimacy from common tribal members. Finally, the governors had some financial resources to carry out the logistics of their office. They could tap the small operating budget of the pueblos, garnered through sales of natural resources to Mexican entrepreneurs, "camping fees" charged to Mexican vacationers on the Yaqui beaches, and an occasional donation from Mexican storekeepers residing in the pueblos.

Apart from organization, the tribe could marshal little additional power. Resources were not sufficient to underwrite an extensive lobbying campaign, nor to appeal to the general public through newspaper advertisements as the other protagonists did repeatedly. And in the one effort to mobilize mass Yaqui support for the tribe's demands—the bus convoy to Echeverría's Obregón rally—the small turnout proved to be somewhat embarrassing.

Ultimately, though, the Yaqui demands failed for lack of *derivative power*. This is the price of Yaqui political autonomy. In contrast to the apparent winners, the campesinos, Yaquis do not fall within the umbrella of the governing PRI. In the dispute, the tribe had no national spokesmen such as the local campesinos found in the leaders of CNC and CCI. Structurally, perhaps, the Instituto Nacional Indigenista, with its national bureaucracy and regional centers, plays a role similar to the CNC, as representatives for indigenous interests in national government. But Yaquis had little faith in the newly organized INI regional center in the zone, and likewise the regional director seemed to keep an exceedingly low profile during the land dispute. The tribe, in short, had not been co-opted into the structure of the governing party, and thus could not expect the political benefits that co-optation entails.

Contrasts with the local campesino groups are telling. In the initial confrontation at San Ignacio, the invaders acted independently of government direction: apparently no national leaders of either the CNC or CCI were on the scene from the start. They arrived quickly, and immediately elevated the dispute to the level of national politics. There, as more-or-less influential members of the governing party's power structure, they could effectively bargain to override state interest. Retaliation against the state government, which had deployed municipal and state police to San Ignacio, was swift. The incumbent governor was ousted and a new state governor was appointed by the party.

Subsequently, campesinos, agrarian leaders, and the PRI coalesced their sources of power. Renewed invasions in November were organized and orchestrated by government personnel. Agrarian officials were on hand to dictate when and where the campesinos were to move. Trucks were provided to take peasants swiftly onto the lands, before pequeños propietarios could defend their tracts with court injunctions. And through the concerted invasions, the power of numbers was invoked: López Portillo, succeeding Echeverría as president, was officially reluctant to revoke the expropriations for fear of "setting the country ablaze."

But the power of numbers, of masses with latent revolutionary potential, was largely derivative, not independent. To be sure, the Frente Campesino Independiente (FCI) followed its own path and, according to one analyst, drove "official agrarian politics a significant step to the left" (Sanderson 1981a:194). But there were limits—imposed from above—to this incipient radicalism. Stimulated by the success of government-backed invasions in Sonora, independent peasants tried to move onto land in the adjoining state of Sinaloa. These invasions, sponsored neither by the PRI nor by national agrarian organizations, were quickly repressed: "State police were called in to move them out, and all but a few thousand hectares are now back in the hands of the legal owners" (*Los Angeles Times,* 6 May 1977). Nation and state clearly retained the power to truncate the independent action of numbers.

Corporately organized and autonomous, the Yaqui tribe lost out to a mass of campesinos, government-financed and organized, and tightly reigned. Through a long and confused series of events in the Yaqui Valley, the federal government and ruling party repeatedly demonstrated the capability and power to interfere, to carefully control the outcome of a struggle for land. The Yaqui polity was no match for the combined power of resources, organization, and numbers displayed in Echeverría's expropriations.

Two questions remain, addressed not to the capability of interference, but to determination. Why were the campesinos supported by the government, and why did the landowners concede? Here we move more directly to the economics, not the politics, of land use in the Yaqui Valley, discussed below. Some proposed, and inadequate, answers to these questions may be examined here.

Throughout the final year of the Echeverría sexenio, commentators in the press speculated on the motivations behind the imminent and, finally, the accomplished expropriations. Two rumors gained widespread currency. One, eventually attributed to conservative businessmen as an effort to provoke reaction to the president (see

Sanderson 1981a:197), held that Echeverría designed the expropriations to create a national state of emergency or fuel a coup d'etat against
the incoming regime of López Portillo, in either case retaining power
for himself. A second rumor held that the outgoing president sought to
firmly establish himself as a leader in Third World nationalist and
revolutionary movements (*New York Times,* 20 November 1976).

In light of the facts, both explanations are strained. Echeverría
moved cautiously with the expropriations. He was cool to the proposal
to reduce maximum holdings to 20 hectares. And he took measures to
assure that the expropriations would be limited to the Yaqui Valley,
leaving much of the large landholding in Sinaloa intact. The larger
proportion of lands expropriated in the Yaqui Valley—65,166 out of
100,000 hectares (*Los Angeles Times,* 6 May 1977)—were grazing lands,
not irrigated farmland. Moreover, some of the demands were met
through an expansion of the irrigation district around Ciudad
Obregón—a district which was already experiencing chronic water
shortages from the overburdened Río Yaqui (Sanderson 1981a).

There were immediate complaints from the presumed beneficiaries of the Echeverría policy, as the *New York Times* reported on
November 26, 1976:

> Of 50,000 landless peasants, only 8,900 received plots last week
> and many felt they had once again been manipulated by the Gov-
> ernment.
>
> In the Roberto Barrios group, one of 150 groups that set up
> improvised camps beside the disputed property for a week before
> the takeover, there were complaints that only the leaders had been
> given land.
>
> "We've been campaigning for land as a group since 1958," one
> angry peasant woman said. "We've been paying our leader 10 pesos
> a week to carry on the fight. Now he's been bought off with a piece
> of land and has abandoned us."

The revolutionary intent of the president may indeed have been
genuine. The limited results spurred new discontent.

As for the pequeños propietarios, their ultimate compliance with
the dictates of the federal government was surprisingly rapid. During
the brief strike in November 1976, they had united a range of powerful
economic interests. Throughout much of the country they were supported by the large private sector of the economy, of business, industry,
and commerce. Prolonging the strike would have dealt a severe blow to
a troubled national economy. But the strike was little more than a call
for sympathy and a show of potential force, of power that was never
again invoked. If in fact the Yaqui Valley expropriations signaled the
demise of a long-entrenched landed elite, the losers only weakly fought
off that downfall.

Hidden for the most part in the land dispute in the Valle Nuevo were the economic realities of commercial agriculture. By gaining ejido lands, the campesinos had in fact won very little. Deprived of their lands, the pequeños propietarios had conceded little: they still retained their capital, their farm machinery, and much of the agricultural infrastructure of the valley—the facilities to process, store, and distribute the products of the land (Hewitt de Alcántara 1978; Haag and Rioseco 1965). They will inexorably regain control over the profits from this land.

CHAPTER 6

The Green Revolution
along the Río Yaqui

As a response to urgent political demands, the expropriation around San Ignacio was a partial, unstable, and, ostensibly, incongruous solution. President Echeverría's actions departed from tradition—which for irrigated northwest Mexico is a tradition of export-oriented latifundismo. The previous chapter focused largely on the politics of this tradition and on efforts to reform it. The emphasis now shifts to the economics of the region. The division is arbitrary. In Mexico, as elsewhere, politics and economics are nearly inseparable. But this serves to underscore another tradition—several centuries of struggle for the economic autonomy of the Yaqui pueblos.

THE ECONOMICS AND ECOLOGY OF EXPROPRIATION

To students of the country, indeed to a large audience concerned with the development—and underdevelopment—of the Third World, the economic growth of northwest Mexico needs little review. The literature in English alone is impressive—indicative, one might argue, of more than simply a scholarly interest in a technological and commercial miracle. Little of the history of the "Green Revolution" need be invoked here: it is available elsewhere (Hewitt de Alcántara 1978; Ceceña Cervantes et al. 1973; Bassols Batalla 1972; Yates 1981; Tuchman 1976; Barkin and Suárez 1982; Norton and Solis M. Leopoldo 1983; Griffin 1974; Esteva 1983; Schramm 1979; Carr 1969; Cleaver 1972; Haag and Rioseco 1965; Hansen 1974; Hicks 1969; Borlaug 1965; Freebairn 1969; Hicks 1967; Wionczek 1982; Markiewicz 1980; and Wellhausen 1976). Little of this history of impressive economic growth was still relevant to coastal Sonora in 1975, when the upheaval began at

San Ignacio. In responding to those events, Luis Echeverría was addressing an economics of decline, not of growth.

In the early visions of men like J. R. Southworth, Carlos Conant, and Davis Richardson, there were few limits to the agricultural potential of southern Sonora. Norman Borlaug and his colleagues from the Rockefeller Foundation enhanced this potential with a carefully integrated technological package of seeds, fertilizers, pesticides, and water. For its part, the Mexican government financed dams and irrigation systems along the coast, with expectations that the resulting export of agricultural commodities would underwrite an expansion of the country's industrial sector.

During the 1960s, these expectations were realized. By the end of the decade, agricultural exports were earning half of all of Mexico's commodity export earnings. By 1975, however, this share dropped to only a quarter and, through internal population growth, the country could no longer feed its own (Norton 1982:102). Quite simply, demand has surpassed supply—the supply of economically irrigable land, which had been largely exploited by 1970 (Norton 1982:104).

Through the agencies of the federal government, President Echeverría and his advisors endeavored to avert a food crisis. Public credit to ejidos increased over 100 percent between 1971 and 1974 (Mogab 1984:217), much of it going to neglected small-scale highland farmers. Support prices for maize were raised significantly in an effort to stimulate greater output. And, out of necessity, imports of basic foods continued. The most noticeable result of these public expenditures was inflation. After more than twenty years of a fixed exchange rate, the Mexican peso had to be devalued by 81 percent in 1976, and has remained unstable since then (Norton 1982:102).

Heavy expenditures on the "reform" sector of Mexican agriculture—the ejidatarios and genuine small farmers of rainfed regions—demanded in turn a renewed emphasis on commodity exports. Mexico's planners and politicians had powerful tools available: the ability to allocate irrigation waters to favored crops, the authority to subsidize farm inputs and domestic market prices, and, significant to the issues at hand, the power to alter—or validate—long-standing patterns of farm ownership along the northwest coast. International market forces also played a key role in what would become—in the 1970s—a major transformation of crop mixes on the coast.

Cotton, long the primary cash crop of southern Sonora, declined substantially in acreage, in response to weak international demand. In its stead, wheat and the oil-seed, *cártamo,* gained dominance (Carlos 1981:32–33). For neither of these crops, however, does Mexico enjoy any significant comparative advantage in international markets (Norton 1982:108). By the 1970s the agriculture of southern Sonora had, quite simply, lost much of its luster (Yates 1981:73–77).

Many of Sonora's agricultural elite had anticipated this relative marginalization: they had invested heavily in Sinaloan tomatoes (Hewitt de Alcántara 1978:156). With more ample water supplies, a more moderate climate, and soils fresher than those of the long-cultivated valleys of the Yaqui and Mayo systems, Sinaloa was quick to respond to the demands placed upon its fields (Cummings 1974; Dunbier 1968).

Vine-ripened Sinaloan tomatoes pass through Nogales into the winter markets of the western and midwestern United States. They compete, with eminent success, against tomatoes from Florida, tomatoes which are artificially ripened in ethylene gas chambers—a process that Florida growers choose to call "de-greening" rather than gassing (*Wall Street Journal*, 3 February 1977).

The Mexican tomato industry, concentrated in the hands of some fifty growers, has survived investigations by the U.S. Treasury Department on antidumping charges, and has become a significant earner of export dollars (*Wall Street Journal*, 3 February 1977; Norton 1982:108; Schmitz, Firch and Hillman 1981; Firch and Young 1968). This industry is also exigent in its managerial skills and consumptive of unskilled, seasonal field labor (Kutcher 1983; Pomareda and Simmons 1983). In short, Sinaloa's agro-industrial complex would have been severely threatened by the changes that President Echeverría introduced to southern Sonora.

Many claimed that the Sonoran expropriations posed an equivalent danger to the supply of domestic wheat and cattle feed. At issue was the perennial debate in Mexican agriculture over the relative efficiency and productivity of ejidos and private farms. There is evidence to support the contention that the "modern" sector outperforms the "reform" sector in production (Yates 1981). Evidence also supports a counter argument: the reform sector, more labor-intensive than private farms, utilizes available inputs more efficiently (Freebairn 1963:1158). Finally, it is evident that the debate is political, not economic. Supporters of the private sector frequently ignore the fact that agrarian reform most often occurs on marginal lands, inherently less productive than those retained by private farmers (Dovring 1970:269), and proponents of the ejido sector frequently leave the claims of the private sector uncontested. As Folke Dovring observes, "It has been widely believed that land reform hurt productivity, and even the defenders of the reform have usually placed more emphasis on its sociopolitical merits than on its economic role as affecting productivity" (1970:264).

Policy analysts typically conclude that more data are needed (Hicks 1967:402). Policy implementors, such as President Echeverría in the final months of his sexenio, are apt to conclude that these data on relative efficiency and productivity are ambivalent enough to warrant the risk of land tenure reform. The president's actions may have been vindicated: for the crop year of 1976–77, wheat yields on the expropriated lands exceeded valley-wide averages by 380 kilograms per hectare, and those of southern Sonora as a whole by more than 1,000 kilograms per hectare (Sanderson 1981a:201–02, citing a memorandum from the Banco Rural).

STRESS AND ADAPTATION IN THE ZONA INDÍGENA

Edward Spicer speaks of the "loss of local initiative" (1980:275) in the contemporary agricultural economy of the Yaquis' Zona Indígena. His reasoning applies equally to the Mexican ejidatarios south of the Yaqui River. Water and capital are essential, and with these inputs come obligations to plant approved crops, market the harvest to specified outlets, and accept the prices offered. This administrative structure of agrarian reform is not altogether displeasing to ejidatarios, Mexican or Yaqui. To many farmers the alternatives to public-sector farming are either unavailable or unattractive. Within the Zona Indígena, Yaquis have explored alternatives, buffered to some extent from the scrutiny of Mexican agrarian officials by the internal governments of the Yaqui pueblos. The results of these economic explorations— these adaptations to a loss of local initiative—have touched all elements of Yaqui society.

Analytically, Yaquis can be classed as *socios, particulares,* or *jornaleros.* In practice, the typology dissolves. Members of agricultural credit societies are frequently found working as private farmers and farm laborers. Private farmers are often indistinguishable from laborers—working their own land for the Mexican *patrón* who finances the operation. And socios, even on their proper ejidos, are in reality simply farm laborers, paid by the bank for the days they toil. While there is an adaptive logic to economic diversification, the contemporary patterns of Yaqui agriculture depart radically from the vision of Lázaro Cárdenas when he decreed the Zona Indígena in 1937.

The Big Ejido

Cárdenas hoped, quite simply, to guarantee a better life for the Yaquis. Spicer outlines the effort:

> The foundations which he laid for achieving such development consisted in the establishment of land ownership in the expectation that this was not only justice for past wrongs but also would prevent the constant conflict in and at the edges of the area occupied by Yaquis. Guaranteed land and water rights were the foundation. However, this was a basis for development, in Cárdenas's view, only if government aid were given for establishing

Yaquis in productive agriculture and provision were made for health and educational improvement. The only rationale given for the government's providing such services was that Yaquis had shown interest in peaceful agricultural development, and Cárdenas thought that this would enable them to contribute in general to a better Mexico (Spicer 1980:277).

Charles Erasmus, another student of Yaqui society, characterizes the Yaqui reserve established by Cárdenas as "one huge *ejido*" (1967:27). More precisely, he observes that there are numerous distinct farm collectives and agricultural credit associations within the bounds of each Yaqui pueblo. The growth of the sociedades following the establishment of the Zona Indígena was slowed by lack of water:

> From 1939 until the completion of the main canal Marcos Carillo in 1956 the majority of Yaquis derived their chief income from individual or family plots. However, some Yaquis were organized into sociedades with Banco Ejidal help prior to 1952, when the new Oviachi dam (Alvaro Obregón) was completed. These Yaquis, mainly in Bataconsica (near Bacum), were supplied water from pumps from the smaller canals of the old dam at Angostura. The other river pueblos had to depend on the same flood river agriculture they had been using for centuries (Bartell 1965:181).

From these initial steps toward cooperative farming, the sociedad system had grown substantially by the early 1960s. Gilbert Bartell estimates that, in 1962, about 75 percent of all family heads of Potam were organized into thirty-two sociedades (1965:186). Similar estimates for the 1970s are difficult to obtain. The renting of sociedad land to private farmers, a practice which is illegal under ejido law, has become widespread. Idle sociedad lands are also abundant, due to salinization, poor productivity, and the failure of socios to obtain adequate financing. And a simple count of socios has become rather misleading: many sociedad members are particulares as well, often deriving more income from private farms than from their collective arrangements. It appears that by 1975 the number of full-time socios had declined substantially from the 1962 estimate of 75 percent of family heads for Potam.

To form a sociedad, a group of men, minimally eight, must petition the Yaqui governors for an available tract of land. Once the governors agree on the availability of the plot, a formal request signed by the petitioners and the signatories of the pueblo is forwarded to the offices of the Banco Rural. Together with the Agrarian Ministry, the Banco decides on the feasibility of irrigating the sociedad's land and financing the farming operation. With the Banco's consent the sociedad may begin cultivation. In recent years the credit available to sociedades has been insufficient, and an unofficial moratorium on new sociedades in the Yaqui Zone has been in effect, an apparent result of the steadily worsening economic situation of the country as a whole. Additionally, there apears to be a feeling among Banco and agrarian officials that most of the available arable land in the Yaqui Zone is already under production in existing sociedades and private farms. New sociedades must await the extension of canal networks, a project which has a lower priority than refurbishing the existing network.

Once officially sanctioned by the Banco, the sociedad proceeds to elect its officials. Each sociedad theoretically consists (see Bartell 1965:177; Erasmus 1967) of two separate governing bodies, the *comisariado ejidal* and the *consejo de vigilancia*. The first, an executive committee of president, secretary, and treasurer, is responsible for the operation of the sociedad and for conducting the necessary affairs with the Banco. The vigilance committee acts essentially as a check on the executive committee, to assure that the president and his chosen officials operate within the stipulations of agrarian law and to see that each socio obtains a fair share of work and profits.

Financing of the sociedad is carried out through the Banco. The initial capital costs are variable. Most sociedades in and around Potam possessed trucks in various states of disrepair, and a few had purchased their own cultivating machinery. These initial acquisitions are funded by the bank, which then extracts a percentage of the sociedad's profits over several years to pay off the debt. Additional costs of production are funded and debited by the Banco in the same manner. In their supervisory capacity Banco officials contract with the Secretariat of Agriculture and Water Resources and with private machinery operators for provision of water, preparation, planting, and harvesting of the land, and transporting crops to the Banco warehouses or the outlets of CONASUPO (Compañía Nacional de Subsistencias Populares). All of these expenses are then deducted from the sociedad profits, along with a tax on yields amounting to 10 percent, out of which the Banco pays the salaries of sociedad officials and covers its own operational expenses.

Individual socios receive payment for their work in two forms. First, they are paid according to the number of days they work for the sociedad, clearing and preparing the land, weeding, and irrigating. Payment is made by the Banco either directly in cash or through the establishment of credit at local stores for the purchase of basic provisions. A second payment comes after harvest, in the form of a "liquidation," a distribution of the profits that remain once the bank has deducted its operation costs and reduced the initial debt of the sociedad.

The income of individual socios is difficult to calculate. Sociedades differ greatly in the size and productivity of their lands, the amount of the original debt, and the number of socios sharing in the work and profits. Moreover, few socios rely entirely on Banco payments for their income; many also operate private farms in conjunction with kinsmen. On the basis of discussions with socios and observations of living standards, though, it is apparent that few farmers realize a great profit through their sociedades. By the same token, socios do not suffer extreme poverty: the general availability of store credit keeps most of them adequately provided for.

Neither realizing nor expecting great profits from their labors, socios nevertheless gain other amenities, most importantly an insurance against disaster. This insurance is of two forms: crops insurance, by which the sociedad will be refunded 25 percent of the market value of their crop in the event of destruction from plagues, wind, and rain; and access to the medical facilities of government-run clinics. Free health care provides an important incentive to sociedad membership, for it extends to the socio's nuclear family.

The contemporary situation of the Yaqui socio must be placed in perspective, both to the economy of the zone prior to the construction of massive irrigation works and to the alternatives open to Yaqui farmers under the current agricultural regime. Financed and advised by the Banco Rural, sociedades no longer have the autonomy to decide what to plant. They must sow the crops dictated by national policy; in the Yaqui Zone, these are usually wheat and cártamo. An oil-seed, cártamo is of no importance in Yaqui subsistence. Wheat is an important element in Yaqui diets, but must be sold to the Banco, processed by non-Yaqui millers, and repackaged for retail back to Yaqui consumers. Thus, under bank policy, Yaqui farmers who are exclusively socios are necessarily tied to the market for their subsistence goods. The dependencies of the past—on uncertain water supplies, low yields, and precarious land tenure—have been replaced by a new dependency on the retail stores and the vagaries of price fluctuations in basic commodities.

An attractive but difficult alternative—or, for some, a complement—to the sociedad system in the Yaqui Zone is "private farming," becoming the client of a wealthy patrón.

Particulares

Ideally, private Yaqui farmers obtain land in a manner similar to socios, by petitioning the pueblo governors, then satisfying agrarian officials as to the feasibility of irrigating and cropping the plot. In practice, particulares have acquired farms through diverse means. Most common is the simple inheritance of arable land from relatives. Land appears to be inherited predominantly through patrilineal relations, but in several observed cases the lands were inherited by wives. Thus, in one instance, a man and his wife's father jointly worked lands that the wife's father had already passed on to this daughter, to be held in trust for her children. In addition to working his wife's land, the man also cultivated a plot several miles away, but near to the fields of his own paternal uncle. In general, land inheritance is less determined by strict lineal descent, and more by the availability of labor to cultivate the farms. In the above case, the man's father-in-law had no surviving brothers or sons to assist him and was no longer associated with his wife. His daughter and her husband, though, had four young sons who would eventually require land. The man and his father-in-law provided adequate labor for cultivating the land until the grandsons were old enough to participate themselves.

Land may be acquired by *particulares* through other means. Frequently, land is borrowed or rented from *sociedades* or other *particulares* who have ceased to cultivate their plots due to the attrition of the labor force through death, curtailing of credit as a result of the malfeasance of *sociedad* officials, lack of adequate financing for a *particular*, alternative occupations such as fishing, or burdensome political and ceremonial duties in the pueblo. These idle lands may be acquired by *particulares* through informal agreements with various stipulations. In some cases, the *particular* will pay the former owner a rent—either cash or a part of the harvest. In others, land may simply be borrowed and worked for several seasons until the original farmer is able to obtain the requisite capital or family labor to work the land himself.

Neither renting nor borrowing is positively sanctioned by Mexican agrarian statutes, nor by traditional Yaqui law. In theory, *ejidal* law precludes renting *sociedad* land to nonmembers. Yaqui law likewise implies that farmers leaving their lands idle should retain no rights over them. These prohibitions are not actively enforced, for reasons not explicitly voiced by either the agrarian officials or the pueblo governors. Informally, the Banco Rural and SARH acknowledge that land may often be more productively and efficiently used by private farmers who irrigate and weed carefully and who do not overtax the Banco's limited credit facilities. And Yaqui officials realize that an individual's ability to continuously farm a plot is now subject to the vagaries of the credit supply and availability of labor, inputs which may fluctuate from year to year. Thus, idle land may represent a farmer's inability, not his unwillingness, to cultivate; for this reason he should not entirely lose his right to these lands.

Once land has been acquired through inheritance, renting, borrowing, or petitioning, the *particular* must obtain the necessary financing and labor to clear and cultivate. As with *sociedad* farming, the labor requirements of the *particular* are heavy only during the stages of initial plot-clearing and periodic weeding demanded by some crops. Capital demands, however, are frequently heavier and more pressing than those encountered by the *sociedades*. Much of *sociedad* farming is carried out on credit, with socios accountable for the costs incurred during production only after the harvest is in. Particulares, on the other hand, are forced in most cases to pay these costs as they arise. Prior to the harvest few Yaquis have the cash on hand for meeting these expenses.

To overcome this capital shortage, successful particulares have entered into clientele relationships with local Mexicans—storekeepers, farm machinery contractors, or other wealthy residents of the Yaqui Zone. Over time, informal contracts evolve in which the Mexican *patrón* sells seed and provides operational capital and credit to the particular in return for a share of the harvest, which is then sold through local stores. Shopkeepers profit by retaining steadily producing clients and often reduce the price of seed below that charged to socios by the Banco. *Patrones* also, in most cases, handle the task of contracting for machinery and water, as well as the transport of the harvest from field to storage or retail outlet. The Yaqui farmer, for his part, bears the responsibility of clearing, weeding, and irrigating, and any additional technical tasks associated with the agricultural cycle.

The percentage of profits extracted by patrons varies widely, ranging as high as 50 percent of the harvest after deducting for his expenditures. By most accounts these relations are beneficial to both patrón and client. These mutual benefits derive primarily from the fact that financiers and growers can select their own mix of crops, free of the dictates of the Banco Rural. Thus, particulares grow many of the subsistence crops shunned by the Banco in favor of commercial export crops. Under the export orientation of Mexico's northwest coast, a local vacuum of subsistence items—corn and beans especially, but also a wide range of vegetables—has been created and is being partially filled by Yaqui particulares. By financing the farming operations of Yaquis, storekeepers can obtain a stock of subsistence goods locally, avoiding the transport costs involved in importing such items from outside the region. At the same time, private Yaqui farmers, even when turning over a sizable portion of their harvest to patrons, can retain enough to substantially reduce the expense of buying subsistence goods in the market.

Particular farming does, however, have several disadvantages. Private farmers seldom qualify for the crop insurance offered by the Banco to sociedades, or the medical treatment automatically available to socios. Moreover, getting started as a particular is more difficult than forming or joining a sociedad. Once a particular finds the necessary land he is faced with the problem of obtaining a creditor willing to back his farming operations. Potential patrons are abundant in Estación Vicam, and less so in Potam. But few are willing to risk their capital on an inexperienced or unproven farmer who is working land of untested quality. When a patrón is found under these conditions, he will be likely to extract an exorbitant percentage of the yields to cover his initial, risky investment. In the event that both farmer and land prove successful, and both patrón and client wish to continue the informal contract, these percentages will become, over time, more equitable for the particular.

One difficulty that faces the particular can become a source of conflict within Potam and other pueblos in the zone. If a client lacks the requisite household labor to clear his land, he must hire outside workers. In the cases observed or reported on, hired laborers were primarily drawn from the farmer's network of compadres, but the terms of employment were not the reciprocal ones traditionally associated with coparenthood. Rather, they were employer-employee ties based on cash. Frequently, though, a particular will not have the cash on hand prior to harvest to pay off his hired help. And few patrons seemed willing to finance this preliminary stage of the agricultural cycle, choosing instead to provide cash or credit only for the subsistence needs of the client and his immediate family. Thus, particulares may be forced into forestalling payment to hired hands, with the nearly inevitable result of festering ill will between employer and employees, between ritual coparents, often residents of the same Yaqui barrio. In addition to the potential disruption of ritual obligations between coparents, these disputes find expression in gossip about the employer, severely reducing his ability to recruit labor in the future.

Other problems beset the untried particular. He will find it difficult to obtain credit at local stores, again due to the risk a patrón-storekeeper faces in financing a new client, working new lands. The particular may also be placed low on the priority scale by machinery contractors who have already established a schedule of plowing, planting, and harvesting for their client sociedades. Additionally, the novice particular may be last to receive his water allocation and may run into conflict with owners of adjacent fields over access to main canals. While all of these difficulties may disrupt the operations of established particulares as well as beginners, it appears that most of the logistical problems have been or can be worked out by a slow process of accommodation with neighboring field owners, with storekeepers, and with machinery operators.

Over the course of several planting seasons a Yaqui particular can achieve a stable working relationship with his patrón and with his neighbors. With time the initially particularistic ties between patrón and client are likely to evolve into multiplistic social ties. Reciprocated social visits become increasingly frequent, coparent relations may occasionally be established, and a great deal of information is exchanged across ethnic lines. Patrons begin to acquire a small vocabulary of Yaqui, usually little more than the traditional phrases of greeting and leave-taking. Yaquis, in turn, acquire a greater facility in the colloquial

Spanish of the northwest. And, through increased social contacts, the relatively strict cost-accounting of a new patrón-client relationship is loosened. Goods and services are more freely exchanged between patrón and client, and the percentage of profits extracted by the patrón is gradually reduced.

Once this stage of the clientele tie is achieved, the Yaqui particular may begin to prosper. And this prosperity, perhaps in the form of cash, a new truck, or house of adobe is evident to young Yaquis, providing an incentive to enter into patrón-client ties and the particular system.

Jornaleros

By choice, by force, or, recently, by lack of employment opportunities in their pueblos, Yaquis have for centuries supplied indispensable labor to the state and national economy. The practice was once adaptive. Fulfilling the demand for workers in colonial Sonora's mines and haciendas, Yaquis forestalled assaults on their river towns (Hu-Dehart 1981). This pattern continued into the nineteenth century, when competition among the state's hacendados for valuable Yaqui laborers fueled internecine power struggles in the region (Hu-Dehart 1984). In the Porfiriato of the early twentieth century, however, the reputation of Yaquis as workers and fighters underwrote the devastating policy of deportation which John Kenneth Turner brought to international attention in *Barbarous Mexico* (1969, original 1911). Unknown numbers of Yaquis were exiled from their Sonoran villages to the henequen plantations of Yucatan to work and, frequently, to die (Hu-Dehart 1974).

Yaquis who survived their servitude in the south or escaped the Sonoran roundups returned to the fields after the Revolution. To some, wage labor on the farms of the Yaqui Valley was a full-time occupation; to others, it provided supplementary income to their own limited agriculture (Moisés, Kelley, and Holden 1971). Cynthia Hewitt de Alcántara observed this pattern in the early 1970s—a "proletariado rural en formación," composed of youthful Yaquis who lacked farm plots and irrigation waters in the Yaqui Zone, and of their fathers who had little work to perform on the increasingly mechanized farms of the reserve (1978:260−61).

The same macroeconomic forces that drove the agrarian unrest of 1975 and 1976 have jeopardized the safety valve of wage labor for the Yaquis. The crop mix in southern Sonora has changed radically since the 1960s. Labor-intensive cotton, with a per-hectare requirement of 72 man-days (Pomareda and Simmons 1983:364), declined in the face of a weak international market and a growing demand in Mexico for cereals and beef. Wheat, the dominant crop in the Valley in the 1970s, requires only 9.6 man-days of labor per hectare; the oil-seed, safflower, similarly requires only 3.9 man-days (Pomareda and Simmons 1983: 364). The incipient rural proletariat that Hewitt de Alcántara remarked upon in the Yaqui Zone had little chance, throughout the 1970s, of finding work.

A Postscript

José López Portillo succeeded President Echeverría with a promise to restore order and tradition to the Mexican countryside. It was not to be the tradition of *agrarismo,* but the more recent trend, agribusiness (see Bartra 1982; Bailey and Link 1981; Sanderson 1981b; Redclift 1980, 1981). Indeed, López Portillo's ministers soon proclaimed an end to the "land redistribution phase" of the Mexican Revolution (Grindle 1981:25). The renewed confidence that the president placed in export-oriented agriculture could not be sustained through the sexenio, however. Total imports of basic food items—corn, beans, wheat, and rice primarily—rose to near-record levels in the second half of the decade (Grindle 1981:17), forcing López Portillo and his advisors to reassess national farm policies. Their solution to the recurrent crisis was two-fold: the Sistema Alimentario Mexicano (SAM) and the Ley de Fomento Agropecuario (LFA).

With SAM, the "Mexican Food System," López Portillo shifted the responsibility of achieving national self-sufficiency in basic food crops from the irrigated zones to "rainfed districts," composed of independent peasant farmers and ejidatarios. Initiated four years into the López Portillo term, SAM

> presented the idea of "shared risk," in which the government committed itself to underwrite a considerable portion of potential loss for the adoption of new technologies. It also announced a new effort to subsidize inputs, research, and extension for technological change at the farm level, and promised to stimulate peasant organization in order to establish an alliance between the state and the *campesino* (Grindle 1981:21–22).

Petroleum revenues funded the expensive undertaking of production and consumption subsidies, expansion of bureaucracies, and the plowing of land previously given over to livestock. The early results of the new program were encouraging. Maize outputs for 1980 and 1981 increased markedly over those for 1979 (Norton 1982:105; Esteva 1983:246–47). But the vulnerability of SAM became evident in 1982. The oil glut severely reduced Mexico's export revenues, plunging the country—and the Sistema Alimentario Mexicano—into prolonged economic crisis (Wessman 1984:257).

In seeming contradiction to SAM, the Ley de Fomento Agropecuario formalized the suspicion López Portillo expressed toward the beneficiaries of Echeverría's expropriations in and around San Ignacio. Designed to facilitate the "penetration of private capital in the countryside" (Wessman 1984:255), LFA gave preference in access to "credits, insurance, fertilisers, seeds, technical assistance and machinery, transport and warehouse facilities" (Anonymous 1979:156) to associations of private capital and public lands. The *Latin American Economic Report* followed the LFA through its early progress in the Mexican legislature:

> In its pursuit of efficiency the bill states that *ejido* and community lands may be rented to agro-industrialists under 'association contracts'; the peasant will provide the land and the investor will provide machinery, technology, marketing and supervision. Profits will be divided 'in proportion to what cash each party to the association has invested' (Anonymous 1979:156).

The policies are young, and the economy of the country is in too much flux to permit a close analysis of SAM and LFA. One early commentator on the reforms, however, denies a contradiction. Together, James Wessman argues, "these policies emphasize that production must occur, in whatever units can get the job done." SAM, with its focus on basic foods, "was a declaration of Mexico's political and economic independence from the United States." LFA, in turn, "was a less publicized tool to guarantee that result" (1984:258).

Locally, SAM and LFA pose unappealing consequences for the fragile agrarian adaptations of the Zona Indígena. By urging association between farmers and private capital, LFA validates the strategy pursued by Yaqui *particulares*. In the process, the competition for private financiers throughout the valley will increase. The unsteady balance of power between the owners of land and the owners of capital—the farmers and their patrons—may tip.

Likewise, SAM, if successful—and there are doubts (Norton 1982)—may fill the local market for basic foods which some Yaquis have endeavored to supply. While it is essential for the country to revive its neglected rainfed districts and its output of basic foods, it is nonetheless ironic that the new direction may place Yaquis in limbo. The tribe reaped few benefits from the great investment in the irrigated northwest. Now, as the focus shifts, their hopes may be dashed.

CONCLUSIONS

Zona Indígena

Historically, Yaquis resisted domination by force of arms. The efforts inevitably failed. Now, as a semiautonomous ethnic group within the nation-state, the tribe must battle the ironies that fall from such incorporation.

Yaquis entered the confrontation for land around Obregón with the strongest political organization of the groups locally involved, yet ultimately lost out to the derivative power and organization of the campesinos. Inquiry into this struggle exposed the Janus-faced character of the Yaqui polity. To the outside, in the political arenas of the region, Yaqui corporate polity displays a single-minded unity of interests—of obtaining land, of seeking a definitive solution to the boundary question. Internally, Yaqui society is beset with conflict—most often between farmer and hired labor, but also between socio and particular over access to limited machinery and over the scheduling of water allotments. And, on a larger level, there is conflict over philosophies. Some Yaquis demand increased economic and technological assistance from the Mexican government. Others seek more limited help, and more limited interference.

In addition to these conflicts, there are several ironies stemming directly from the fundamentals of commercial agriculture. First, in symbol and in fact, Yaquis retain political control over the lands of the zone, yet they lack economic control; they are at the mercy of the outside financiers. Secondly, those Yaquis who appear to be making an adequate living are doing so by imposing subsistence crops onto a commercial export market. Those who make it, do so by operating outside the realm of national agrarian institutions, outside of the ejido. They make it, in short, by contravening both the national ideal of agrarian revolution and the tribal ideal of political and economic autonomy; they make it by working for Mexican patrons.

Internally weakened over the issue of capital inputs, the polity is externally strengthened over the issue of land. Yaquis can unite, as they perennially do, around the demand for territory, because that demand does not implicate the more crucial and rupturing issue of finance.

Valle del Yaqui

The violent events of San Ignacio in the autumn of 1975 have been used as a point of entry into the role of agrarian politics in national development and into the economic niche occupied by Yaqui farmers in the larger scheme. The discussion has strayed from the central theme of Yaqui Indian ethnicity, but for a purpose. Leo Despres has postulated a link between ethnicity and politics, as has George Collier (1975) for the Tzotzil of highland Chiapas. The link has been rightly criticized for inadequate attention to the *outcome* of ethnic political action (Smith 1977b). The lengthy digression here into agrarian policy, economy, and ecology has sought to respond to this critique.

The results of Yaqui political mobilization in 1975 and 1976 were patently discouraging. The demands of the governors were not only unfulfilled, they were virtually ignored in the volatile aftermath of San Ignacio. An explanation for the failure of the Yaqui corporate polity to win this battle for resources can be found largely in the nature of their co-competitors, the Mexican campesinos, and in the alliance established between campesinos and a lame duck president, Echeverría. In the limited expropriations at the end of his sexenio, Echeverría sought to appease both his constituency of peasants and his ideology of agrarian populism. That he was equally committed to an ideology of *indigenismo* is undoubted. In southern Sonora, resources of land and water were simply insufficient to satisfy all claimants.

There was a geography of expropriation as well as a sociology. In Sinaloa, Echeverría stopped short of implementing his reform, mindful of the key role of vegetable exports to a faltering national economy. To the north, in Sonora, the miracle of the Green Revolution had already worn thin by the 1970s. There, wheat production could no longer keep up with internal demands, let alone supply an international market. To be sure, the president ran a risk of further shortening the supply of basic foodstuffs to the internal market by redistributing land to campesinos. But the persistent inconclusiveness in the data—of the relative productivity of private farms and ejidos—served to minimize the political costs of this risk.

Contrasts between Sinaloa and Sonora add little to our understanding of why Mexican ejidatarios prevailed over Yaqui ejidatarios in the local struggle for San Ignacio. The contrasts do, however, establish the salience of natural resources to political decisions. This theme will be carried into the next chapter, where a comprehension of the distribution and abundance of shrimp in the Gulf of California helps to explain a significant political success for the Yaquis against a group of Mexican estuary shrimpers. This success was achieved at Bahía de Lobos, close to the mouth of the Río Muerto.

CHAPTER 7

The Politics of the Estuary

From the middle of August to Christmastide, Guásimas and Lobos on the coast become centers of intense fishing. The year-long residents of Guásimas and the seasonal occupants of the Lobos camp set out soon after daybreak in motor-powered, fiberglass boats (*canoas* or *pangas*) of about eighteen feet, to net-cast for shrimp. Returning to shore around noon, the crews of two or three decapitate the catch, weigh it, and pack it in refrigerated trucks for transport to Guaymas, then on to processors across the border in San Diego. Once the catch is packed and shipped, the fishermen return to their houses—mostly tarpaper shacks at Lobos, cinderblock houses up the coast at Guásimas—and relax, eat, gossip, and mend their *attarayas* (cast nets).

The Yaqui shrimp cooperative, the Sociedad Cooperativa de Producción Pesquera, "Communidades Yaquis," has, since its tentative beginning in the 1950s, achieved modest financial success, expanded to encompass two large bays and a number of estuary camps, diversified its operation to include its own ice-making plant and fish flour grinder, and continued to maintain virtual autonomy from Mexican interference. Thus, Yaqui shrimping stands in direct contrast to Yaqui agriculture. Yaqui fishermen and the cooperative directors control the production and distribution processes and, through presidential decrees, have attained exclusive rights to the marine resources of the Yaqui Zone. With its success in the arena of resource competition between Yaqui and Mexican, the fishing co-op has become a source of pride for the whole tribe, a symbolic expression of long-held, frequently unrealized values of autonomy and territorial integrity. Paradoxically, Yaqui fishermen are neither the most active supporters of, nor frequent participants in obvious manifestations of Yaqui identity—the ceremonial and political systems, the traditional dress, the Yaqui language. Contrary to the expectations of Despres (1975) and others, the fishing co-op provides evidence for an almost inverse relation between competitive success and the cultural content of ethnicity. This chapter will seek to explain this deviation from expectations.

The comparative dimension here concerns Yaqui fishermen and Yaqui farmers. As in the previous chapter, however, an understanding of broader political and economic dynamics is indispensable. Discussion will center on two contrasting relationships: one between shrimpers of the *estero* and of the *altamar* (estuary and open water), and the other, between the inshore cooperatives of Sonora and those of Sinaloa and Nayarit to the south.

DEMISE OF THE SINALOA-NAYARIT COOPERATIVES

Cooperative shrimp fishing in the lagoon of Sinaloa and Nayarit began auspiciously in the 1930s. Anthropologist James McGoodwin has traced the history of these cooperatives, a history of failed expectations and internal turmoil. Initially, the co-ops surpassed government expectations, which centered on three goals: (1) to increase living standards of rural fishermen, (2) to augment national food supplies, and (3) to generate export income in the aftermath of the protracted and costly Mexican Revolution. The condition of these cooperatives three decades later was quite another story:

> Production has dropped to less than half its level at the time they were founded, and they had surpluses of unwanted, unproductive members. They were plagued with internal conflicts and dissention. Corrupt officials ran many of them with an iron hand. They were also embroiled in conflicts with other rural people in their regions, as well as with the government officials who regulated them. Furthermore, although their production was traded for large sums of money in the international marketplace, comparatively little of that income returned to their members (McGoodwin 1980a:39–40).

A shifting government policy precipitated this demise. Responsible initially for organizing, capitalizing, and regulating the inshore cooperatives, federal fisheries agents never relinquished their control. Moreover, these regulators became more responsive to the problems and prospects of offshore fishermen than to those of the estuarine fishermen. Attuned to the premium prices offered for Mexican shrimp on the international market, policymakers systematically fostered the growth of capital-intensive, mechanized trawler fleets, exploiting the altamar off the coast, and establishing shrimp as the leading primary commodity export, representing slightly under 50 percent of all such exports. But this dependence on foreign markets also had unfavorable repercussions:

When world prices for shrimp fall, the Mexican government has to pass the price reduction down to its producers. From the government's point of view, cutting prices paid to the inshore cooperatives is less problematic than cutting those paid to its offshore cooperatives. Cutting prices paid to the inshore cooperatives results mostly in income losses for their members, whereas cutting prices paid to the offshore cooperatives seriously jeopardizes the latter's ability to repay longterm loans made to them by the government's National Bank for Promoting Cooperatives. Such loans constitute a considerable capital commitment on the part of the government for financing the construction of offshore trawlers as well as modern freezing and packing plants. Thus, when a price squeeze comes it is the inshore cooperatives which usually suffer the most (McGoodwin 1980a:44−45).

The vagaries of international marketing and national financing tie the fates of inshore and offshore fishermen closely to one another. So, too, does the life cycle of the penaeid shrimp. Hatched in the open waters of the gulf, the larvae grow to subadults in the protected coastal estuaries and lagoons. Subsequently, they emigrate back to the sea for spawning. The inshore cooperatives are in a position to intercept this movement with estuarial weirs.

McGoodwin argues that the marginalization of inshore cooperatives ultimately stems from these intricate biological and economic facts. Empowered to regulate fishing, government agencies deflect the troubles of the offshore trawler industry onto the inshore cooperatives. Diminishing returns to offshore trawlers are translated into shorter seasons for inshore fishermen and constant reprimands on the destructive economic consequences of estuarine shrimp-trapping. Wracked by internal dissension, the inshore cooperatives are unable to contravene these external pressures to curtail their fishing effort.

In his disheartening picture of demise along the coast of Nayarit and Sinaloa, McGoodwin puts heavy emphasis on the ecology of shrimp. This is by no means misplaced, yet it warrants more precise analysis. In the following sections, I will review the known details of three species of the genus *Penaeus* in the Gulf of California and southward along the Mexican coast, and discuss several important environmental differences between the northern and southern regions. Major points of contrast on the north-south axis can be usefully previewed here: (1) ecological factors contribute to a pattern by which southern shrimpers, inshore and offshore, exploit the same shrimp stocks, whereas northern lagoonal fishermen capture a species distinct from that of their offshore counterparts; (2) economic factors have placed the offshore fleets in the south in an unfavorable position vis-á-vis the northern fleets and have heightened the desire of the southern fleets to exploit inshore shrimp stocks; and (3) geomorphological factors underlying lagoon formation prohibit the use of estuarine traps in the north, thus removing a stimulus for conflict between offshore and inshore fishermen.

THE GULF OF CALIFORNIA

Scholars of the gulf describe it as a "caricature of oceanography," an exaggeration of fundamental geologic and hydrologic processes (Thomson, Findley, and Kerstitch 1979:1). Soundings through the long finger-shaped body of water provide the starkest evidence of this. At irregular intervals the gulf floor is punctuated by massive basins, cutting down to 3700 meters below sea level. Land-derived sediments are carried into these basins through a series of submarine canyons, piercing through the offshore shelf of the major rivers.The coastal shelf itself, demarcated at roughly the 100-meter depth line, is variable in breadth throughout the gulf. On the peninsular side it forms a narrow band, the consequence of a virtual absence of sediment-carrying rivers in Baja California. On the opposite side, substantial rivers having their origins in the Sierra Madre Occidental have deposited a deep covering of sediments, creating a shallow floor extending up to 50 kilometers offshore (Maluf 1983:26–27).

The upper gulf highlights these processes in the extreme. Cut off only in the present century by water storage facilities and agricultural development, the Colorado River historically contributed over 50 percent of the total flow of freshwater into the gulf. With this flow came some 180 million tons of sediment annually (Maluf 1983:30). The geologic results are not surprising: a massive delta and an extensive, shallow evaporation basin, where the area above the 100-meter depth line covers some 50,000 square kilometers (see map). In the upper gulf, bottom topography enhances the tidal ranges, salinity gradients, and water temperatures characteristic of the lower gulf and the open Pacific. Mean tidal range at Guaymas is 1.5 meters, decreasing to 1 meter at the mouth of the gulf. By contrast, in the upper gulf the mean range is 6.6 meters, with extremes recorded of 9.6 meters where the Colorado River joins the gulf. This vertical displacement of water, ranking among the largest in the world, interacts with the gently sloping, shallow bottom to create extensive intertidal zones, in places up to 5 kilometers wide (Maluf 1983:36).

Salinity and water temperature gradients, important factors in the behavioral ecology of shrimp, follow a similar trend. In the upper gulf, where evaporation exceeds freshwater inflow, salinities are higher than in the lower gulf (Brusca 1973:8; Maluf 1983:38). Extreme fluctuations in sea temperatures are also experienced in the upper gulf. Affected by

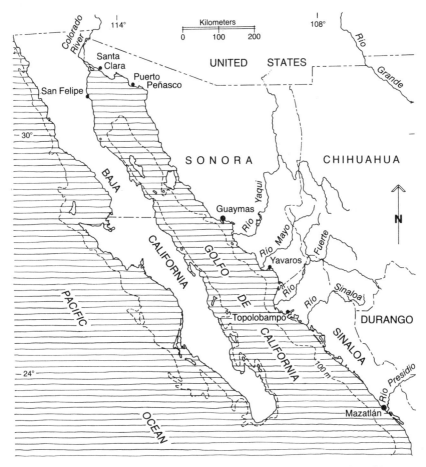

The Gulf of California. *Adapted from Thomson, Findley, and Kerstitch, 1979.*

the substantial seasonal variation in air temperature of the adjacent Sonoran Desert, shallow shoreline waters are rapidly warmed and cooled. Surface water temperature in Puerto Peñasco reaches 30°–32°C (88°–91°F), plunging as low as 10°–11°C in the winter. Offshore, however, temperatures remain fairly constant, with a seasonal flux on the order of 2° to 5°C (Brusca 1973:78, Maluf 1983:38).

Lagoon Morphology

The coastal zone between water and land also takes its shape through the complex interaction of hydrographic and terrestrial processes. In the Gulf of California, these forces have resulted in a differential distribution of lagoon morphologies: open lagoon in the north and closed lagoon in the south. F. B. Phleger (1969:9–10; see also Edwards 1978a), summarizing the processes underlying lagoon formation, notes that the number and size of inlets connecting lagoons and estuaries to the open sea are determined by the amount of water exchanged through these openings. Water volume derives from two sources: the ebb and flow of oceanic tides and the disgorging of rivers into the lagoons. As a rule, the greater the water flow through the lagoon openings, from either source or both combined, the broader and deeper the openings.

Complications arise when this model is applied to the coastal zone of Pacific Mexico. One source of water volume—the tidal range—is greater in the northern gulf than in the south; thus lagoons are generally more open in the former area. River flow, however, makes relatively little contribution to water volume in the open lagoons to the north, along the deltas of the Yaqui, Mayo, and Fuerte systems. For decades, these once-destructive rivers have been dammed and parcelled out to irrigators. Down the coast, the rivers of southern Sinaloa and Nayarit still flow to the sea. But their volume is insufficient to expand the narrow breaches of the region's closed lagoons. This differential distribution of lagoon types underwrites a crucial difference in shrimping technologies; the narrow inlets of the southern estuaries are easily closed by traps, an infeasible method on the more open lagoons of the upper gulf. This trap technology has become the point of contention for the beleaguered offshore trawlermen of the south.

Shrimping Technology: Offshore

Staggered by years of revolution in the early twentieth century, Mexico's economy rebounded slowly in the 1930s and 1940s. The history of the Pacific coast trawler industry reflects this tentative process. In the early 1920s, several foreign firms displayed interest in the resources of the Gulf of California, yet attained little success. At Guaymas a California company designed a temporary shrimp-packing plant, but ceased construction when it realized that shrimp were available only seasonally. Attempting to operate at Topolobampo on the Fuerte River, where shrimp were purportedly more abundant, the firm was once again stymied. Discouraged investigators for the United States Department of Commerce reported the cause of the new failure:

> The Mexican customs officials insisted upon collecting an export duty of 2 cents per kilo . . ., not only on the shrimps, but also on the wooden containers in which the 5-gallon cans were placed and the ice in which they were packed, 40 pounds of fresh shrimps requiring about 100 pounds of ice for railway shipment to the border (Bell and MacKenzie 1923:192).

Yet interest in the development of gulf fisheries persisted both inside and outside of Mexico. The impediments to progress clearly lay not in the absence of shrimp, but in the lack of technological infrastructure. An American expatriot in Mazatlán recorded a thriving traditional lagoonal fishery for the Commerce Department investigators:

> Shrimps are plentiful in many places along the coast of Sinaloa. . . The canners can expect about one poor year in five, but even in a poor year there is thought to be enough in the run to put up a food pack. Some nights as high as 50 tons can be taken at one trap gateway, but such runs occur only a few times during the season. . . On account of the very delicate nature of the shrimps, and because of the hot climate, it would be necessary to locate a cannery very near to the selected place on the lagoon which was known to have a large run, or else means would have to be provided to collect the shrimps from other lagoons, with ice packs; the means of transportation are lacking, as boats large enough to carry several tons of shrimps could not navigate these shallow lagoons. . . (A. Russell Crowell, quoted in Bell and MacKenzie 1923:192–93).

In the 1930s, Japanese fishermen and processors capitalized on this underexploited abundance. Conducting extensive operations on the Pacific shrimp grounds between 1936 and 1939, the foreign fleet stimulated development of coastal-based processing plants and utilized refrigeration ships to hold their excess catches (Edwards 1978b:146). Their efforts ended abruptly in 1939, however, when the prospect of war induced Japan to withdraw its fleets from far-flung and potentially hostile waters (McGoodwin 1980b:28).

In the ensuing vacuum, Mexico's own efforts to develop the fishery would finally succeed. The state-owned development bank provided the financial impetus for both inshore and offshore cooperatives, and the industries expanded rapidly. By 1955, five hundred trawlers fished from off of the Pacific coastline and up into the Gulf of California. With some lag, the shore-based processing facilities caught up with the fleet's capacities (Edwards 1978b:146). As profits accrued to the Mexican shrimp industry, fleets continued to expand and modernize. Older trawlers are frequently of less than 250 horsepower, while more recently constructed ones have main engine capacities of 350 horsepower. In recent years, some of the fleet have been equipped with "twin trawls," two otter trawls attached to each boom. With these four nets a vessel sweeps 60 meters of seabed in a single tow. Thus equipped, boats can obtain yields of 2 to 6 tons of shrimp for the week-long trips during the height of the season, September to December. Toward the end of the season, in May or June, the effects of natural and fishing mortality are felt, and a single trip may yield only 1 ton (Edwards 1978b:147).

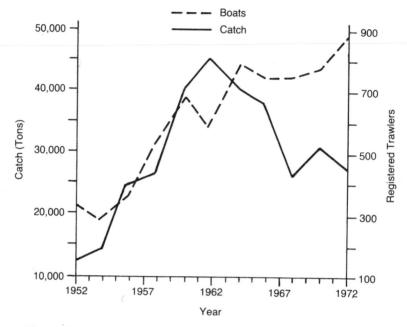

Fig. 7.1 Total Shrimp Catch and Registered Trawlers in the Gulf of California,
1952–1972. Adapted from Edwards 1978b, citing Lluch 1974.

Expansion, modernization, and technological change have led to overexploitation of the resources of the genus *Penaeus* along the Pacific coast and the Gulf of California. Summarizing catch statistics presented by Lluch (1974) and Mathews (1974), R. R. C. Edwards (1978b:154) gives a concise picture of this decline (fig. 7.1). From a peak catch of around 45,000 tons (tail weight) in the 1960–61 season, yields have declined irregularly through the early 1970s. Yet the number of operating trawlers has risen substantially through these decades. By 1970, 850 vessels fished along the Pacific coast, with 820 of these within the confines of the Gulf of California (Edwards) 1978b:146). This expansion continues apace in the 1980s; on opening day of the 1980–81 season, the Sonoran shrimp fleet, based at Yavaros, Guaymas, and Puerto Peñasco, totaled 640 vessels (*La Voz del Puerto*, 25 September 1980); a decade earlier, these ports dispatched only 358 boats (Chávez and Lluch 1971:148). With this unbridled growth, the average catch per boat has inevitably decreased.

Expansion of the fleet does not tell the complete story. In 1961, much of the Pacific shrimp industry adopted trawls with smaller mesh size, 38 millimeters, as opposed to the older stretched mesh size of 64 millimeters. This technological change substantially reduced the size of capture from approximately 140 millimeters total length for the 64-

millimeter net to 110 millimeters for the 38-millimeter net (Edwards 1978b:149). While the reduction in mesh size may account for the surge in catches in the early 1960s, the economic returns were not proportionate to this increase in catch. In the marketplace, the price of shrimp is not linearly related to shrimp size: larger tails bring a higher price per kilogram than smaller tails. Thus, the reduction of mean length has reduced the market value of the catch (Edwards 1978b:149).

Compounding the effects of reduced mesh size and fleet expansion, many of the newer vessels have increased horsepower, which gives them wider range and reduces the travel time to and from port. The impact of this increased efficiency, however, is far from clear. Some speculations can be drawn from the port-by-port comparison for 1970 (table 7.2), presented by Chávez and Lluch (1971:148). Taking the mean value of investment per vessel as an indication of fleet modernization, there is a slight tendency (Spearman $r_s = +.321$, n.s.) for larger mean catches to be associated with newer fleets. But the data are suspect, for in the aggregate level presented by Chávez and Lluch no indication of variation in vessel investment within each port's fleet is given. Indeed, these authors report that the fleets out of Mazatlán and Guaymas, although ranking above the mean investment for all ports, have not been modernized in recent years. There is some hint elsewhere of "overcompensation" by older vessels in the fleet. Edwards notes that "older vessels with less powerful engines (below 200 hp) caught more shrimp and made more trips than the more powerful vessels in the new fleets" (1978b:155).

More astonishing, but equally intractable, is the pattern of extreme variation in the value of shrimp from port to port. Tentatively, Chávez and Lluch (1971:155) suggest that the price differentials reflect mesh size differences. They single out Puerto Peñasco as an example of utilizing large-mesh nets to capture larger, more valuable shrimp. Unfortunately, they do not validate the suggestion with mesh size data for each port. Nonetheless, their explanation is plausible, and the figures themselves highlight the weak economic position of the southern fleets dispatched from Mazatlán, Topolobampo, and Yavaros.

Yet these data only hint at the irony of the trawler industry, a prime example of resource management gone awry. Biologists generally agree that population sizes of shrimp stocks bear only an insignificant relation to sizes of the previous year. More important determinants of abundance are the numerous ecological conditions that foster or preclude spawning and development. Thus, wide fluctuations in recruitment can occur from year to year, irrespective of the level of fishing effort in past seasons. With their tremendous reproductive capabilities, shrimp stocks are almost immune to biological overexploitation. But herein lies the peculiar management problem: no population equilibrium curve for the fishery can be drawn, hence the long-term maxi-

Table 7.2   Vessel and Catch Comparison, Gulf of California Shrimp Ports, 1970

Port	Number of Vessels	Mean Value of Vessels (pesos)	Tons Captured	Mean Tons Captured Per Vessel	Value Per Ton (pesos)	Mean Value of Catch Per Vessel (pesos)
San Felipe, B.C.	37	470,703	505	13.65	29,901	408,108
Santa Clara, Son.	18	122,333	204	11.33	16,176	183,333
Puerto Peñasco, Son.	85	441,176	1704	20.08	29,994	602,353
Guaymas, Son.	259	420,270	5082	19.62	18,654	366,023
Yavaros, Son.	14	350,000	412	29.43	9,951	292,857
Topolobampo, Son.	69	523,000	1689	24.48	7,993	195,652
Mazatlán, Sin.	229	526,878	5144	22.46	8,359	187,773
Mean =		407,766	2105.7	20.15	17,290	319,443
S.D. =		139,946	2139.8	6.2	9,518.3	153,820

Adapted from Chávez and Lluch 1971

mum economic yield position is indeterminate. A short succession of good years, based on fortuitous environmental factors, can lure increased capacity into the fishery; random poor years can idle this capacity or depress returns on investments (Anderson 1977:103–04).

A rational management goal, economist Lee Anderson suggests, is to maintain sufficient capacity to harvest the maximum economic yield for the average year at minimum cost, while making provisions at the same time for short-term increases or decreases in effort (1977:104). Mexican fisheries strategy for the Pacific trawler industry, however, consists primarily of seasonal regulations (*vedas*) designed to protect spawning shrimp. Little attention is given to problems of unrestricted entry into the fishery, or of changes in gear selectivity. These two factors may be at the root of the economic decline in the industry, as graphed in Figure 7.1. At first glance, the divergence in catch sizes and vessels after 1960 looks like a familiar case of biological overexploitation. But, taking into account the independence of subsequent shrimp stocks from fishing effort, it appears that increasing numbers of shrimpers, equipped with small-mesh trawls, are rushing to capture a share of the stock before it is lost to others. Consequently, the overall catch falls far short of maximum seasonal biomass.

Shrimping Technology: Inshore

The financial troubles of the offshore trawler fleets underlie the endemic conflict between this industry and its inshore counterpart. Faced with declining yields per unit of effort, the trawlermen are contemptuous of any efforts to block the recruitment of shrimp to the offshore stock. The *tapos* or weirs spanning the inlets of many of the semiclosed lagoons of the southern coast are immediate targets of this wrath.

Describing this time-tested technology, Edwards reviews recent efforts to modernize the traps (1978b:157–59). Traditional traps were constructed entirely of locally available materials. Two wings of densely packed brush, running up onto shore, direct shrimp into the central trap. The traps consist of a removable fence of mangrove poles and heart-shaped collectors designed to concentrate the shrimp against the trap. Fishermen situated on platforms around these collectors capture the shrimp with scoop-nets or cast-nets (see Hubbs and Roden 1964:179).

Innovations have replaced the upright wooden supports of the traditional design with concrete posts, and have substituted a double wire mesh for the old mangrove screens. The new galvanized screen allows for easier maintenance, since one screen can remain in place while its pair is removed and cleaned. Modern traps are also stronger, making them less prone to flood damage, but they are substantially more expensive to build and maintain.

Weirs are sealed in mid-August, when lagoonal shrimp populations are at their peak, and remain closed until April. Fishing does not commence until early to mid-September, allowing the juveniles trapped in the estuary to grow to commercial sizes. Catches are largest during the months of October and November, declining thereafter as a result of natural mortality, fishing mortality, and decreased recruitment to the lagoon population from the sea (Edwards 1978b:169).

No precise measure of the comparative efficiency of the two designs has been made, but both traps appear effective in interrupting the emigration from the lagoons. At peak emigration periods during new moons, shrimp have been reported to form *golpes* or shock waves against the barriers, and may yield catches of up to 5 kilograms with each cast of the net (Edwards 1978b:168).

Despite the apparent efficiency of the inshore fishery, the resulting level of production remains only a small proportion of total shrimp yields on the Pacific coast. Chávez and Lluch (1971:146) present data on regional catches from 1952 to 1970 (table 7.3), indicating that inshore production has fluctuated around a mean of 10.5 percent of the total yields. These data, however, should be treated with some caution. They conflict in detail (though not in trend) with figures from alternative sources presented by McGoodwin (1980b:31), and they do not account for home consumption and illegal local sales by fishermen, which some observers estimate to be 3 percent of reported catches for lagoonal fisheries (Edwards 1978b:169). A comparable correction factor for offshore trawlers has not been estimated and remains cloaked in the dangerous secrecy of *changüerismo*, the unlawful selling of shrimp on the open sea (Lozano 1972). However suspect these catch statistics may be, they nonetheless indicate the relative shares of the industry garnered by inshore and offshore technologies. And however minor the estuarine share is, it is a contentious issue for the offshore fleet, faced with the uncertainties of world prices and the realities of declining yields.

Penaeid Ecology and Distribution

Along the Pacific coast of Mexico, the problems of marine resource management are complex. Three penaeid species are of major economic importance, distributed differentially along some 2000 kilometers of coastline, living under differing ecological circumstances, and exploited, often simultaneously, by both inshore and offshore shrimpers. Some of this complexity can be unraveled by looking first at a generalized model of the penaeid life cycle, and then examining interspecific differences.

The Politics of the Estuary

135

Table 7.3 Shrimp Production in Offshore and Lagoon Fisheries, Gulf of California, 1952–1970

Year	Total Catch (tons)	Offshore (tons)	Lagoons (tons)	Lagoon Catch as Percentage of Total Catch
1952	11,118	9,016	2,102	18.91
1953	12,594	12,223	281	2.25
1954	11,948	9,843	2,105	17.62
1955	16,290	13,935	2,355	14.46
1956	8,629	7,966	663	7.68
1957	14,036	12,099	1,937	13.80
1958	17,866	14,746	3,120	17.46
1959	20,821	18,700	2,121	10.19
1960	24,454	23,316	1,138	4.65
1961	29,538	27,791	1,747	5.91
1962	28,785	27,360	1,425	4.95
1963	29,154	26,489	2,665	9.14
1964	25,894	24,861	2,033	7.85
1965	20,624	19,624	1,000	4.85
1966	25,016	23,187	1,829	7.31
1967	25,613	23,098	2,515	9.82
1968	19,161	16,864	2,297	11.99
1969	17,297	15,464	1,833	10.60
1970	21,399	17,909	3,490	16.31
Mean =	20,008	18,078	1,929.3	10.5
S.D. =	6,486.4	6,346.6	791.6	4.9

Adapted from Chávez and Lluch 1971

The species of the genus *Penaeus* are among the most fecund of shrimp and prawn, releasing 100,000 to 1 million eggs in a single spawning. The early phases of growth, from egg through several larval and postlarval stages, proceed rapidly. Eggs that survive until their first molting cycle, when they are vulnerable to predation and cannibalism, reach juvenile length in about two months. For the next two to four months, growth continues to adult sizes when fishing mortality joins the natural death rate as a major limiting factor. Most penaeid species follow a well-defined migration pattern through this life cycle, consisting of oceanic and estuarine phases. Spawning, which takes place offshore, may occur throughout the year but generally manifests several seasonal peaks. Postlarval shrimp then move inland to brackish lagoons and estuaries, where much of their development through juvenile stages occurs. Subsequently, the surviving subadults and adults emigrate back to the offshore waters.

The mechanisms triggering the inward migration are poorly known, although a consensus favors the assumption that postlarvae actively seek out the low salinity of lagoons in the wet season for development. Some support for this view comes from a correlation, established by numerous observers, between high rainfall and high seasonal shrimp catches. Speculating on the possible factors involved in this correlation, Edwards warns that there is little evidence to support any one of them (1978b:171) Years of high rainfall and increased runoff of freshwater from rivers may reduce salinities in coastal waters at farther distances from shore, thus enlarging the "attraction area" for postlarvae seeking low-salinity water. Moreover, during years of increased rainfall, estuaries cover a greater area, inundating and decomposing peripheral vegetation zones and producing a rich detrital substratum for shrimp to feed on. Finally, the increased runoff into the lagoon caused by high rains introduces nitrates and phosphates from surrounding agricultural lands, enhancing the primary productivity of the water.

Emigration to offshore waters is also poorly understood. Some evidence suggests that salinity tolerances in shrimp decrease with age. Thus postlarvae and juveniles are more able than adults to withstand the wide fluctuations in salinity experienced in estuaries (Temple 1973:18). It is the seasonal migration of late juveniles and adults, seeking the more stable conditions of open water, that the lagoon traps are designed to intercept.

This generalized model of the penaeid life cycle is inadequate in accounting for the complexities of the Gulf of California and the Pacific littoral. While it is true that most of the *Penaeus* shrimp spend some portion of their developmental cycle in estuarine systems, the length of this phase varies markedly among species. Joseph Kutkuhn (1966:20−21) places the Pacific coast shrimp on opposite ends of a continuum. *Penaeus californiensis* characteristically spends little time in estuaries, whereas the two other exploited species, *P. stylirostris* and *P. vannamei,* spend substantial time inshore, *P. stylirostris* remaining in estuaries longer than *P. vannamei.* Kutkuhn's rankings are only relative, but Edwards's studies of the Sinaloa-Nayarit estuarine zone show that *P. vannamei,* the primary estuary species there, spends between six and twelve weeks during the wet season in the lagoon habitat (Edwards 1978b:167; see also Edwards 1977; Menz and Bowers 1980). With the onset of the dry season and its attendant high salinities inshore, the maturing shrimp attempt their escape to the open water.

In the open lagoon systems of Sonora and northern Sinaloa, the patterns of distribution and movement are different. Here, *P. stylirostris* replaces *P. vannamei* the dominant inshore catch, and characteristically inhabits the estuaries longer than *P. vannamei* does to the south. This longer inshore phase can be attributed primarily to lagoon morphology: the open feature in the north allows easy water exchange between lagoon and the gulf, so that their salinities are almost comparable (Edwards personal communication 1981). Thus, unlike the *P. vannamei* exodus from hypersaline, dry-season lagoons in the south, *P. stylirostris* does not need to seek out the waters of the gulf. Where *P.*

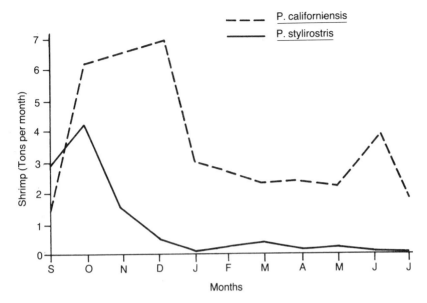

Fig. 7.4 Shrimp Species Composition by Month, Guaymas Landings. *Adapted from Chapa Saldaña, Guilbot Taddei, and Romero Rodriquez 1968.*

stylirostris does occur, in greatly reduced numbers in the south, it appears to behave like *P. vannamei*, evacuating the salty estuaries in favor of open water during the dry season.

The distribution and abundance of *P. californiensis* throughout the gulf and adjacent waters are equally complex. Predominantly an offshore species, it appears to thrive in the relatively hypersaline conditions of the upper gulf, and decreases markedly in the catches landed at Mazatlán and southward. For offshore trawlers landing their shrimp at Guaymas, *P. californiensis* accounts for over 80 percent of the yearly catch. In contrast, *P. californiensis* composes only 62 percent of the catches landed at the southern port of Mazatlán (figures 7.4 and 7.5). Edwards, however, warns against the facile conclusion that *P. californiensis* is more tolerant of high salinities than are *P. stylirostris* and *P. vannamei*. Its relative dominance in the upper gulf simply reflects the fact that the other species are less abundant there (Edwards personal communication 1981).

In sum, the distribution of the three penaeid species is as follows. South of Mazatlán, the low salinities of closed lagoons during the wet season favor the development of *P. vannamei*, which dominates both inshore and offshore catches. Further north, *P. vannamei* decreases in abundance due to the absence of favorable low-salinity periods in the open lagoons. Its relative importance in the total catch is taken over by *P. californiensis*, whose life cycle is not dependent on a period of low

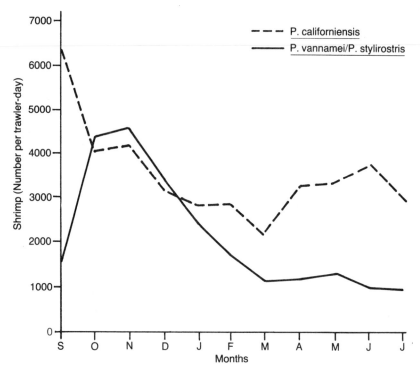

Fig. 7.5 Shrimp Species Composition by Month, Mazatlán Landings. *Adapted from Edwards 1978b.*

estuarine salinity. *P. californiensis* nonetheless is a significant element in the offshore catch as far south as Mazatlán, for it can still take advantage of the dry-season hypersalinity of the lagoons, shunned in that season by *P. vannamei*. *P. stylirostris* enters the picture in significant fashion only to the north of Mazatlán. As an estuarine competitor with *P. vannamei*, but not as dependent on a low-salinity phase, *P. stylirostris* largely replaces *P. vannamei* in the open lagoons of the north. Finally, the relatively constant salinities of the open lagoons in the north throughout the year do not encourage the mass emigration to open seas of *P. stylirostris*. This behavior contrasts with the forced march of *P. vannamei* from the hypersaline closed estuaries in the south.

Summary

From Mazatlán southward, the preconditions for intense economic conflict between estuarine and offshore shrimpers are present. The trawler fleets of that region are in a less viable position, measured in terms of the value of catch per vessel, than are the shrimpers to the north. To supplement their declining yields, the southern trawlers must rely on a larger haul of the predominantly estuarine species, *P. vannamei* and *P. stylirostris*. And, due to the peculiarities of lagoon formation, the highly efficient trap technology is more readily employed on the semiclosed estuaries of the southern coast, thus compounding the economic woes of the offshore fishermen and giving them a visible target for their protestations.

In their cumulative effect, these factors provide the necessary elements for explaining the comparative success of the Yaqui shrimp cooperative on the coastal estuaries of southern Sonora. But arguments for ecological and economic determinism are precarious: this cluster does not provide sufficient reason for the Yaqui success nor, by itself, the reason for the relative failure of the inshore cooperatives of Sinaloa and Nayarit. Cognizant of this, McGoodwin looks to the contributing factors of population pressure on resources, ineffectual cooperative political organization, and the deleterious impact of *caciques* (1980a:39–40). It is precisely this set of conditions for failure that has been absent, attenuated, or actively overcome in the Yaqui shrimping cooperative.

THE POLITICAL ECONOMY OF YAQUI SHRIMPING

Since 1957, with the founding of the cooperative at Guásimas, the littoral resources of the Yaqui Zone have played an enhanced role in the tribe's subsistence. Previously, fish and shellfish of the coastal estuaries and mudflats provided, at best, only supplementary nutrition and income to an economy based on agriculture, the wild resources of the desert, and day labor in the surrounding Mexican settlements. Several Yaquis had become professional fishermen in the 1950s, employed on trawlers out of Guaymas. Motivated by the productive possibilities of the Yaqui coast and by the existence of this nucleus of knowledgeable Yaqui fishermen living outside the reserve, Dolores Matus petitioned to form the cooperative at the fishing camp of Guásimas. Matus won the backing of the traditional Yaqui authorities and of the Mexican officials resident in the zone. Acceding to the request, the Federal Maritime Commission provided an initial subsidy of 1.5 million pesos for the purchase of boats, motors, fishing equipment, and housing; the Secretariat of Water Resources supplied a pump and dug a well; the Education Department built and staffed a school; and an infirmary went into operation at Guásimas in 1962 (Bartell 1965:259–61).

Since this original founding and financing, the co-op has had a substantial twenty-year growth period. Gilbert Bartell counted thirty-three family heads as original members (socios), 90 percent of whom were drawn back to the reserve from wage-labor jobs on the outside. By

1962 there were fifty-two Yaquis and thirty Mexicans fishing from Guásimas, the latter permitted to fish there as long as they supplied their own fishing equipment and agreed to market their shrimp through Yaqui channels (Bartell 1965:261). By the 1970s Yaqui socios totaled well over three hundred, although the number fishing in a given year averages two hundred. The remaining socios work either as non-fishing employees of the co-op, or reside in the river towns, assisting their relatives in agriculture. This increase in members over the last twenty years can be accounted for primarily by internal growth, not absorption of Yaquis living outside the zone. Most of the newer socios are sons or brothers of established co-op members, who began to fish during or shortly after their high school education.

Organizationally, the co-op has diversified. When originally incorporated, it followed the ejido pattern of dual administration, headed by presidents of the Consejo de Administración and the Consejo de Vigilancia. Elected by the socios, these officials are responsible for the major economic decisions of the co-op, and each group, in theory, serves as a check upon the actions of the other. Additional offices of secretary and treasurer, appointed by the president of administration, have been created to conduct the paperwork of the co-op and to keep an accounting of profits and disbursements. The governors and other elected officials of the Yaqui pueblo of Belem, in whose territory Guásimas is located, hold authority over the fishing cooperative. While their power seldom intrudes into the daily affairs of the fishermen, it can be activated in times of crisis. Should an imbalance develop between the consejos within the co-op, these officials can step in to correct the situation and, if necessary, bring disputes to the deliberation of governors from all eight Yaqui towns. This Yaqui tribal organization serves to dampen the debilitating *caciquismo,* common to the atomistic shrimp cooperatives of the Sinaloa-Nayarit region.

With growth in the number of socios, the co-op infrastructure has expanded. Offices have been moved from Guásimas to Guaymas, outside the Yaqui Zone, where financial affairs are now handled. Export and marketing arrangements are organized there, bills paid, weekly disbursements to socios made, and payment for medical care for fishermen and their families authorized.

Due in part to this centralization of administration in Guaymas, and in part to the increased activity of the cooperative, a number of additional positions have become available to Yaquis. At the fishing station on Bahía de Lobos, a "field boss" (*jefe de campo*) oversees production and handles minor disputes. Both Guásimas and Lobos employ receivers, responsible for weighing and recording daily catches. Both sites also have men to dispense gas, truckers to drive the catch to Guaymas, and packers in charge of ice-packing the daily catches into co-op trucks. In addition, Yaquis are employed in the ice-making plant at Guásimas, as mechanics for the co-op's equipment, and as laborers in the Guaymas fish-freezing plant which handles the co-op's products. Finally, two Yaquis work as auxiliary fisheries inspectors for the Secretariat of Fisheries, charged with enforcing the licensing of commercial and sport fishermen and the regulations on closed seasons, minimum capture sizes, and catch limits. These and other employees are drawn from the membership of the co-op. Only a few, such as mechanics and truck drivers, require special skills. For some positions, notably election as co-op president or president of the vigilance committee, demonstrated fishing success is an important asset. Other positions are frequently given to temporarily disabled fishermen.

Capital investment in the cooperative has expanded rapidly since its founding in 1957. With government assistance, a modern ice-making plant was built at Guásimas in the mid-1960s, with a daily capacity of 4 tons of ice. More recently, a deep freeze storage room with an 8-ton capacity of shrimp and fish has been completed adjacent to the ice plant. A similar storage facility has been constructed at Lobos. Together, these facilities allow a more efficient processing of the Yaqui catch, for it is no longer necessary to transport shrimp daily to Guaymas in often poorly refrigerated trucks. Now, catches can be immediately frozen and stored on site until sufficient to warrant delivery to the processing center.

A great portion of the co-op's profits over the last twenty years has been reinvested in fishing equipment. Approximately 270 fiberglass boats, 6 meters in length, are now operated by socios. A small number of outboard motors, most in good repair, belong to the co-op. A more constant co-op expense is for nylon cast nets. At a cost of 300 pesos each (at the 1975 exchange rate of 12 pesos to the U.S. dollar), these nets seldom last more than one season and must be continuously repaired and replaced. Taking 1972 as a representative season, co-op expenses totaled 8,041,000 pesos: 3,726,000 pesos (46 percent) for costs of production, including a substantial investment in new equipment; 1,822,000 pesos (23 percent) for operational costs which include salaries of co-op officials, legal expenses, taxes, and travel expenses for co-op representatives; and 2,493,000 pesos (31 percent) in direct payments to fishermen for their catches. Income from shrimp, scale fish, and fish byproducts totaled 5,147,000 pesos, thus necessitating loans of 2,894,000 pesos to pay the balance of operation and production costs. At the end of the succeeding year, the co-op had managed to pay off a portion of the 1972 loans, and showed a profit of 60,290 pesos after expenses. Through the first half of 1974, the profits banked by the co-op had risen to 155,750 pesos.

A closer look at itemized but partial 1974 expenses (January through July) indicates that success is not adequately reflected in the small profits carried over from year to year. Aside from salaries to co-op officials (109,443 pesos for six months), a respectable portion of income from the sale of shrimp and fish products goes back into social services and direct loans to members. Twenty-four Yaquis received loans ranging from 200 to 8,450 pesos, with a total loaned out by the co-op of 32,533 pesos. *Gratificaciones,* bonuses paid to socios and officials during the Lenten season, totaled 18,800 pesos. Finally, 217,350 pesos were spent on social welfare—insurance payments, hospital expenses, education, and fiestas. Nonetheless, shrimping remains a seasonal occupation, and Yaqui fishermen do not get rich. Without the delayed bonuses paid out during the religious weeks leading up to Sabado de Gloria and Easter Sunday, many fishermen would fail to meet ceremonial expenses. In the off-season, they must find work in the fields as day-laborers or, through membership in cooperative ejidos in the Yaqui Zone, share proceeds from the cultivation and sale of export crops.

Indigenous Resource Management

The *veda,* designed to protect critical growth stages of the penaeid, closes the inshore shrimp season from mid-April to the end of July. As one of the few governmental intrusions into the affairs of the Yaqui cooperative, it meets little opposition. Indeed, fishermen curtail their activities well before the nominal end of the open season. By mid-December, natural mortality and the results of intensive fishing in the estuaries have diminished yields to an unprofitable point. The chill of the desert winter and the strong, constant winds of Lent further discourage shrimping past December. Finally, the debilitating heat of summer, slacking somewhat by the end of August, adds to the acceptability of the veda.

From early autumn to December indigenous methods of resource management replace the formality of government regulation. More by chance than design, these methods address the gaps in federal policies toward shrimp fisheries. First, they restrict unlimited access to the local fishery and thus reduce the possibility for economic overexploitation and its consequence—miniscule individual yields. Second, they slow the pace of fishing, prolonging the season through four or five months. This enhances the biotic and economic potential of the fishery: *camarón chica,* uncaptured early in the season, can grow into *camarón grande* and fetch a higher market price.

Surprisingly, these results have been achieved without recourse to an acclaimed solution to the dilemma of the commons, the establishment of territoriality (see Acheson 1975, 1979; Forman 1970; Edel 1973:48–51). The behavioral ecology of *Penaeus stylirostris* ironically offers an ideal foundation for creating exclusive rights to specific fishing spots. Within Bahía de Lobos and the Yasícuri estuary at Guásimas, shrimp abound on the shallow detrital substratum near shore and along the food-bearing currents. To Yaqui fishermen, these optimum fishing grounds are common knowledge, generally predictable, and easily demarcated. Despite such preconditions for stable territoriality, however, Yaquis congregate. Boats getting good returns from preliminary casts will summon other fishermen to those areas (Bartell 1965:265), thereby increasing the potential for overexploitation.

Surprisingly, too, excessive fishing seems to have been avoided in spite of technological development. For the first decade of operation, the length of daily fishing at the cooperative was restricted by marketing arrangements. Lacking its own freezing facilities, the co-op sold its catch to buyers working for Guaymas processors or to individual retailers. Each day at noon, the buyers' trucks would pick up the catch directly from Yaqui fishermen at the estuaries. To meet the schedule, fishermen had to cease fishing in midmorning (Bartell 1965:270). With the construction of ice-making and freezing facilities at Guásimas, the co-op was no longer under the constraint of this schedule. The potential for longer days on the water was precluded, however, by the dangers of small-boat fishing in the afternoon chop on the bays. Thus, even with the technological capacity to process and preserve catches throughout the day, fishing regularly ceases between noon and 1:00 P.M.

Several additional factors limit access to the Yaqui fishery. *Pangas* are in plentiful supply, but the outboard motors necessary to propel them are in frequent disrepair. Permanent housing for fishermen and their families is in short supply at Guásimas, thus restricting the number of socios able to work the Yasícuri estuary. And at Lobos, tarpaper shacks that house the seasonal fishermen can be constructed rapidly, yet the relative remoteness of the camp from the established Yaqui settlements precludes an unwanted influx of temporary fishermen. Finally, membership in the cooperative is drawn on ethnic lines: no non-Indians can obtain membership.

The cumulative impact of individual decisions is as significant as ethnic boundaries, choppy water, housing restrictions, and broken motors in determining the level of fishing effort in the cooperative, however. The two-man boat crews, frequently composed of brothers or father-son combinations, remain relatively stable throughout the season, but composition may change from day to day as individual socios choose not to fish. Thus, both the number of fishing days per season and the size of individual catches vary. During the season of 1972, the single year for which I obtained disaggregated records (fig. 7.6), the totals for the 178 active socios ranged from 13 to 755 kilograms, with a mean individual catch of 336.7 kilograms.

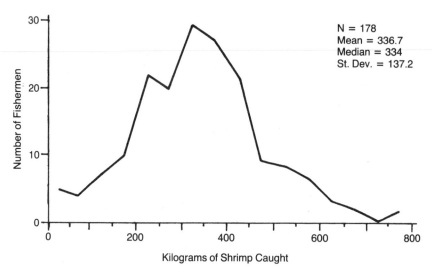

Fig. 7.6 Frequency Distribution of 1972 Shrimp Catch by Yaqui Fishermen

To explain the variance in the distribution, Yaqui fishermen most often invoke the factor of persistence. For a number of reasons—family matters, fatigue, and illness—socios do not fish continuously throughout the season. Many of those catching only small amounts are sick or injured during part of the season; occupational hazards are by no means rare to Yaqui shrimping. Despite adequate knowledge of their equipment and environment, Yaquis are prone to colds and pneumonia induced by exposure, to muscle strains resulting from the handling of heavily ladened nets, and to heart problems brought on by overexertion.

The success of the few fishermen catching large amounts can be attributed to continuous work throughout the season. A middle range of 300–350 kilograms may be obtained through relatively persistent fishing; no particular expertise beyond practice at casting and retrieving the net is needed. Luck is seldom a factor in this variability. Shrimp locations are generally predictable, thus obviating the need for trial-and-error searches across the lagoon.

A rough measure of the underutilization of labor can be computed from available data. By fishing five days a week through the four-month season (mid-August to mid-December), an individual socio could reasonably be expected to bring a seasonal catch of 800 to 1200 kilograms, assuming a realistic daily catch of 10 to 15 kilograms. For the 178 socios actively working during the 1972 season, the hypothetical total catch would be from 142,400 to 213,600 kilograms. This range greatly exceeds the actual total of 59,571 kilograms for that season.

An individual shrimper bases his daily decision to fish or remain on shore on a host of personal considerations. The statistical effect of these choices, however, is felt at a different level. Fishing effort is paced through the season, enhancing the biotic yield of the fishery. Moreover, with substantially less than the full co-op manpower out on the lagoon on any given day, the deleterious potential in the Yaqui strategy of congregating over productive spots is dampened.

These factors appear to prevent excessive exploitation of the shrimp along the Yaqui littoral and to ensure respectable individual yields. Nevertheless, a perceived imbalance between fishermen and shrimp during the 1960s played a major role in the expansion of activities from the initial site at Guásimas to the larger, more productive bay at Lobos.

Expansion and Competition

Although groups of Yaquis and Mexicans shrimped and fished in the Yasícuri estuary around Guásimas prior to the founding of the co-op, it is doubtful that such exploitation was intensive. Few in number, with motorless boats, these fishermen shrimped for subsistence rather than commercial production. With the founding of the co-op in 1957, the purchase of new equipment and motorized craft, the construction of permanent housing, and the establishment of dependable means of transport to the growing luxury markets of Guaymas and the United States, fishing effort increased at Guásimas. Unfortunately, the effects of this expansion and intensified fishing on the economic yield of the Guásimas fishery are unknown, since prior to 1971 few accurate records were kept. It is safe to assume that individual yields declined in some proportion to the increase in number of socios exploiting the resources of the littoral. Consequently, from the 1960s to the early 1970s, attention focused on Lobos, along the coast south of Guásimas (see map).

Bahía de Lobos was not an unexploited virgin fishery. Two Mexican small-boat cooperatives were already fishing the bay in the 1960s, housed in the permanent village of Liliba straddling the irrigation drain into the bay (Hinojosa, Paralta, and Vega 1972). The yields of these Mexican co-ops may have been substantial, since Lobos presents a better ecological setting for shrimp than Guásimas. There are more feeding grounds of greater size in the convoluted bay of Lobos than in the open Yasícuri estuary of Guásimas. Moreover, the drain plays an important role in the ecology of Lobos, emptying the nutrients washed from cultivated fields of the Yaqui Irrigation District directly into the bay. The shape of the predominant current at Lobos contributes to a high mass of shrimp. Entering south of the sandbar that protects Lobos from the gulf, it carries across the entire length of the bay, bringing a continuously renewed supply of feed for shrimp. By contrast, the current at Guásimas enters and leaves by the same opening into the gulf, and its course within the Yasícuri lagoon is more confined. The fishing potential of Lobos drew many Yaquis away from the crowded conditions of Guásimas. During the early 1970s a seasonal fishing camp had been firmly established at Lobos, across from the existing Mexican village. By informants' accounts, use of the Lobos fishery proved immediately profitable for the Yaqui co-op, temporarily relieving the growing pressure on housing and resources at Guásimas. But this success heightened tensions between Yaqui fishermen and the permanent Mexican residents across the drainage canal. The Yaqui authorities' quick response was to demand the complete removal of Mexicans from Lobos.

Demands and Concessions

At the peak of the 1972 shrimping season, Yaqui officials simultaneously delivered two petitions to the highest levels of Mexican government. One, addressed to the Subsecretary of Fishing, affirmed the Yaqui desire to work through legal channels, but strongly insisted on exclusive access to the Bahía de Lobos through the Resolución Presidencial of 30 September 1940 (Autoridades Tradicionales de sus Ocho Pueblos, Tribu Yaqui 1972a). By demarcating the Yaqui Zone's southern boundary as the southeastern tip of Isla de Lobos, the directive placed all but one edge of the bay within Yaqui territory. Yaquis complained through the petition that the Mexican boats of Liliba, across the canal from the Yaqui camp at Lobos, were illegally exploiting a Yaqui littoral zone.

A more deferential petition was dispatched to President Luis Echeverría:

> After extending the most cordial and respectful greeting from us and on behalf of the other members of the Yaqui tribe, once more we are resorting to you to solicit your valuable intervention, so that the fisheries authorities will not continue to dally in granting the exclusive right which belongs to our fishing cooperative . . .
> In the Bahía de Lobos there exists a cooperative called "*Pescadores del Yaqui,*" made up of members foreign to our race, who are now in open disobedience not only against the rights of our fishermen but also against the dispositions of the fisheries authorities. If no violent act has occurred, it is because we have succeeded in keeping our fishermen calm, confident that this situation will be resolved by the competent authorities of our Supreme Government, honorably represented by yourself (Autoridades Tradicionales de sus Ocho Pueblos, Tribu Yaqui 1972b).

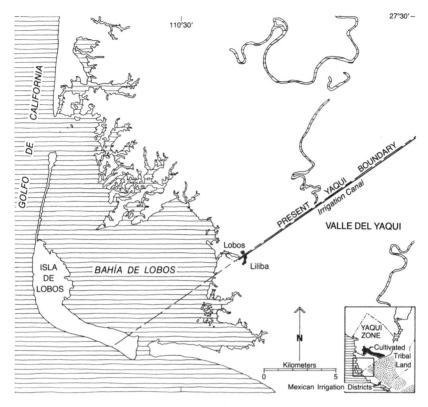

Bahía de Lobos

The Yaqui demands brought results. Fourteen months later, President Echeverría visited Guásimas to issue a directive for exclusive Yaqui access to marine resources within the Yaqui Zone. As reported in the Sonoran newspaper, *El Imparcial*, the decree contained three main articles:

1. Members of the Yaqui tribe and of the *Sociedad Cooperativa de Producción Pesquera "Comunidades Yaquis"* will solely and exclusively be allowed to fish in the waters of the estuaries and bays of the Yaqui Zone.

2. The Secretary of Industry and Commerce will grant and renew the permits and concessions for fishing, in accordance with the federal law for the improvement of fisheries, to the *Sociedad Cooperativa "Comunidades Yaquis."*

3. The Yaqui tribe, its members, and the *Sociedad Cooperativa* remain obligated to allow the free transit of boats, persons, or materials on the waters of the estuaries and bays and also to respect all

the provisions relating to the government of the federal zone of the littorals referred to in this resolution (*El Imparcial,* 19 December 1973:1).

Since 1973 fishing by "foreigners" has decreased, held in check by the vigilance of the Yaqui fisheries inspectors and a small contingent of Mexican naval guards. Yaquis have found little government support for the complete removal of Mexican residents from Liliba, where they continue to live and work in nearby wheatfields. Nevertheless, with its expansion into the Bahía de Lobos, the cooperative reversed the decline in individual yields during the 1960s. By 1972, prior to the expulsion of Mexican shrimpers from the bay, 178 active Yaqui socios at Lobos and Guásimas obtained mean individual catches of 336 kilograms. A decade and a half earlier, individual yields for the eighty fishermen of the newly founded cooperative at Guásimas were on the order of only 200 kilograms per year (Bartell 1965:272).

The victory over the issue of exclusive access, limited as it is by the continued presence of Mexican agricultural laborers on the shore of Bahía de Lobos, has no counterpart in the troubled fisheries of Sinaloa and Nayarit. Internally weakened by power struggles, those cooperatives were unable to wage a unified political struggle to ameliorate their marginality. In this comparative frame, then, the Yaqui political organization appears to have played a determinant role in the tribe's successful pursuit of exclusive use of the littoral zone. As duly elected spokesmen for the tribe's interests, the village governors pressed a set of unified demands through official channels. As recognized representatives of the tribe, the governors warranted and received official governmental response to the petition.

Yet these same "autoridades tradicionales," the pueblo signatories, served as petitioners in the unsuccessful fight for farmlands near San Ignacio. As a contrast, then, the corporately organized political authority of the tribe cannot be used to explain the very different degrees of success achieved by farmers and fishermen in the interethnic competition for resources. An explanation may be hidden, though, in the possibility of varying degrees of real political unity underlying the facade of corporateness put forward by the pueblo authorities in their formal petitions. I have suggested, for example, that the externally perceived unity of agricultural demands—for more land, more autonomy—masks some festering tensions between farming socios and particulares, hired laborers and their employers, and developmental policies. Can Yaqui fishermen and their co-op leaders be seen as more united in their interests and demands?

On several occasions in the field I received unsolicited commentary on the affairs of the fishing cooperative: *puro pleito,* "pure dispute." The disputes, however, are structured differently from the horizontal feuds of the agricultural villages, which pit Yaqui farmer against Yaqui farmer, elected governors against pretenders. In the shrimp co-op, tensions are more vertical: working fishermen against their leaders. The co-op disputes are generated from modest prosperity, not from the debilitating dependency on outside administrators experienced by Yaqui farmers. Internal tension in the shrimp co-op is a consequence of successful resource competition and exploitation.

A crucial manifestation of co-op prosperity, the business office was moved to Guaymas in the early 1970s. The move was a pragmatic one: closer to the networks of communication and more accessible to marketing information, the co-op could more efficiently distribute its increasing yields. Yet the relocation had rather profound internal consequences for the co-op, for it removed co-op business from daily monitoring by working fishermen.

Contentiousness has increased along with prosperity. Fishermen are now quick to observe and remark on patterns of "conspicuous consumption" displayed by co-op leaders. Several past leaders have constructed relatively substantial adobe homes in the Yaqui villages or have moved into comfortable residences in Guaymas. Some have become wealthy farmers and ranchers on Yaqui land. And, on any given day, the co-op president and head of the vigilance committee may be observed driving between Guaymas and the fishing camps in new co-op pick-up trucks, conducting necessary co-op business, but also at times taking advantage of the subsidized transportation to haul cheaper groceries from the urban markets to their houses in the zone. Fishermen are also quick to notice that co-op officials, not individual workers, garner most of the funds set aside from co-op profits for loans to needy members facing immediate crises.

Partly a surfacing of resentment against the powerful, the accusations directed toward co-op officials represent a more significant development as well: the uneasy "institutionalization of suspicion." Suspicion, as Ronald Dore points out, is a concomitant to the successful operation of modern cooperatives in traditional societies. Such organization cannot be based on "diffuse sentiments of solidarity." Rather,

They must be predicated on a belief in original sin. Man, the assumption is, has an inevitable tendency to corruption. Therefore organizations must build in checks and balances such as the audit and the periodic re-election of officers . . . institutionalized suspicion in the long run benefits all, including those against whom it is directed. Thus the treasurer welcomes the audit—even though the audit makes sense only on the assumption that the treasurer might have been dishonest—because it clears him of suspicion. That justice should be done may be in the interests of the members; that it should be seen to be done is in the interest of the elected officials (Dore 1971:54–55).

Underlying this argument, of course, is the fact that organizations held together by ties of personal affect—rather than an impersonal sense of responsibility to play by the rules—are ripe for corruption, nepotism, and ultimately, the withdrawal of participation by members. Yet suspicion, the accepted application of checks and balances, is extremely difficult to instill, and the modernizing cooperative will likely face desperate growing pains. As Dore contends:

> Either the objective rules, with their suspicious assumptions or original sinfulness, are scrupulously applied—with the likelihood . . . of arousing such animosity between those who apply the rules and those to whom they are applied that the organization is burst asunder—or else the rules are not scrupulously observed and the non-observance eventually becomes so flagrant that the losers in the game of influence withdraw from the cooperative, or it founders in the factional struggle for advantage (Dore 1971:56–57).

The Yaqui co-op is currently experiencing the growing pains of modernization. While the immediate stimulus for conflict and dispute may be a perceived and sometimes real misuse of funds and equipment by co-op leaders, another level of tension seems to underlie these issues. This tension is between managers and workers; the point of contention is one of reinvestment in equipment versus increased individual earnings. Co-op officials argue for expenditures on new equipment and maintenance of existing boats, motors, and trucks. Fishermen recurrently demand a greater share of the co-op profits. By its nature, the issue cannot be definitively resolved but must be renegotiated as the need for new equipment arises. And, although I made no firsthand observations of the process of renegotiation, it appears that the results are acceptable to both managers and fishermen. The potential costs of modernization—withdrawal from the enterprise by disgruntled members or the surfacing of truly debilitating factionalism—have been avoided.

Freedom from Intervention

Free from government administration, the Yaqui co-op has also avoided intervention by local Mexican entrepreneurs and financiers. Unlike commercial agriculture in the Yaqui Valley, where Mexican-controlled technology is essential for indigenous farming, Yaqui small-boat shrimping and Mexican offshore fishing are technologically incompatible. Shallow draft, open pangas are unsuitable for offshore shrimping, just as the large, mechanized Mexican trawlers cannot pursue shrimp in the shallow estuaries of the littoral. Technologically constrained to their offshore niche, Mexican shrimpers and their financial backers have stayed out of the Yaqui estuaries.

Nor do the Guaymas processing plants attempt to intervene financially in the Yaqui co-op. The offshore shrimp season extends through most of the year, but the peak yields coincide with the brief estuary season. If the estuary and offshore seasons were complementary, processors would have more incentive to oversee Yaqui shrimping in order to assure a continuous supply.

While the location and seasonal availability of Yaqui shrimp underwrite a degree of economic autonomy for the co-op, investment opportunities for outsiders are also lacking. In contrast to commercial agriculture in the Yaqui Valley, coastal shrimping is more labor-intensive and technologically manageable by the Yaquis alone. Efficient farming demands carefully managed water allocation, mechanized plowing, planting, and harvesting, precisely controlled application of fertilizer, and regular cropdusting from airplanes. Neither Yaqui particulares nor socios have the capital to apply these agricultural inputs, and hence are at the mercy of non-Yaqui financiers—government or private—and technicians. Fishing, on the other hand, requires rudimentary boat-handling skills and easily acquired net-casting techniques. Little outside technical aid is necessary. And, given the initial capitalization of the fishing co-op by the federal government, subsequent investment in new equipment has been taken from the substantial co-op profits. Technologically and financially, the shrimping co-op remains more self-sufficient than Yaqui farmers.

Patron-client ties between Yaqui fishermen and Mexican financiers are less likely to develop under these circumstances. A major obligation of patrons is to support their farming clients while crops are growing, up to harvest. Fishing, by contrast, is a daily activity, and the returns are immediate: Yaqui fishermen working for the co-op are paid a portion of their catch as it is landed on the beach, giving them ready cash. The balance of the payment, minus the co-op's percentage, is then paid to the fishermen at intervals throughout the shrimp season. Active fishermen thus have little need to seek financial support from patrons during the season, and most seem to save enough cash to carry them through the closed periods.

Mexican patronage is sought, however, for off-season nonshrimp fishing. Some Yaqui fishermen exploit *pesca de escama* (scale fish) in coastal estuaries during the Lenten season, when a demand for fish exists in local markets. Individual Yaqui fishermen, who are not co-op members, may obtain permission to use co-op equipment—boats, motors, and gas cans. Additionally, they will need a *chinchorro*, the 50' to 100' long, 5' high net stretched across an estuary mouth, and a truck for transporting men and equipment to the coast. Few Yaquis can afford the chinchorro and must seek outside financing through Mexican shop-owners. Storekeepers wishing to meet the Lenten fish demand will partially finance the net, provide transportation for the

Yaqui fishing crew and equipment, and usually bring along food and drink for the three- or four-day expeditions. Division of the catch is informal. Each Yaqui on the crew will take enough for his own immediate needs and for distribution to friends and relatives, while the storekeeper takes the remainder for sale or personal consumption. As fish preserve poorly, even when cleaned, salted, and dried, the catch is distributed and consumed quickly. Chinchorro fishing thus does not provide a long-term food supply for the fisherman and his family.

Through capital inputs into these expeditions, local Mexican shopowners can thus gain access to exclusive Yaqui resources. But this access does not extend into the more profitable co-op shrimping industry: chinchorro technology is distinct from the attaraya-casting used for shrimp. And the profits from the limited local market for fresh fish are not substantial enough to support a widespread system of fishing patronage. The few patrons and clients involved in off-season fishing are, frequently, already tied through agricultural production. Expeditions to the coast seem more a secondary diversion than a primary economic activity for Mexican shopowners and their Yaqui clients.

THE FORTUITY OF SUCCESS AND FAILURE

Through measures of internal political and financial stability, maintenance of a rough equilibrium between population and marine resources, and the resolution of territorial demands, the Yaqui shrimp cooperative has achieved modest success. Two relative failures—the Yaqui efforts to shore up their claims to farmlands near San Ignacio, and the marginalized shrimp cooperatives on the coast of southern Sinaloa and Nayarit—help to factor out the complex reasons for this success.

For the co-ops of Nayarit and Sinaloa, the odds against success are great. Offshore trawlermen, faced with heavy capital investment and declining returns, have effectively created a condensed symbol of their own plight: the inshore shrimp trap. Regulatory powers at the national level have, by and large, accepted this statement of cause and effect and marshal their efforts to curtail estuarine shrimping. Internal organizational abilities of the cooperatives are insufficient to overcome these outside pressures. The process of marginalization runs its course.

Success or failure in the competition for resources, however, does not turn wholly on organizational capabilities. Yaqui governors are repeatedly frustrated in their petitions for a responsive hearing on the boundary dispute. In the volatile regional matrix of anachronistic hacendados and landless masses, tribal demands are quickly shunted aside. Yaqui fishermen called up these same organizational capacities to win an important local skirmish over shrimping rights to Bahía de

Lobos and the coastline of the reserve. But here, the economic stakes were different, both from the wheatfields and range around Ciudad Obregón and from the fisheries of Sinaloa and Nayarit. Trawlermen out of Guaymas, economically more successful than their counterparts to the south, and exploiting a stock distinct from that of the lagoons, maintain a relatively peaceful coexistence with Yaqui shrimpers from the open Sonoran estuaries. The lines of battle are drawn not between the altamar and the estero, but between the organized tribal fishermen and a small group of politically impotent Mexican estuarine shrimpers.

RESIDENCE, CEREMONY, AND ETHNICITY

Yaqui fishermen have been successful in gaining exclusive access to coastal resources in the zone, and have also avoided the entangling dependence on outside capital, whether public or private. They have, in short, come closer than Yaqui farming pueblos to the tribal ideal of economic, political, and territorial integrity. Yet Yaqui fishermen show few of the markers of ethnic identity. A number of them are monolingually Spanish; many of the women opt for Mexican-style dress; their children seem more fully integrated into the Mexican school system and Mexican peer groups; and fishermen, by and large, seem content to be irreligious.

Based on historical roots, this comparatively weak interest in Yaqui ethnicity is now reinforced by patterns of residence and ceremonialism. The founders of the co-op were not drawn randomly from the towns of the Yaqui Zone. Rather, many were already living outside the reserve and outside the focus of Yaqui tradition. They were fishermen from Guaymas and Empalme, trained on Mexican shrimpers in the Gulf of California and forced into close interaction with urban Mexican society (Bartell 1965:258). At present, most Guásimeños continue this association with the cities along the federal highway. Women do most of their shopping in the supermarkets of Guaymas. Fishermen make use of the medical and dental facilities of the city. Highschool students are bused to schools there, and the paydays at the co-op's Guaymas office draw crowds of Yaqui socios and their families to town.

Residentially, however, the two Yaqui fishing villages are more solidly Yaqui than the larger pueblos along the river bed. Few non-Yaquis live at Guásimas, and virtually none live in Lobos proper. Across the irrigation drain from Lobos is a sizable Mexican settlement, but the social tensions of past conflicts over the Bahía de Lobos serve to keep the two villages separated.

There is a coincident absence of ceremonial activity at Lobos and Guásimas. Lack of ritual at Lobos stems largely from the complementarity of shrimping and Catholic religious schedules: shrimp are caught in the fall, a season with few major Catholic ceremonial dates. For the remainder of the year, the Lobos camp is abandoned and Yaqui fishermen return to homes along the river. At Guásimas, inhabited year-round, the pattern of ritual observation is somewhat more complex. Several elderly men and women have struggled to build up the ceremonial organization to observe Lent and have succeeded in constructing a small church. Key ceremonial positions are staffed for the most part by residents of other Yaqui pueblos, who move to Guásimas for the duration of the religious season. Yet this influx of ritual specialists is nearly balanced by a pilgrimage of the few traditional Guásimeños out of the village. They go to larger river pueblos to observe and participate in the more spectacular pageantry. The potential audience at Guásimas is thereby depleted, and the ceremonialism remains largely uninspired.

Exploiting a marginal but lucrative resource, Yaqui fishermen have more successfully lived up to the tribal ideal of autonomy—an ideal which Yaqui farmers, forced into dependence on outside capital, can honor only in the breach. Their economic success contrasts, however, with cultural ideals; Yaqui fishermen are less involved in patterns of ethnicity than their counterparts in the Ocho Pueblos along the river. The final chapter will draw some conclusions from these observations.

CHAPTER 8

Resources, Power, and Ethnicity in Southern Sonora

Yaqui ethnicity has been the professed concern of this monograph. Much of the analysis, though, has focused on the Mexican political economy: how and why the national government interferes in the economics of Sonora's commercial agriculture, and how and why the same government chooses a laissez faire policy toward Yaqui fishing operations. De-emphasizing ethnicity as a pre-eminently cultural phenomenon, another theme emerges: ethnic identity as, primarily, a subject of politics and economics. More instrumental than categorical, it deals with group advantage, not simply with primordial sentiments or individual allegiances.

Concern here with regional and national politics and economics also responds to a long-standing critique of Middle American ethnography: it is excessively oriented to the community and fails to link indigenous villages to regional centers and metropolises (Chambers 1977). This last chapter will tie together these themes, demonstrating links among ethnicity, politics, and economics, and among nation, region, and village.

Corporately organized ethnic groups have advantages in the competition for resources over those ethnic populations that are not corporately organized. The advantages lie essentially in the corporate polity's ability to express unified demands and to carry out the politics requisite to meeting these demands. Abner Cohen, following Max Weber, adds the element of efficiency or rationality to such organizations: neither time nor energy need be wasted in endowing nonpolitical functions—ceremony or the gathering of friends—with political purpose. And, fostered by corporate organization, successful resource competition will be conducive to the maintenance of ethnic boundaries and the assertion of ethnic identities.

In treating ethnicity as primarily instrumental, Leo Despres provides a necessary counterpoint to static analyses of ethnicity as primordial sentiment. Under such analyses, ethnic identity is nonproblematical: individuals belong because they feel a need to belong (for a critique of such views, see Williams 1978; for some support, see Parsons 1975). But Sonoran Yaqui ethnicity offers direct support for neither the instrumental nor the sentimental. The Yaquis constitute an organized corporate polity, an "ethnic group." But to Yaqui farmers, this polity provided little advantage in the struggle for resources. Territorial expansion failed, as did demands for a definitive survey of the tribal boundary. Yet, contrary to the implications of Despres's propositions, social boundaries between Yaqui and non-Yaqui persist and underwrite distinct ethnic identities. Despres's predictions fall short because the impetus for Yaqui boundary maintenance rests not on pecuniary advantage, but on a more involuted process, on the complex symbolic reciprocity that centers on Yaqui ceremonial performances and audiences. This is where propositions of primordial sentiment need to be amended. Such sentiments exist, but are perhaps more a consequence than a cause of persistent Yaqui ceremony. Finally, and again in contradiction to Despres, the day-to-day assertion of ethnic identity, whether to other Yaquis or to outsiders, is minimal. Yaquis do not instrumentally manipulate their group membership and identity, but neither do they sentimentally uphold the ideals and traditions of Yaqui culture and history.

CORPORATE POLITY AND RESOURCE COMPETITION

In recent years, Yaquis have been eminently successful in the competition for marine resources, but have repeatedly failed in their demands for more agricultural land. In both cases, the same Yaqui polity, the gubernatorial organization of the Eight Pueblos, articulated the demands and pursued the negotiations. Success and failure cannot be attributed, per se, to political organization within the Yaqui Zone. Instead, it is to the larger outside forces of economics and politics in the region and the nation that we must look. F. G. Bailey's notion of "composite interference" is of assistance here. The Mexican government has substantial *capability* to interfere in the affairs of its ethnic enclaves and its subordinate socioeconomic classes. The question thus becomes: why did it show its *determination* to block Yaqui demands for land at the same time that it granted Yaqui demands on the coast?

Littoral resources in the Yaqui Zone, as suggested in chapter 7, are at once marginal to national economic interests and inaccessible to regional fishing technology. Governmental treasuries would receive little boost by taxing the yields of the Yaqui co-op. Hence, it is not worth the administrative effort to closely regulate the small-scale indigenous enterprise. Nor do the offshore Mexican fishermen seek such regulation and interference in the operation of the Yaqui co-op. Their boats are too large to ply the Yaqui estuaries and their processors are already busy during the Yaqui shrimping season. Secondarily, too, the national government can derive political capital by the very act of noninterference: the co-op is held up as a model of successful Indianist developmental policy. Guásimas is now a routine stop for presidential candidates and party hopefuls.

The comparison is not perfectly symmetrical. Irrigation land in the Yaqui Zone is as important as the estuaries are marginal, but this does not fully account for the failure of Yaqui governors to regain land and settle the boundary issue. The regional politics and the economics of commercial agriculture are more complex.

Farmland on both sides of the Río Yaqui—the Mexican Valle Nuevo and the Yaqui Zona Indígena—are made to contribute substantially to the economic development of the entire country. Through financing and marketing facilities, the government seeks to control production decisions and exports from the delta. Government agencies are effective in regulating Yaqui farming, but only to the limits of their ability to finance it. In the face of credit shortage, Yaqui farmers have turned to local patrons and to the subsistence-food market generated by governmental crop policies in the region.

Were the selection and distribution of crops the only issues at stake along the Yaqui River, then the boundary dispute might just as quickly have been settled in the tribe's favor as in the campesinos'. The economics of irrigation agriculture point to one dominant fact: the question of who owns and works the land is of less importance than that of who finances production and controls distribution. Yaquis could farm the San Ignacio plots as easily as campesinos could; in either case, the crucial capital inputs would have to come from elsewhere, from public and private sources.

Land was awarded to campesinos, not retained by latifundistas or regained by Yaquis. This was ultimately a complex political statement, not an economic one. Yaquis lost the political gambit because they relied merely on organizational power, on their corporate polity. Campesinos won, politically if not economically, because they relied not merely on the power of numbers, but on the derivative power of the outgoing president as well. And latifundistas lost, politically if not commercially, because they relied too briefly, during a short economic strike, on their power of resources.

Ironically, then, the Yaquis turned out to be too organized and too autonomous. Corporate organization has replaced the threat of mass Yaqui action; political autonomy places them outside the ruling party.

By long refusing co-optation into the government structure, the tribe had given up its right to the derivative power emanating from the apex of control in the nation. And it had given up the corresponding duty: to unconditionally support the presidency and the ruling party.

ETHNIC BOUNDARIES AND CEREMONIAL PERFORMANCES

The failure of the Yaqui polity to win its immediate demand—to extend the territorial boundary—has not destroyed the social and cultural boundaries between Yaqui and Mexican. Nor have such boundaries been particularly attenuated in the face of prevailing under-assertions of ethnic identity. In other words, the persistence of boundaries is not motivated by political success of the corporate polity, nor are such boundaries simple derivatives of ethnic assertiveness. Instead, these boundaries are founded upon an active and persistent ceremonial system whose fundamental and ironic feature is its openness, its lack of compartmentalization.

Yaqui Catholicism is curiously indigenized and universalistic. Yaqui and Mexican alike are allowed and encouraged to attend, observe, and participate, and thus win the favor of the santos. Mexicans and Yaquis do attend the ritual performances for this reason, but also for others. Ceremonies periodically interject into the dusty coastal setting the exciting burlesque of the pascolas, the camaraderie of friends, and the color of religious pageantry. Yaqui rituals build upon these individual motivations for attendance and participation and proceed to take on a symbolic and communicative life of their own. They contain messages of cultural distinctiveness and social boundaries. Mexicans see that the Yaqui santos are very Catholic but also very indigenous, and pascolas host both audience and gods, performing in the universal language of pantomime, but speaking like Yaquis. Mexicans in the audience vaguely comprehend but are recurrently reminded of how much of the Yaqui culture and society they do not understand. Yaquis in attendance as performers or simply as observers can watch as these boundaries—social and cultural—are drawn and redrawn. They can see the Mexican audience as a body of interested and, to a degree, reverent admirers of local Catholicism. But the Yaquis ultimately see Mexicans in the audience as a group of outsiders, not privy to the pascolas' verbal wit and unknowing of the fact that Jesus was, in the ancient past, a Yaqui curandero.

ETHNIC IDENTITY: ASCRIPTION AND ACHIEVEMENT

In daily interaction across ethnic boundaries and within such boundaries, individual ethnic identity is seldom asserted or actively communicated. Nor is such assertion customarily demanded or elicited by others. On occasion—usually when confronted with counter-claims —some Yaquis will profess their tribal identity and allegiance. For the most part, Yaquis do not symbolically manipulate the attributes of group membership and individual belonging. Moreover, a number of Yaquis do not even possess the range of ethnic markers typically associated with Yaqui identity. They also appear to make little effort to affirm their identification.

Yaqui group membership, with its attendant rights and duties, rests fundamentally on ascription, not on achievement. An individual is or is not a member of the tribe, based on his descent. For many persons whose families have maintained long residence in the zone, the criterion is never formally applied. For those returning to the region after an extended absence and petitioning for access to Yaqui resources, this criterion may be actively implemented. Pueblo governors must collect a biography of the individual in question and judge his ascriptive membership. Such judgments may be casuistical, for many Yaquis have, through several generations of displacement and forced interaction with non-Yaquis, developed only tenuously Yaqui biographies or genealogies. Importantly, though, such casuistical judgments are not flexible enough to allow outsiders to "become" Yaqui, to "achieve" Yaqui membership and the ensuing rights and duties in the zone. In short, group membership—as I have strictly defined it and as pueblo governors strictly determine it—rests upon descent and not on performance.

An ethnic performance—an assertion of ethnic identity—is neither necessary nor sufficient for attaining group membership. This fact, though, does not *logically* preclude the active assertion of identity or the conscious manipulation of Yaqui ethnic symbols in situations of interethnic contact and communication. Group membership, as both Despres and Barth have pointed out, is a different level of phenomenon than interaction, the face-to-face, give-and-take of social action across ethnic lines. Empirically, though, the general irrelevance of ethnic performance on Yaqui group membership may help to explain—or more loosely, may have something of a spill-over effect on—the infrequency with which ethnic symbols are activated in social interaction across ethnic lines. Internally, in interaction with other Yaquis, an individual is under little compulsion to "perform," to assert his ethnic identity. This seems to carry over into external contacts: as individuals and as a group, Yaquis feel little compulsion, and little need, to tell Mexicans who and what they are.

Such an interpretation is difficult to verify in a single case, a single multiethnic society. But comparative material may bear this out: where an individual's group membership is based more fundamentally on achievement or performance than on ascription, there will be coincident manipulation of ethnic symbols in interethnic transactions.

A MODEL OF POLITY AND ETHNICITY

Disregarding for the moment the complex historical development of polity, economy, ceremony, and ethnicity in southern Sonora, a synchronic model of Yaqui persistence as an ethnic group may be presented. The key elements of the model have been summarized above: Yaquis form a corporate *ethnic group*, not simply an aggregate or *ethnic population*; membership in the group is *ascribed,* not *achieved;* ethnic identities are not strongly asserted—they are *undercommunicated,* not *overcommunicated.* And a fourth element, ignored in the preceding summary, must now be incorporated. In Yaqui society, there is a disjunction of the three dimensions of status—wealth, power, and prestige. Chapter 4 presented evidence for this point. Economic wealth seems neither necessary nor sufficient for political power and social prestige. Power, likewise, does not stem directly from prestige, nor prestige from power. In short, the convertibility of one status dimension into another is, among Yaquis, attenuated. This is not a new finding, for Spicer (1954:181) observed a similar disconnection among ritual, politics, and the marginalized economy of the 1940s. What needs to be done at this point is to trace the linkages between such status disjunctions and the other elements of Yaqui ethnicity—of group membership, organization, and the communication of identity. I suggest the following ties:

(1) *The existence of a corporate Yaqui polity "allows" group membership to be based on ascription rather than achievement or performance.* Genealogical relations are, in the abstract, clear and incontrovertible means of group recruitment and exclusion. In practice, and especially in the historical context of Yaqui mobility—of migrations, expulsions, intermarriages — genealogies have become complex and clouded. As legitimate authorities within their respective pueblos, Yaqui governors have the right to judge the validity of an individual's claimed descent and rights within the zone. The existence of such rights and duties demands a definitive classification of persons. Ethnic populations, as noncorporate aggregates, do not possess the legitimate authority to make such classifications.

(2) *Membership by ascription in turn fosters the disjunction of wealth, power, and prestige.* An individual Yaqui does not have to achieve group membership through a demonstrated allegiance to, interest in, or knowledge of Yaqui culture—except that pertaining to his own family history. He does not have to participate in Yaqui ceremony, nor in Yaqui politics. He is not compelled by strong sanctions of ostracism to funnel wealth into these activities. The majority of Yaquis do maintain such allegiance, interest, and knowledge, but not for purposes of gaining membership in Yaqui society.

(3) *The relative isolation of status dimensions, one from another, fosters a continuation or persistence of ritual participation and ritual attendance.* Wealth is not essential to ritual participation, and involvement, expenditure, or sponsorship are not invariably demanded of those who are wealthy. The import of these factors—of the resiliency of Yaqui ritual to both poverty and affluence—must be viewed in comparative perspective. In the traditional civil-religious hierarchies of southern Mexico and Guatemala, wealth, power, and prestige are tightly intertwined. An individual on his cargo career converts wealth into a series of linked ceremonial and political offices and in the process gains social prestige and political power. Intense social pressures of gossip and ostracism are brought to bear on nonparticipants. Should these pressures prove insufficient, the outgoing officers have the legitimate power to appoint their successors. In colonial Mesoamerica, this combination of positive reinforcement and negative sanction seemed adequate to assure participation and the maintenance of an isolating, tradition-oriented set of ceremonies and offices (see Smith 1977a).

In modern Middle America, the civil-religious system is a double-edged sword: it can just as quickly cut through ethnic boundaries as uphold them. As local political authority weakens in the onslaught of national institutions and forces of incorporation and as new alternatives for wealth become available and attractive, the traditional rich may channel their wealth in other directions: into consumer goods, into entrepreneurships. As the rich increasingly refuse to participate in traditional ritual, the burden of ceremonial support falls more heavily on the poor. They also refuse to participate, not from an arrogance of wealth and power, but from the simple inability to finance the crumbling but expensive system.

Yaqui ritual organization, by contrast, is relatively immune to these pressures of poverty and wealth. The local rich are not coerced to participate by the threat of expulsion. Local poor are not forced into crushing expenditures; they can contribute labor or simply attend the performance, and they can achieve social prestige.

(4) *The persistence of ritual serves to maintain ethnic boundaries between Yaqui and Mexican.* As an indirect consequence of the ceremonial openness and the attractiveness of Yaqui ritual performances, cultural boundaries are preserved. The argument here is dramaturgical. Yaqui rituals are designed in part to attract audiences. Large audiences frequently attend, heightening the interest and enthusiasm of performer and observer, and both gain renewed respect for Yaqui ritual and symbol. Mexicans in attendance continuously regenerate Yaqui ceremony and, at the same time, observe the strength of this cultural persistence, largely unconscious of their own role. In ritual persistence, there may be cause for the unassertiveness of individual Yaqui ethnic

identity. Ritual, in a sense, performs the task of boundary maintenance, a chore that individual Yaquis do not have to perform in daily
interaction across ethnic lines.

Analytically, this chain of connection is set off by the existence and
operation of the Yaqui corporate polity. Verification of such a model
must rest, however, on a close examination of Yaqui history, a task
outside the scope of the present report. Moreover, the issues involved
are ones of ethnographic interpretation, not history alone: are there
significant and predictable differences in the ethnic system of Potam
and the Yaqui Zone in the 1940s, when Spicer made his observations
and recorded them, and in the 1970s?

CHANGE AND PERSISTENCE IN THE YAQUI ZONE

Massive economic change has occurred in the Yaqui Valley over the
last thirty years. Yaqui pueblos have been transformed into burgeoning
outposts of commercial agriculture. Yaqui polity has changed as well,
from a struggling staff forced to share jurisdiction with the armies
occupying the zone, to a semiautonomous government within a state.
Corresponding changes have occurred in the Yaqui ethnic system
which are congruent with the foregoing interpretation of Yaqui
ethnicity and polity in the 1970s.

Much of this interpretation rests on an apparent weakening of
traditional sanctions, an apparent attenuation of tradition knowledge. I have claimed that the strengthening of the Yaqui corporate
polity may in large measure account for these observations. A legitimate corporate body, with the authority to define group membership,
frees individual Yaquis from the need to perform according to traditional values and standards, and to conform strictly to traditional
sanctions. Comparable aspects of Yaqui ethnicity in the 1940s—as I
interpret these patterns from Spicer's writing—are not fortuitous.

During that era Yaquis were tied closely to a set of values and
sentiments that had taken shape in the struggles of the nineteenth
century and had been reinforced by the events of the twentieth. By
1940, Yaquis had repossessed several of their traditional pueblos and
had been granted a degree of territorial and religious autonomy under
the Cárdenas decrees. Throughout the 1940s, though, the Yaqui polity
remained comparatively weak. Mexican military units occupied the
zone, and Mexican commanders actively interfered with internal tribal
affairs. In the face of these assaults to their political integrity, Yaquis
were able to preserve their ethnic integrity by vitalizing traditional
values and sentiments.

But such change—in political strength and in the manifestation of
traditional culture—is intractable to precise measurement. Historical

comparison appears to give some independent support to my views of contemporary Yaqui ethnicity, but the analysis remains an interpretation. Its assessment may finally rest not on measurement but on ethnographic method and theoretical perception.

In the field during the 1940s Spicer faced the task of description, of recording the structural and cultural outlines of a poorly understood society. He accomplished this and more—he filled in many of the pieces of everyday life. And much of his cultural and structural description rests carefully on such pieces of everyday life. In the end, though, *Potam* (Spicer 1954) stands as an account of the rules or norms of Yaqui society, not of patterned deviations from those rules.

Because this structural and cultural description had been accomplished, I looked for deviations and quickly found them. I proceeded to construct an interpretive framework that would account for such deviation and also acknowledge the persistence of Yaqui culture, ritual, and ethnic identity. This interpretation differs from Spicer's in the direction, though not in the magnitude of Oscar Lewis's restudy of Tepoztlán. Lewis, in the words of one Redfieldian, emphasized "connivance, violence, hatred, suspicion, promiscuity, betrayal, suffering, and death" (Leslie 1976:158) in *Life in a Mexican Village* (1951) and other writings. Robert Redfield, Lewis's predecessor and protagonist in the Tepoztlán ethnology, was portrayed as one who "distorted reality to fit his idyllic conception of folk societies" (Leslie 1976:158). Redfield, as Charles Leslie notes, was publicly quiet throughout these assaults on his method and theory (1976:154), so the controversy was never fully resolved.

Fortunately, Eric Wolf has addressed the controversy, and his sketchy resolution (1960) points to history, not to interpretive bias. In Wolf's view, the internal integration and harmony of peasant communities vary inversely with the political and economic strength of the nation. When the nation is strong, peasants and Indians are pressured to contribute to this strength at the expense of their own demands and desires. When the nation is weakened, as it was in the aftermath of the Mexican Revolution, this external and disintegrating pressure is removed. Redfield examined Tepoztlán during such a period of national instability and observed "internal organization and consistency" (Wolf 1960:4). Lewis, in his critique, supports a contrary view with evidence from the Porfiriato and from the 1940s—two periods of national economic ascendancy and, consequently, "wholesale assaults on the Indian redoubts" (Wolf 1960:4).

In *Potam* (1954) Spicer constructs a model of internal consistency not unlike Redfield's. But this consistency was built firmly on opposition to the outside, to impinging economic and political forces. Those forces weakened momentarily under the indigenismo ideology of Lázaro Cárdenas, and the autonomy—however partial—which Yaquis had sought for centuries, received some legitimacy. This polity was still nascent when Spicer studied the pueblo in the 1940s. By the 1970s, it had grown more confident, to the point of guaranteeing the flexibility of Yaqui ethnic identity. In and of itself, Yaqui political organization will not be sufficient to ensure victories against the state. It may prove adequate, however, to ward off the cycle of hope and despair that rocks Tepoztlán.

Bibliography

Acheson, James M.
1975 The Lobster Fiefs: Economic and Ecological Effects of Territoriality in the Maine Lobster Industry. *Human Ecology*, 3:183−207.
1979 Variations in Traditional Inshore Fishing Rights in Maine Lobstering Communities. In *North American Maritime Cultures: Anthropological Essays on Changing Adaptations*, ed. Raoul Anderson, 253−76. The Hague: Mouton.
Acuña, Rodolfo F.
1974 *Sonoran Strongman: Ignacio Pesqueria and His Times*. Tucson: University of Arizona Press.
Adams, Richard
1970 *Crucifixion by Power: Essays on Guatemalan National Social Structure, 1944–1966*. Austin: University of Texas Press.
Almada, Francisco R.
1952 *Diccionario de Historia, Geografía, y Biografía Sonorenses*. Chihuahua, Chih., Mexico.
Anderson, Bo, and James D. Cockcroft
1969 Control and Co-optation in Mexican Politics. In *Latin American Radicalism: A Documentary Report on ·Left and Nationalist Movements*, ed. Irving Louis Horowitz, Josué de Castro, and John Gerassi, 366−89. New York: Vintage Books.
Anderson, Lee G.
1977 *The Economics of Fisheries Management*. Baltimore: The Johns Hopkins University Press.
Anonymous
1979 New Mexican Policy Opens Door to Agro-Industry. *Latin American Economic Report* 7 (20): 156−57.

Autoridades Tradicionales De Sus Ocho Pueblos, Tribu Yaqui
    1972a Letter to Hector Medina Neri, Subsecretario de Pesca,
        Mexico City, from Vicam Pueblo, Sonora, 24 October. Copy
        in possession of author.
    1972b Letter to Luis Echeverría Alvarez, Presidente Constitu-
        cional de los Estados Unidos Mexicanos, Mexico City, from
        Vicam Pueblo, Sonora, 24 October. Copy in possession of
        author.

Bailey, F. G.
    1969   *Strategems and Spoils: A Social Anthropology of Politics.* New
        York: Schocken Books.

Bailey, John J., and John E. Link
    1981   Statecraft and Agriculture in Mexico, 1980–82: Domestic
        and Foreign Policy Considerations in the Making of Mexi-
        can Agricultural Policy. Working Papers in U.S.-Mexican
        Studies No. 23, Program in United States-Mexican Studies.
        San Diego: University of California.

Banco Nacional De Credito Ejidal, S.A.
    1945   El sistema de producción colectiva en los ejidos del Valle del
        Yaqui, Sonora, México: Banco Nacional de Crédito Ejidal.

Barkin, David, and Blanca Suárez
    1982   El Fin de la Autosuficiencia Alimentaria, Editorial Nueva
        Imagen, S.A., México, D.F.

Bartell, Gilbert D.
    1965   Directed Culture Change Among the Sonoran Yaquis.
        Ph.D. diss., University of Arizona, Tucson.

Barth, Fredrik
    1966   Models of Social Organization. *Occasional Papers of the Royal
        Anthropological Institute* 23.
    1969   *Ethnic Groups and Boundaries.* Edited by Fredrik Barth.
        Boston: Little, Brown and Company.
    1975   *Ritual and Knowledge Among the Baktaman of New Guinea.*
        New Haven: Yale University Press.

Bartra, Roger
    1982   Capitalism and the Peasantry in Mexico. *Latin American
        Perspectives* 9:36–47.

Bassols Batalla, Ángel
    1972   *El Noroeste de México: Un Estudio Geográfico-Económico.* In-
        stituto de Investigaciones Económicas, Universidad Na-
        cional Autónoma de México, México, D.F.

Beals, Ralph L.
    1945   The Contemporary Culture of the Cahita Indians. *Bureau
        of American Ethnology, Bulletin 142.*

Beene, Delmar L.
    1972   *Sonora in the Age of Ramon Corral, 1875–1900.* Ph.D. diss.,
        University of Arizona, Tucson.

Bell, P.L., and H. Bentley MacKenzie
  1923 *Mexican West Coast and Lower California: A Commercial and Industrial Survey.* Bureau of Foreign and Domestic Commerce, Special Agents Series 220. United States Department of Commerce.
Bellah, Robert
  1964 Religious Evolution. *American Sociological Review,* 29:358–74.
Bennett, John W.
  1975 *The New Ethnicity: Perspectives from Ethnology.* Edited by John W. Bennett. American Ethnological Society Proceedings, 1973.
Berreman, Gerald
  1962 *Behind Many Masks: Ethnography and Impression Management in a Himalayan Village.* Society for Applied Anthropology, Monograph 4.
Bierstedt, Robert
  1950 An Analysis of Social Power. *American Sociological Review.* 15:730–38.
  1967 Power and Social Class. In *Social Structure, Stratification, and Mobility,* ed. Anthony Leeds, 77–83. Washington, D.C.: Pan American Union.
Boon, James
  1973 Further Operations of Culture in Anthropology: A Synthesis of and for Debate. In *The Idea of Culture in the Social Sciences,* ed. Louis Schnieder and Charles Bonjean, 1–32. London: Cambridge University Press.
Borlaug, Norman E.
  1965 Wheat, Rust, and People. *Phytopathology* 55:1088–98.
Braroe, Niels Winther
  1975 *Indian and White: Self-Image and Interaction in a Canadian Plains Community.* Stanford: Stanford University Press.
Breton, Yvan
  1979 The Introduction of Capitalism in Yucatecan Coastal Fishing. In *New Directions in Political Economy: An Approach from Anthropology,* ed. Madeline Barbara Leons and Frances Rothstein, 141–58. Westport, Conn.: Greenwood Press.
Brusca, Richard C.
  1973 *A Handbook to the Common Intertidal Invertebrates of the Gulf of California.* Tucson: University of Arizona Press.
Burke, Kenneth
  1973 *The Philosophy of Literary Form: Studies in Symbolic Action.* Berkeley: University of California Press.
Cancian, Frank
  1965 *Economics and Prestige in a Maya Community: The Religious Cargo System of Zinacantan.* Stanford: Stanford University Press.

Cancian, Frank (*Continued*)
  1967   Political and Religious Organization. In *Handbook of Middle American Indians* 6:283–98, ed. Manning Nash. Austin: University of Texas Press.

Carlos, Manuel L.
  1981   State Policies, State Penetration and Ecology: A Comparative Analysis of Uneven Development In Mexico's Micro Agrarian Regions. *Working Papers in U.S.-Mexican Studies No. 19*, Program in United States-Mexican Studies, University of California, San Diego.

Carr, Raymond
  1969   Mexican Agrarian Reform 1910–1960. In *Agricultural Change and Economic Development: The Historical Problems*, ed. E.L. Jones and S.J. Woolf, 151–68. London: Methuen and Company, Ltd.

Ceceña Cervantes, José Luis, Fausto Burgueño Lomelí, and Silvia Millán Echeagaray
  1973   *Sinaloa: Crecimiento Agrícola y Desperdicio*. Instituto de Investigaciones Económicas. México, D.F.: Universidad Nacional Autónoma de México.

Chambers, Erve
  1977   Modern Mesoamerica: The Politics of Identity. *American Anthropologist* 79:92–97.

Chapa Saldaña, H.C. Guildot Taddei, and H. Romero Rodriguez
  1968   *Ensayo de Interpretación de las Tallas Comerciales de Camarón en los Litorales de Sonora, México*. F.A.O. Fisheries Report 57, 2:357–72.

Chávez, E. A. and D. Lluch
  1971   Estado Actual de la Pesca de Camarón en el Noroeste de México. *Revista de la Sociedad Mexicana de Historia Natural* 32:141–56.

Clifton, James A.
  1972   The Southern Ute Tribe as a Fixed Membership Group. In *The Emergent Native Americans: A Reader in Culture Contact*, ed. Deward E. Walker, 485–500. Boston: Little, Brown and Company.

Cleaver, Harry M.
  1972   The Contradictions of the Green Revolution. *Monthly Review* 24:80–111.

Coatsworth, John
  1974   Railroads, Landholding, and Agrarian Protest in the Early Porfiriato. *Hispanic American Historical Review*, 54:48–71.

Cohen, Abner
  1974   *Two-Dimensional Man: An Essay on the Anthropology of Power and Symbolism in Complex Societies*. Berkeley: University of California Press.

Collier, George A.
1975   *Fields of the Tzotzil: The Ecological Bases of Tradition in Highland Chiapas.* Austin: University of Texas Press.

Compañia Constructora Richardson
1904   Richardson Construction Company Papers, Special Collec-
-27   tions, University of Arizona Library, Tucson.

Cordell, John
1974   The Lunar-Tide Fishing Cycle in Northeastern Brazil. *Ethnology* 13:379–92.

Crumrine, N. Ross
1964   The House Cross of the Mayo Indians of Sonora, Mexico: A Symbol of Ethnic Identity. *Anthropological Papers No. 8.* University of Arizona, Tucson.

1977   The Mayo Indians of Sonora: A People Who Refuse to Die. Tucson: University of Arizona Press.

1981   The Ritual of the Cultural Enclave Process: The Dramatization of Oppositions Among the Mayo Indians of Northwest Mexico. In *Persistent Peoples: Cultural Enclaves in Perspective,* ed. George Pierre Castile and Gulbert Kushner, 109–31. Tucson: University of Arizona Press.

Cummings, Ronald G.
1974   *Interbasin Water Transfers: A Case Study in Mexico.* Baltimore: The Johns Hopkins University Press.

Dabdoub, Claudio
1964   *Historia de el Valle del Yaqui.* Manuel Porrúa, México, D. F.

Despres, Leo
1975   *Ethnicity and Resource Competition in Plural Societies.* Edited by Leo Despres. The Hague: Mouton Publishers.

Dore, Ronald F.
1971   Modern Cooperatives in Traditional Communities. In *Two Blades of Grass: Rural Cooperatives in Agricultural Modernization,* ed. Peter Worsley, 43–60. Manchester: Manchester University Press.

Dovring, Folke
1970   Land Reform and Productivity in Mexico. *Land Economics* 46:264–74.

Dozier, Craig L.
1963   Mexico's Transformed Northwest: The Yaqui, Mayo, and Fuerte Examples. *Geographical Review,* October:548–71.

Dunbier, Roger
1968   *The Sonoran Desert: Its Geography, Economy, and People.* Tucson: University of Arizona Press.

Duncan, Hugh D.
1962   *Communication and Social Order.* London: Oxford University Press.

Edel, Matthew
1973   *Economies and the Environment.* Englewood Cliffs, N.J.: Prentice-Hall.

Edwards, R. R. C.
1977   Field Experiments on Growth and Mortality of *Penaeus vannamei* in a Mexican Coastal Lagoon Complex. *Estuarine and Coastal Marine Science* 5:107−21.
1978a Ecology of a Coastal Lagoon Complex in Mexico. *Estaurine and Coastal Marine Science* 6:75−92.
1978b The Fishery and Fisheries Biology of Penaeid Shrimp on the Pacific Coast of Mexico. In *Oceanography and Marine Biology: An Annual Review,* ed. Harold Barnes, 16:145−80. Aberdeen, Scotland: Aberdeen University Press.
Eisenstadt, S. N.
1964   Social Change, Differentiation and Evolution. *American Sociological Review* 29:375−86.
Erasmus, Charles
1967   Culture Change in Northwest Mexico. In *Contemporary Change in Traditional Societies,* Vol. 3: Mexican and Peruvian Communities, ed. Julian H. Steward, 1−131. Urbana: University of Illinois Press.
1970   Comments on "Resistance to Change" and Radical Peasant Mobilization: Foster and Erasmus Reconsidered by Gerrit Huizer. *Human Organization* 29:314−20.
Escudero, Jose Agustin De
1849   *Noticias Estadísticas de Sonora y Sinaloa.* Tipografía de R. Rafael, México.
Esteva, Gustavo
1983   *The Struggle for Rural Mexico.* South Hadley, Mass.: Bergin and Garvey Publishers, Inc.
Fabila, Alfonso
1940   *Las tribus Yaquis de Sonora y su anhelada auto-determinación.* Departamento de Asuntos Indígenas, México.
Firch, Robert S., and Robert A. Young
1968   An Economic Study of the Winter Vegetable Export Industry of Northwest Mexico. *Agricultural Experiment Station Technical Bulletin No. 179.* Tucson: University of Arizona.
Forman, Shepard
1970   *The Raft Fisherman: Tradition and Change in the Brazilian Peasant Economy.* Bloomington: Indiana University Press.
Fortes, Meyer
1969   *Kinship and the Social Order: The Legacy of Lewis Henry Morgan.* Chicago: Aldine Publishing Company.
Freebairn, Donald K.
1963   Relative Production Efficiency Between Tenure Classes in the Yaqui Valley, Sonora, Mexico. *Journal of Farm Economics* 45:1150−60.
1969   The Dichotomy of Prosperity and Poverty in Mexican Agriculture. *Land Economics* 45:31−42.
Geertz, Clifford
1973   *The Interpretation of Cultures.* New York: Basic Books, Inc.

Giddings, Ruth W.
1959   Yaqui Myths and Legends. *Anthropological Papers No. 2.* Tucson: University of Arizona Press.

Goffman, Erving
1959   *The Presentation of Self in Everyday Life.* Garden City, New York: Doubleday and Company.
1963   *Stigma: Notes on the Management of Spoiled Identity.* Englewood Cliffs, N.J.: Prentice-Hall.

Goodenough, Ward
1969   Rethinking 'Status' and 'Role': Toward a General Model of the Cultural Organization of Social Relationships. In *Cognitive Anthropology*, ed. Stephen A. Tylor, 311–29. New York: Holt, Rinehart and Winston.

Gouy-Gilbert, Cécile
1983   *Une Résistance Indienne: Les Yaquis du Sonora.* Lyon, France: Fédérop.

Grindle, Merilee S.
1981   Official Interpretations of Rural Underdevelopment: Mexico in the 1970s. *Working Papers in U.S.-Mexican Studies No. 20*, Program in United States-Mexican Studies. San Diego: University of California.

Griffin, Keith
1974   *The Political Economy of Agrarian Change: An Essay on the Green Revolution.* Cambridge: Harvard University Press.

Haag, Herman and German Rioseco
1965   Marketing of Grains and Other Farm Products in the Yaqui Valley, Sonora, Mexico. *School of Agriculture Publication No. 21*, Southern Illinois University.

Hammel, E. A.
1969   *Power in Ica: The Structural History of a Peruvian Community.* Boston: Little, Brown and Company.

Hansen, Roger
1974   *The Politics of Mexican Development.* Baltimore: The Johns Hopkins University Press.

Hernandez, Fortunato
1902   *Las Razas Indígenas de Sonora y la Guerra del Yaqui.* La Casa Editorial J. de Elizalde, México, D. F.

Hewitt de Alcántara, Cynthia
1978   *La Modernizacion de la Agricultura Mexicana, 1940–1970.* Siglo Veintiuno Editores, S.A., México, D. F.

Hicks, George L. and David I. Kertzer
1972   Making the Middle Way: Problems of Monhegan Identity. *Southwestern Journal of Anthropology* 28:1–24.

Hicks, W. Whitney
1967   Agricultural Development in Northern Mexico, 1940–1960. *Land Economics* 443:393–402.

Hicks, W. Whitney (Continued)
1969   Primary Exports and Economic Development: An Appli-
       cation of the Staple Theory to Sonora, Mexico. Canadian
       Journal of Agricultural Economics 17:46–62.
Hinojosa, Alicia, Olivia Peralta and Alicia Vega
1972   En Bahía de Lobos.Revista 2:3–5. Hermosillo: Universidad
       de Sonora.
Horowitz, Donald L.
1975   Ethnic Identity. In Ethnicity: Theory and Experience, eds.
       Nathan Glazer and Daniel P. Moynihan, 111–40. Cam-
       bridge: Harvard University Press.
Hubbs, Carl L. and Gunnar I. Roden
1964   Oceanography and Marine Life along the Pacific Coast of
       Middle America. In Handbook of Middle American Indians, ed.
       Robert C. West, 1:143–86. Austin: University of Texas
       Press.
Hu-Dehart, Evelyn
1974   Development and Rural Rebellion: Pacification of the
       Yaquis in the Late Porfiriato. Hispanic American Historical
       Review 54:72–93.
1981   Missionaries, Miners, and Indians: Spanish Contact with the
       Yaqui Nation of Northwestern New Spain, 1533–1820. Tucson:
       University of Arizona Press.
1984   Yaqui Resistance and Survival: The Struggle for Land and Au-
       tonomy, 1821–1910. Madison: University of Wisconsin
       Press.
Huizer, Gerrit
1970a Peasant Organization in Agrarian Reform in Mexico. In
       Masses in Latin America, ed. Irving Louis Horowitz,
       445–502. New York: Oxford University Press.
1970b La lucha campesina en México. Centro de Investigaciones
       Agrarias, México.
Johnson, Jean B.
1943   A Clear Case of Linguistic Acculturation. American Anthro-
       pologist 45:427–34.
Kapferer, Bruce
1976   Transaction and Meaning: Directions in the Anthropology of Ex-
       change and Symbolic Behavior. Edited by Bruce Kapferer.
       Philadelphia: Institute for the Study of Human Issues.
Kelley, Jane Holden
1978   Yaqui Women: Contemporary Life Histories. Lincoln: University
       of Nebraska Press.
Kroeber, Clifton B.
1983   Man, Land, and Water: Mexico's Farmlands Irrigation Policies,
       1885–1911. Berkeley: University of California Press.
Kutcher, Gary P.
1983   A Regional Agricultural Programming Model for Mexico's

Pacific Northwest. In *The Book of CHAC: Programming Studies for Mexican Agriculture*, ed. R. D. Norton and L. Solís M., 317–51. Baltimore: The Johns Hopkins University Press.

Kutkuhn, Joseph H.
1966   The Role of Estuaries in the Development and Perpetuation of Commercial Shrimp Resources. In *A Symposium on Estuarine Fisheries*, ed. Roland Smith, Albert Swartz, and William Massmann, 16–36. American Fisheries Society, Special Publication No. 3.

Leach, Edmund
1964   *Political Systems of Highland Burma: A Study of Kachin Social Structure*. Boston: Beacon Press.

Leslie, Charles
1976   The Hedgehog and the Fox in Robert Redfield's Work and Career. In *American Anthropology: The Early Years*, ed. John V. Murra, 146–66. St. Paul, Minn.: West Publishing Company.

Lewis, Oscar
1951   *Life in a Mexican Village: Tepoztlán Restudied*. Urbana: University of Illinois Press.

Lluch, David
1974   La pesquería de Camarón de Altamar en el noroeste: un analysis biologica pesquera. *Serie Informativa*. México: Instituto Nacional de Pesca.

Lozano, Salvador
1972   El Camarón: Eterno Conflicto. *Técnica Pesquera* 5:23–32.

Maluf, Linda Yvonne
1983   The Physical Oceanography. In *Island Biogeography in the Sea of Cortez*, ed. Ted J. Case and Martin L. Cody, 26–45. Berkeley: University of California Press.

Markiewicz, Dana
1980   *Ejido Organization in Mexico, 1934–1976*. Los Angeles: University of California, Latin American Center Publications.

Mathews, C.
1974   Cuánto resistirá el Camarón? *Ciencias Marinas* 1:86–91.

McGoodwin, James R.
1980a   Mexico's Marginal Inshore Pacific Fishing Cooperatives. *Anthropological Quarterly* 53:39–47.
1980b   The Human Cost of Development. *Environment* 22:31–42.

McGuire, Thomas R.
1979   *Politics, Economic Dependence, and Ethnicity in the Yaqui Valley, Sonora*. Ph.D. diss. University of Arizona, Tucson.
1983   The Political Economy of Shrimping in the Gulf of California. *Human Organization* 42:132–45.

Menz, A., and A. B. Bowers
1980   Bionomics of *Penaeus vennamei* Boone and *Penaeus styliros-*

Menz, A., and A. B. Bowers (*Continued*)
   tris Stimpson in a Lagoon on the Mexican Pacific Coast.
   Estuarine and Coastal Marine Science 10:685–97.
Mogab, John
   1984   The Mexican Experience in Peasant Agricultural Credit.
   Development and Change 15:203–21.
Moisés, Rosalio, Jane Holden Kelley, and William Curry Holden
   1971   *The Tall Candle: The Personal Chronicle of a Yaqui Indian.*
   Lincoln: University of Nebraska Press.
Montes De Oca, Rosa Elena
   1977   The State and the Peasants. In *Authoritarianism in Mexico,*
   ed. Jose Luis Reyna and Richard S. Weinert, 47–63.
   Philadelphia: The Institute for the Study of Human Issues.
Moore, Sally Falk and Barbara G. Myerhoff, eds.
   1975   *Symbol and Politics in Communal Ideology: Cases and Questions.*
   Ithaca: Cornell University Press.
Nadel, S. F.
   1957   *The Theory of Social Structure.* London: Cohen and West, Ltd.
Nash, Manning
   1985   Political Relations in Guatemala. *Social and Economic Studies*
   7:65–75.
Norton, Roger D.
   1982   Future Prospects for Mexican Agriculture. *The Southwestern*
   Review 2:101–28.
Norton, Roger D., and Leopoldo Solís M., editors
   1983   *The Book of CHAC: Programming Studies for Mexican Agricul-*
   ture. Baltimore: The Johns Hopkins University Press.
Padgett, L. Vincent
   1966   *The Mexican Political System.* Boston: Houghton Mifflin
   Company.
Paine, Robert
   1974   Second Thoughts About Barth's Models. *Occasional Papers*
   of the Royal Anthropological Institute 32.
Parsons, Talcott
   1975   Some Theoretical Considerations on the Nature and
   Trends in Change of Ethnicity. In *Ethnicity: Theory and Ex-*
   perience, ed. Nathan Glazer and Daniel P. Moynihan,
   53–83. Cambridge: Harvard University Press.
Peacock, James L.
   1968   *Rites of Modernization: Symbolic and Social Aspects of Indonesian*
   Proletarian Drama. Chicago: University of Chicago Press.
   1969   Society as Narrative. In *Forms of Symbolic Action,* ed. Robert
   F. Spencer, 167–77. Proceedings of American Ethnological Society.
Phleger, F. B.
   1969   Some General Features of Coastal Lagoons. In *Lagunas*
   Costeras, Un Simposio, 5–25. UNAM-UNESCO. México.

Plotnicov, Leonard
1962 Fixed Membership Groups: The Locus of Culture Processes. *American Anthropologist* 64:97–103.
Pomareda, Carlos, and Richard L. Simmons
1983 A Risk Programming Model for Mexican Vegetable Exports. In *The Book of CHAC: Programming Studies for Mexican Agriculture,* ed. R. D. Norton and L. Solís M., 352–74. Baltimore: The Johns Hopkins University Press.
Redclift, Michael
1980 Agrarian Populism in Mexico—The "Via Campesina." *The Journal of Peasant Studies* 7:492–502.
1981 Development Policymaking in Mexico: The Sistema Alimentario Mexicano (SAM). *Working Papers in U.S.-Mexican Studies No. 24,* Program in United States-Mexican Studies. University of California, San Diego.
Redfield, Robert
1930 *Tepoztlán: A Mexican Village.* Chicago: University of Chicago Press.
Royce, Anya Peterson
1982 *Ethnic Identity: Strategies of Diversity.* Bloomington: Indiana University Press.
Salisbury, Richard
1976 Transactions or Transactors? An Economic Anthropologist's View. In *Transaction and Meaning: Directions in the Anthropology of Exchange and Symbolic Behavior,* ed. Bruce Kapferer, 41–59. Institute for the Study of Human Issues, Philadelphia.
Sanderson, Steven E.
1981a *Agrarian Populism and the Mexican State: The Struggle for Land in Sonora.* Berkeley: University of California Press.
1981b The Receding Frontier: Aspects of the Internationalization of U.S.-Mexican Agriculture and Their Implications for Bilateral Relations in the 1980s. *Working Papers in U.S.-Mexican Studies No. 15,* Program in United States-Mexican Studies. University of California, San Diego.
Schmitz, Andrew, Robert S. Firch, and Jimmye S. Hillman
1981 Agricultural Export Dumping: The Case of Mexican Winter Vegetables in the U.S. Market. *American Journal of Agricultural Economics* 63:645–54.
Schramm, Gunter
1979 Input and Market Constraints in Irrigation Planning: Mexico. *Land Economics* 55:431–43.
Shibutani, Tamotsu and Kian M. Kwan
1965 *Ethnic Stratification: A Comparative Approach.* New York: Macmillan Company.
Smith, Carol
1975 Examining Stratification Systems Through Peasant Mar-

Smith, Carol (*Continued*)
  keting Arrangements: An Application of Some Models
  from Economic Geography. *Man* 19:95–122.
1976 Exchange Systems and the Spatial Distribution of Elites:
  The Organization of Stratification in Agrarian Societies. In
  Regional Analysis, Vol. 2: Social Systems, ed. Carol Smith. New
  York: Academic Press.
Smith, Waldemar R.
1977a *The Fiesta System and Economic Change*. New York: Columbia
  University Press.
1977b Class and Ethnicity in the Fields of the Tzotzil. *Peasant
  Studies* 6:51–56.
Sonnichsen, C. L.
1976 *Colonel Greene and the Copper Skyrocket*. Tucson: University of
  Arizona Press.
Southworth, J. L.
1897 *Sonora Ilustrado: El Estado de Sonora, México — Sus Industrias,
  Comerciales, Mineras y Manufactureas*. Nogales, Arizona: The
  Oases Printing and Publishing House.
Spicer, Edward H.
1940 *Pascua: A Yaqui Village in Arizona*. Chicago: University of
  Chicago Press.
1943 Linguistic Aspects of Yaqui Acculturation. *American Anthro-
  pologist* 45:410–26.
1954 Potam: A Yaqui Village in Sonora. *American Anthropological
  Association Memoir 77*. Menasha, Wisconsin.
1958 Social Structure and Cultural Process in Yaqui Religious
  Acculturation. *American Anthropologist* 60:433–41.
1961 Yaqui. In *Perspectives in American Indian Culture Change*, ed.
  E. H. Spicer, 7–93. Chicago: University of Chicago Press.
1962 *Cycles of Conquest: The Impact of Spain, Mexico, and the United
  States on the Indians of the Southwest, 1533–1960*. Tucson:
  University of Arizona Press.
1971 Persistent Cultural Systems. *Science* 174:795–800.
1974 Highlights of Yaqui History. *The Indian Historian* 53:2–9.
1976 The Yaquis: A Persistent Identity System. Paper presented
  at the Seventy-fifth Annual Meeting of the American Anthropological Association.
1980 *The Yaquis: A Cultural History*. Tucson: University of Arizona
  Press.
Stagg, Albert
1978 *The Almadas and Alamos, 1783–1867*. Tucson: University of
  Arizona Press.
Tax, Sol
1953 Penny Capitalism: A Guatemalan Indian Economy. *Institute of Social Anthropology Publication 16*. Smithsonian In-
  stitution, Washington, D.C.

Temple, Robert F.
1973   Shrimp Research at the Galveston Laboratory of the Gulf Coastal Fisheries Center. *Marine Fisheries Review* 35:16—20.
Thomson, Donald A., Lloyd T. Findley, and Alex N. Kerstitch
1979   *Reef Fishes of the Sea of Cortez.* New York: John Wiley.
Thompson, Richard A.
1974   *The Winds of Tomorrow: Social Change in a Mayan Town.* Chicago: University of Chicago Press.
Troncoso, Francisco P.
1905   *Las Guerras con las Tribus Yaqui y Mayo del Estado de Sonora.* Departamento de Estado Mayor, México.
Tuckman, Barbara
1976   The Green Revolution and the Distribution of Agricultural Income in Mexico. *World Development* 4:17—24.
Turner, John Kenneth
1969   *Barbarous Mexico.* Austin: University of Texas Press.
Turner, Victor
1969   Forms of Symbolic Action: Introduction. In *Forms of Symbolic Action,* ed. Robert F. Spencer, 3—25. Proceedings of American Ethnological Society.
Voss, Stuart F.
1982   *On the Periphery of Nineteenth-Century Mexico: Sonora and Sinaloa, 1810–1877.* Tucson, University of Arizona Press.
Wallace, Anthony F. C.
1970   *Culture and Personality.* New York: Random House.
Weber, Max
1946   Class, Status, Party. In *From Max Weber: Essays in Sociology,* eds. H. H. Gerth and C. Wright Mills, 180—95. New York: Oxford University Press.
1947   *The Theory of Social and Economic Organization.* Translated by A. H. Henderson and Talcott Parsons. Edited by Talcott Parsons. Glencoe: Free Press.
Wellhausen, Edwin
1976   The Agriculture of Mexico. *Scientific American* 235:128—50.
Wessman, James W.
1984   The Agrarian Question in Mexico. *Latin American Research Review* 19:243—59.
Williams, Glyn
1978   Industrialization and Ethnic Change in the Lower Chubut Valley, Argentina. *American Ethnologist* 5:618—31.
Wionczek, Miguel
1982   The Roots of the Mexican Agricultural Crisis: Water Resources Development Policies (1920—1970). *Development and Change* 13:365—99.
Wolf, Eric
1955   Types of Latin American Peasantry: A Preliminary Discussion. *American Anthropologist* 57:452—71.

Wolf, Eric (*Continued*)
1960   The Indian in Mexican Society. *Alpha Kappa Deltan,* Winter:3 – 6.
Yates, P. Lamartine
1981   *Mexico's Agricultural Dilemma.* Tucson: University of Arizona Press.

Newspapers

Ciudad Obregón *Diario del Yaqui*
Ciudad Obregón *Tribuna del Yaqui*
Guaymas *La Voz del Puerto*
Hermosillo *El Imparcial*
Los Angeles Times
Miami Herald
New York Times
New York *Wall Street Journal*
Washington Post

Index